TORTURE AND STATE VIOLENCE IN THE UNITED STATES

TORTURE AND STATE VIOLENCE IN THE UNITED STATES

A SHORT DOCUMENTARY HISTORY

Edited by ROBERT M. PALLITTO

The Johns Hopkins University Press · Baltimore

© 2011 The Johns Hopkins University Press
All rights reserved. Published 2011
Printed in the United States of America on acid-free paper
9 8 7 6 5 4 3 2 1

The Johns Hopkins University Press
2715 North Charles Street
Baltimore, Maryland 21218-4363
www.press.jhu.edu

Library of Congress Cataloging-in-Publication Data

Torture and state violence in the United States : a short
documentary history / edited by Robert M. Pallitto.
    p. cm.
   Includes bibliographical references and index.
   ISBN-13: 978-1-4214-0248-2 (hardcover : alk. paper)
   ISBN-10: 1-4214-0248-3 (hardcover : alk. paper)
   ISBN-13: 978-1-4214-0249-9 (pbk. : alk. paper)
   ISBN-10: 1-4214-0249-1 (pbk. : alk. paper)
   1. Torture—United States—History. 2. Torture—Govern-
ment policy—United States. I. Pallitto, Robert M., 1964–
   HV8599.U6T678 2011
   364.6'7—dc22

                                        2011008228

A catalog record for this book is available from the British
Library.

*Special discounts are available for bulk purchases of this
book. For more information, please contact Special Sales at
410-516-6936 or specialsales@press.jhu.edu.*

The Johns Hopkins University Press uses environmentally
friendly book materials, including recycled text paper that
is composed of at least 30 percent post-consumer waste,
whenever possible.

To John, Daniel, and Isabel

CONTENTS

LIST OF DOCUMENTS

Chapter 3. Imperialism, Jim Crow, and World War

Chapter 4. The Cold War, Vietnam, and Torture by the Police

Chapter 5. The War on Terror

ACKNOWLEDGMENTS

This book benefited immeasurably from a wealth of kind support and assistance from many people. Suzanne Flinchbaugh and the late Henry Tom at the Johns Hopkins University Press maintained faith in the project through many twists and turns and guided and shaped it into its present form. Although Henry did not see the book come to completion, his many contributions to scholarly literature are readily apparent in the works he shepherded and in the esteem of his colleagues. The anonymous reviewers of the book manuscript provided thoughtful, informed, and constructive suggestions that significantly improved the final product.

My research assistant, Mayo Alao, deserves special thanks. He tracked down obscure source material, accepted every new request cheerfully, and always responded promptly. I cannot imagine a more able or conscientious researcher. He sets a high standard indeed for research assistance.

I am deeply grateful for the use of several archival collections. It would be difficult, if not impossible, to cover the span of nearly four hundred years represented by the documents in this book without access to those collections. I was fortunate to utilize materials at the Luzerne County Historical Society's Bishop Library, the Rutgers Oral History Archive, the National Security Archive at George Washington University, the Justice Robert Jackson Archive, the Boston Public Library Rare Books Collection, and the state archives of New Jersey, Massachusetts, Connecticut, Georgia, and South Carolina.

A number of people commented on drafts and provided suggestions regarding design and content of the project. I want to thank David Plotke, Josiah Heyman, John Feffer, Roman Santillan, John Motoviloff, Kathryn Motoviloff, Robert Pallitto, Christina Pallitto, and Bob Murray for their valuable input. In particular, I thank my brother, John Motoviloff, for patiently answering many questions (sometimes repeated questions) both from the writer's viewpoint and the editor's. Any errors, of course, are my own.

For three years now, I have had the ideal professional home in the political science department at Seton Hall. I am fortunate to work with a wonderful group of people who have been unfailingly helpful, supportive, and encouraging in all of my work. I am grateful to the members of Seton Hall's philosophy department and to Vice Provost Kathleen Boozang for their support as well.

For the inspiration of their scholarship, I would like to thank Bill Weaver, Torin Monahan, Louis Fisher, David Adler, Nancy Fraser, Ana Castillo, and Patricia J. Williams.

Friends and family members helped in so many ways that it is difficult to remember all the acts of assistance, large and small. The subject matter of this book made it a difficult book to write, but those around me assured me that what made writing about torture difficult also made it important. For helping me to see it through, I am indebted to Ellen, Roger, and Andrew Miller; Ana Melendez; Ben Smith; Kerry Motoviloff; Emily Bregman; Gwyn Murray; Jessica Loy; Danielle Escontrias; Joe Medina; Shelli Soto; Chris Moyer; Mark Gorman; Kristin Gosselink; Leo Gayten; Larry Perfetti; and Richard Gutierrez.

Finally, I am grateful to Laura Melendez for too many things to name here. Most of all, though, I am inspired by the example of her life. By bringing kindness and compassion to wherever she sees cruelty, she has shown me that hope for a better world is best pursued through action.

It is the general impression of the people of that country that the only way to fight them is to fight as they fight; kill their women and children and kill them. At the same time, of course, we consider it a barbarous practice.

MAJOR SCOTT ANTHONY, testifying before Congress on the 1864 killings of Cheyenne and Arapaho at Sand Creek, Colorado

Liberalism and Torture

Judith Shklar believed that, for liberals, "cruelty is the worst thing we do."[1] Yet state-enacted cruelty appears all too often in the record of U.S. history. If torture stands as the most extreme form of cruelty and torture is documented throughout the nation's history, we may well question the status of the liberal commitment to avoid cruelty. This book examines the relationship—indeed, contradiction—between the liberal-democratic vision enshrined in the U.S. Constitution and the state's support and use of torture and other state violence in the name of national security and freedom. To explore this subject, I draw on historical examples and documents far older than the "war on terror" and even the Cold War, including some that date back to the early years of the republic, and trace the attitudes about the treatment of the actual bodies of torture victims that have developed against the background of a purportedly liberal political order.

As I assess the gap between liberal commitments and actual state practices, I want to emphasize that I use the word *liberalism* here in a sense that is quite different from its common usage in political rhetoric, where it is often "identified narrowly with the growth of government and with the welfare state."[2] In what follows, *liberalism* refers instead to the political doctrine that aims, as Shklar puts it, "to secure the political conditions that are necessary for the exercise of personal freedom."[3] Of the multiple articulations of liberalism within modern political theory, Shklar's "liberalism of fear" is most relevant to a discussion of torture. The liberalism of fear seeks above all to prevent cruel treatment; "the freedom it wishes to secure is freedom from the abuse of power and intimidation of the defenseless."[4] She sees a resurgence of

1

such cruelty with the coming of the two world wars; liberals' historical memory of world war and its aftermath generated an ongoing fear and urgency about guarding against repetition of various forms of cruel treatment. The impulses of liberal thought are refocused, and the components of liberal governance are enlisted, in the project of preventing state cruelty. Rule of law, for one, "is the prime instrument to retrain governments."[5] Democracy, too, is a bulwark against abuse, as it brings accountability and recourse for oppressive government actions. These familiar concepts gain urgency when employed in the liberalism of fear.

To say that liberalism *ought* to guard against state cruelty is not at all to suggest that it has, in fact, done so. Efforts to halt and prevent torture have not always been successful, to be sure, and in many instances such efforts are not even made at all. State actors professing adherence to liberal commitments often act in ways that belie such adherence. Moreover, groups and individuals who could practice the liberalism of fear often focus instead on aspects of liberalism that Shklar sees as "less urgent," such as the unfettered development of the self. Nonetheless, the emphasis on preventing cruelty is crucial as torture continues to proliferate in the world.

In fact, Shklar underestimates the extent to which cruelty has been continuous in U.S. history, as the documents collected in this book will show. There is no "cruelty-free" phase of the nation's history. Indeed, Darius Rejali sees a more complex relationship between cruelty (torture in particular) and democracy. Taking torture as a constant, he documents the relationship between human rights monitoring (growing out of democratic political practices) and the production of "clean" tortures. As monitoring emerges, states continue to torture, but they employ methods that leave no evidence on the body. Thus, rather than bringing torture to an end, democracy is actually *productive* of certain forms of torture—forms that are even harder to detect and regulate.[6] This insight is worth keeping in mind as we encounter, in the documents, official bans on practices that *do* leave marks, such as flogging or branding.

Torture continues, but the public no longer sees its results inscribed on the victims' bodies. Meanwhile, commentators suggest, in consequentialist terms, that torture should be permitted because it may yield benefits, such as useful intelligence, in some cases. In response to such arguments, Daniel Rothenburg draws out one implication of what Rejali calls "stealthy" torture by comparing torture to the practice of displaying mutilated bodies publicly, or "public presentational" torture.[7] We know that such public displays have been staged in the United States, most frequently in cases of lynching. If contemporary policy makers are willing to consider the former (stealthy torture) but not the latter (publicly displayed corpses), what could one conclude? That there are some things the state is not willing to trade in order to achieve greater efficacy in counterterror operations? Granted, the "communicative logic of broken bodies" serves a different purpose as compared to coercive interrogation—to create fear and thereby secure obedience—but if we assume that the display does in fact effectively secure obedience or preserve order, then the question remains: do those ends justify the practice?[8] If torture is permitted because it is perceived as effective, but public display of "broken bodies" is not permitted *despite* the fact that it is effective, can we still say that the resort to torture is fully explained by efficacy? Or is it more accurate to conclude that the operative concept is secrecy: that the state has more to lose by being discovered as cruel than it has to gain by collecting counterterror intelligence?[9]

At times, especially currently, policy makers suggest that torture is justified by the need to preserve the nation or protect its people. Rather than prohibiting torture absolutely, some would permit its use based on a claim of necessity, despite the fact that torture violates liberal understandings of individual rights. The most pertinent theoretical construct here is the notion of the "state of exception," which originates with the political theorist Carl Schmitt and has been cited by a number of scholars in the context of U.S. anti-terror policy after 9/11. The sovereign claims the power to act outside the "normal" law-bounded political order; this claim can be grounded in a specific constitutional provision, or it can be based on a commitment to preserve the very state itself, a commitment that is analytically prior to the constitutional rules governing "ordinary" situations. In either case, the state of exception provides a space for state action that suspends legal rules protecting individual rights and restricting state power. As with all exceptions to otherwise applicable rules, the state of exception creates a problem of scope. How can the scope of the exception be limited, and when does frequency of its invocation cause the exception to swallow the rule of "normal" constitutional politics? One commentator has claimed that "when exceptional circumstances arise justifying actions taken under the rule of necessity, and when the executive has the authority to decide when those circumstances exist, there is a risk that such exceptions may become increasingly normal."[10]

One textual source for exception from applicable rules is, of course, the suspension clause of Article I of the Constitution.[11] That clause authorizes suspension of the writ of habeas corpus, meaning that detained individuals may not challenge the legality of their confinement via habeas corpus petitions in civilian courts. However, it is Congress, not the executive, that may invoke this suspension. In fact, when the Bush administration argued that habeas corpus was not available to detainees at Guantanamo Bay (i.e., that it had been suspended), the Supreme Court rejected that claim. "The test for determining the scope of this provision," Justice Anthony Kennedy wrote for the majority, "must not be subject to manipulation by those whose power it is designed to restrain."[12] Clearly, then, there are strong normative grounds on which to object to a grant of "exception" or "necessity" power to the executive.

Regardless of what one thinks about the normative status of a rule of exception, however, Schmitt's "state of exception" is illuminating as a way to describe what actually happens when the state employs violence. In this study, I document instances of torture and state violence through U.S. history. Moreover, the documents included in this book all originate with the government, so that they describe policies and practices whose occurrence is not in doubt. Even a glance at the table of contents leads one to wonder whether these exceptions to the "normal" liberal-constitutional political order simply happen too frequently to accurately be called exceptions. Violent events, often displaying patterns of repetition, are so numerous as not to appear exceptional at all. We can see, through the work of Schmitt and others on the "state of exception," how the executive accomplishes the normalization of a "necessity regime."[13] The next question is whether liberalism still accurately describes the politics of the U.S. state as it wages the "war on terror," and if not, what is to be done? Is it enough to argue, on the level of constitutional interpretation, for a strict and cabined conception of executive power that will foreclose the "state of exception"? This would be to assume that the remedy for excessive executive power culminating in violence is persuasion—advocates of a strong executive must be persuaded that their interpretation of the constitution is wrong or dangerous (or both). Or must we look deeper than liberal-constitutional critique and try to understand how state power generates perpetual occasions for violence, both violence as an instrument and violence as an end in itself? It is my hope that this collection of documents becomes a step toward a more thoroughgoing investigation of the workings of power in purportedly liberal-democratic societies. Critical analysis of power relations is not a replacement for constitutional critique but rather a supplement to it. Effective reform—whether generated through judicial opinion, legislative enactment, or protest—requires an understanding of actual power practices, of the realities "on the ground."[14]

Understandings of "Torture": Historical, Socially Constructed, Legal

Before delving into the documents themselves, it is important to clarify the ways in which "torture" is understood. A survey of the usages of the term suggests that it has been overdetermined by the accumulated references within so many discourses, so many deployments for different purposes. It is reasonable to assume that torture usually carries a negative connotation; thus, in the words of one commentator, "To call something torture is almost always to condemn it, with the result that we have to confine the term, lest we be forced either to reexamine the legitimacy of our other coercive practices or to accept the fact of coercion as a routine aspect of our personal, social, and political arrangements."[15] The word *torture*, then, is used to distinguish prohibited practices from other practices, such as "cruel, inhuman or degrading treatment," which are arguably permitted by law. As we will see, that definitional move is used often in contemporary torture discourse. However, as Frankenberg points out, it would be inaccurate to say torture is always considered taboo; we have also seen a return of the word *torture* used forthrightly and without condemnation by commentators who posit counterfactual conditions in which torture should be permitted. By virtue of apologists' use of the term, torture has become a "domestic animal."[16] Among this range of usages, we can specify three dimensions of understanding of the concept of torture (and, by extension, other types of state violence): historical, socially constructed, and legal. The categories overlap, of course, but it is nonetheless useful to consider them separately, to see what each category can contribute to a discussion of torture.

Torture as a Historical Phenomenon

It is important to ask, in historical terms, what sorts of cruelty have been inflicted on others, for what reasons. This inquiry helps us to understand the *historical* dimension of torture. Not all cruelty amounts to torture, and state discourses of violence continually draw lines between forms of violence, deeming some acceptable and condemning others. Torture usually lies on the unacceptable side of the line—as, for example, in the debate over ratification of the U.S. Constitution, when some legislators argued forcefully in support of a clear constitutional provision outlawing torture. Here, "torture" seemed to signify an illiberal practice that was incompatible with commitments to limits on state force and respect for individual liberty. Document 1.12 in chapter 1 reflects an attempt to uphold those commitments. At the same time, however, slaveholding society openly recognized as legitimate the denial of all rights to persons held as slaves. Moreover, maiming and mutilating slaves was considered acceptable and was not described as torture (see, e.g., document 2.14 in chapter 2). Classification of certain practices, such as punishing slaves, was more reflective of existing power relations than of adherence to liberal principles.

We remain aware of the history of "torture" as we grapple with its place in U.S. state practices, and historical resonances can be found in the discourse. When ruling on the legality of the police practice of stomach pumping to find evidence of crime, for example, Justice Frankfurter found that tactic "too close to the rack and the screw," and therefore unconstitutional.[17] Here, Frankfurter sounds like Patrick Henry, who asked, "What has distinguished our ancestors?" and then supplied the answer: "That they would not permit of tortures, or of cruel and barbarous treatment" (document 1.12 in chapter 1). The point here is that both men were aware of the historical commitment to avoiding torture. Whether that commitment has been honored, of course, is another matter.

Torture as a Social Construction

A second dimension of understanding torture in the U.S. context has to do with social constructions of "torture." Exploring the meaning(s) of "torture" as it circulates in discourse, as it is part of discourse, is aligned with the historical inquiry just outlined but is also distinct. The communicative usages of the word bear and shape meaning at the same time that state practices inscribe "torture" into bodies. It would be misleading to suggest a dichotomy between language and action, and it is not my intention to do so. Instead, I simply suggest that torture practices reflect talk about torture and shape that talk as well, such that there is a mutually reinforcing relationship between those practices and the construction of meaning through language. The electric chair can be used as an actual method of execution because it is not considered torture (under Supreme Court decisional law), and at the same time, it is not considered torture, in definitional terms, because it is actually used by the state as a tool of criminal justice administration (it is official, routinized, and public).

When we think about torture, violent images from the premodern past confront us: crucifixion by the Romans, the Inquisition, the Salem witch trials, and Foucault's spectacularly horrifying description in *Discipline and Punish* of execution by dismemberment. These practices are premodern in temporal terms, but they exhibit important continuities with contemporary practices. Some seek to extract information, while others are meant to deter or to punish certain behaviors in the general population, and we can see all of these goals—information, punishment, and deterrence—lying behind torture as it is practiced today. A distinction is sometimes made between judicial and political torture.[18] Judicial torture is employed to extract confessions of crime, whereas political torture is a tool for gathering intelligence. The police practices documented in the Wickersham Report (excerpts of the report are included in chapter 3) seem to fit with judicial torture, whereas the interrogation of Khalid Sheikh-Mohammed (chapter 5) appears to be political torture. In both cases, though, infliction of physical and psychological pain is instrumental to discovering information. In *A Question of Torture*, Alfred McCoy powerfully and carefully documents the fifty-year relationship between the academic research community and the U.S. intelligence operatives seeking better interrogation methods. McCoy shows that the CIA-funded research on the application of psychological stress—alone or in combination with physical pain. From the early years of the Cold War to the fall of the Soviet Union, the United States and its clients around the globe applied researchers' discoveries to interrogation subjects, and McCoy demonstrates that the 9/11 terror attacks revived vigorous U.S. government interest in aggressive interrogation practices.[19]

As important as it is, however, to understand the recent history of interrogation-related torture, we must remember that torture has also been practiced, historically, for reasons besides interrogation. If interrogation is inquisitory in nature, lynchings are exemplary: they signal to the population the costs of transgression of political or social norms, and they regulate by example. Lynching was employed as "a social ritual and means of political administration" in the Jim Crow–era American South, for example.[20] But lynching and other instances of violence in American history are exemplary at the same time as they are punitive. The targeting, killing, and mutilation of noncombatant Cheyenne and Arapaho at Sand Creek, Colorado, in 1864 was intended by the U.S. Army as punishment for killings of white settlers by unidentified raiders, but it also served as a warning to other tribes as to the treatment they could expect if such raids continued.[21] In David Luban's terminology, lynching was designed to create "terror." Luban also notes a category of torture he calls "victor's pleasure," in which "tyrannical rulers . . . take their pleasure from the degradation of those unfortunate enough to be subject to their will."[22] The "victor's pleasure" category is meant to evoke premodern practices (Luban uses a Mayan mural as a reference point), but we need not assume that it never figures as a motive for torture in modern history.[23]

Of course, purposes and effects intertwine in histories of state violence, and the terror felt by observers and victims alike in the presence of state-sponsored brutality is an important element in the use of brutality. Political administration of terror works most effectively when the publicly displayed results are horribly cruel. The recent exhibition of collected lynching photos, *Without Sanctuary*, is a powerful and unforgettable demonstration of how cruel and how horrifying the public lynchings actually were.[24] The photographs are difficult to look at now, but we must remember that the victims' bodies themselves stood on public display as a warning, vastly more horrifying than the photographs. Additionally, psychological methods are sometimes seen as the most efficient means to the torturer's end, especially when information is sought. The Cold War history recounted by McCoy centers on psychological abuse (though physical abuse was often used concurrently). He points out that many people believe—mistakenly—that psychological abuse does not constitute torture. The effects of sensory deprivation and sexual humiliation that he depicts, however, leave little room to argue that the devastating, permanent damage wrought by the CIA's psychological interrogation techniques is not torture. Yet some would still draw the definitional line around torture to exclude nonphysical methods.[25]

"Torture" is often constructed in opposition to other forms of state violence. One could ask, for example, whether the execution of a condemned prisoner is torture. Foucault's reference to the public dismemberment of a convicted murderer is meant to show not only that such punishment was horribly painful but also (and more importantly) that by contrast modern punishment sought to eliminate the spectacle of public infliction of pain. Thus, modern penology moved away from such grotesque displays, and its methods appeared less like torture. But certainly the more "sanitized" versions of discipline and punishment still amount to state violence, even if they are not readily understood as torture. Execution by lethal injection and shooting wounded prisoners in the Iraq War are examples of state violence that do not fit with conventional notions of torture. Some documents presented in the following chapters describe episodes of state violence that most observers would not classify as torture; I have included them, though, because they shed light on what "torture" means—both in opposition to, and as extension of, the notion of state violence.

The boundaries of this study, then, describe state violence generally; torture is in some senses the most egregious of state violence, but at the same time I am less interested in defining precisely, for all contexts, what is and is not properly classified as torture, and more interested in depicting state violence in the forms it appears in U.S. history. The common feature, of course, is that the state or its agents have committed the acts in question.

Torture as a Matter of Law

Notwithstanding my decision to examine a range of violent state actions in this study, the legal definition of torture itself is still important. It matters, in a legal sense, what we classify as "torture," because law operates according to definitional rules. While the liberalism of fear concerns itself with cruelty, broadly speaking, definitions become important in efforts to set limits to state behavior. If torture is to be prohibited and punished, there must be a legal line demarcating what is prohibited. And while there is a certain amount of discomfort in talking abstractly, constructing definitions, about viscerally disturbing events, it is nonetheless necessary in order to set the bounds of the inquiry at the outset. In particular, the legal definition is important because it generates consequences for transgression. Clearly, a prohibition without legal sanctions is of little effect in constraining behavior, especially in the case of a long-used, oft-used technique such as torture.

The Geneva Conventions of 1949 prohibit torture and cruel treatment. Using even more specific terms, the 1984 Convention against Torture (CAT) declares the right to be free of torture and cruel, inhuman, and degrading treatment a human right. The CAT supplies a legal definition of torture but does not clearly state how "cruel treatment" is to be regulated. The United States signed and ratified the CAT but submitted reservations concerning the scope of the CAT's torture ban. In 1994 Congress passed implementing legislation that made torture a federal crime, but the U.S. Code provision further narrowed the definition.

The definitional question of what constitutes torture, legally speaking, has taken on a new importance with the initiation of the "war on terror." Both U.S. law and international conventions prohibit torture, but harsh interrogation methods have nonetheless been used, and proclaimed necessary, in the fight against terrorism. The Bush administration sought to construct a legal defense for its treatment of detainees by arguing, first, that the detainees were not subject to the protections of the Geneva Conventions and then by claiming that only the most severe actions—such as inflicting pain equivalent to "organ failure"—constituted torture.[26] At his 2007 confirmation hearing, Attorney General Michael Mukasey disavowed any intention to utilize torture if confirmed but then hedged about what specific actions amount to torture. Senate Judiciary Committee members criticized Mukasey's refusal to answer the question, but the nominee's evasiveness indicates the need for government officials to categorize their actions in a way that comports with liberal principles of limited state force and respect for individuals (and to avoid criminal liability), even as "the most severe" actions are authorized and carried out.

In 2002 Assistant Attorney General Jay Bybee advised in the now-infamous "torture memo" to presidential counsel Alberto Gonzales that many of the interrogation tactics used by the United States and its surrogates abroad did not constitute torture. The memo, which is reproduced in part and discussed later in this book, has been criticized for its legalism and strained argumentation. Harold Hongju Koh, for example, said the memo was "perhaps the most clearly erroneous legal opinion I have ever read."[27] Interpreting, for example, the requirement that only actions producing "severe" pain can qualify as torture, the memo looks to a federal health care statute (one that governs payment for emergency medical care) in an attempt to define severe pain—and to raise the bar for what level of pain is "severe."[28] Reading this argument, one realizes what a legal stretch it is to cite a statute written to authorize payment for medical treatment as authority for inflicting pain on a person. In fact, the U.S. Code provision outlawing torture, which the Bybee memo sought to interpret so narrowly, was, in the words of one commentator, "intended to be an additional expression of the repugnancy of the practice of torture, and was most definitely not intended to serve as a guideline for proper interrogation by or acceptable behavior of U.S. officials. Removing the prohibition on torture from its context and analyzing it in a legal vacuum is a contributing factor to this pseudolegal outcome."[29]

Yet repeatedly, Bybee and others in the Bush administration sought to draw a line between the *many* harsh interrogation tactics allowable under U.S. law (arguing that they do not amount to torture) and the *few* that met the administration's narrow definition of torture and were therefore prohibited. The Bybee memo was withdrawn and replaced late in 2004 by the Levin memo, which rejected some of the arguments of its predecessor; the later memo is also presented in chapter 5.

The rationales of the Bybee memo have drawn criticism from many quarters since the memo became public. That criticism is appropriate on legal, logical, and humanitarian grounds, of course, but it can obscure an important fact about torture-related state practices: the striking similarity between Bybee's analysis and earlier interpretations of "cruel and unusual punishment" in American law. Colin Dayan demonstrates compellingly that two continuities are clearly present in this regard throughout American history. First, there is a dividing line, seen throughout case law and public statements, between harsh punishment (which is legal) and excessive punishment (which is illegal). Dayan notes pointedly that punishment of slaves, for example, involved horrible acts such as dog mauling and mutilation, which were permitted by law *as long as they were not done excessively.* Thus, illegal punishment has long been a question of degree rather than kind. Second, the question of excessive punishment or torture always concerns the bodies of those who stand outside the law, who are dead to the law: convicted prisoners and slaves historically and now "illegal enemy combatants."[30] The question How much is too much? arises only when the bodies of certain marginalized victims are at stake; it is not a question that is ever asked about "ordinary," fully included, and legally recognized citizens. Viewed in this light, the administration's statements of justification for torture are more than opportunistic excuses for extreme behavior. They are also a continuation of discourses of punishment that create maximum space for state violence within a liberal ethos. The repetition of state discourses about the treatment of bodies—specifically, discourses about the extent of harsh treatment permissible and the identities of its victims—is an important theme of the analysis in the following chapters.

The Convention against Torture, which the United States ratified in 1984, provides a definition of torture that would appear to restrict state actors seeking to inflict harsh treatment on persons in their custody. The convention defines "torture" as

> any act by which severe pain or suffering, whether physical or mental, is intentionally inflicted on a person for such purposes as obtaining from him or a third person information or a confession, punishing him for an act he or a third person has committed or is suspected of having committed, or intimidating or coercing him or a third person, or for any reason based on discrimination of any kind, when such pain or suffering is inflicted by or at the instigation of or with the consent or acquiescence of a public official or other person acting in an official capacity. It does not include pain or suffering arising only from, inherent in or incidental to lawful sanctions.[31]

This legal definition contains several points worth noting. First, it encompasses both physical and mental suffering, thereby contradicting the often-expressed claim that only physical pain amounts to torture. Psychological pain is explicitly recognized and included. Second, it recognizes that torture may be perpetrated for a number of different purposes, as I indicated previously (not only interrogation). Third, it requires that state actors be involved. While it is, of course, true that torturous acts occur outside the context of state actions, I am concerned here only with torture conducted, facilitated, or sponsored by the state. Fourth, the definition excludes "lawful" punishment from its definitional purview, creating a space for permissible infliction of severe pain authorized by law, and "insert[ing] local permissions and norms into what is meant to be an absolute prohibition."[32] As Dayan notes, this move shifts the inquiry from the kind of pain to the degree of pain, so that a range of tactics is permitted so long as they are not "taken too far." As noted, this "exception" threatens to swallow the rule so long as the sovereign is permitted to define the scope of the exception. If lawful punishment is an exception to the torture ban, then the sovereign will define its actions as lawful, thereby creating a "state of exception" authorizing torture. This was the project of the Bush administration.

The inclusiveness of the federal law definition is helpful in gaining a grasp on what sorts of practices ought to be prohibited, and that statute will appear in chapter 5, notwithstanding the fact that its explicit exception for "lawful" punishment raises problems that require much discussion, to be sure. Thus, all the examples provided in the following chapters involve state actors applying mental or physical harm to subjects for inquisitory, exemplary, and/or punitive ends. That description applies to a range of violent state actions in U.S. history: interrogation and killing of North Vietnamese by U.S. military and intelligence, lynching of African Americans, public punishment of slaves, treatment of Civil War prisoners, and the 1864 Sand Creek Massacre.

Those who argue for a precise definition of torture as an act involving physical pain are concerned with effective regulation. As Rejali puts it,

> There are good reasons to keep the commonplace distinction between psychological fears and physical pain, not the least of which because one would want to distinguish between torture and frivolous sentimental claims. If one does not distinguish between psychological fears of pain and pain itself, it is just as logical to argue that sticking someone's head under water is simply playing on their psychological fear of death. And when torture becomes such a slippery word, analytic discussion becomes meaningless.[33]

There are two points worth noting here. First, "frivolous sentimental claims" may diminish the significance of—or even trivialize—the pain produced by the many physical torture techniques Rejali documents. Second, just as "analytic discussion becomes meaningless," so does effective policy making become more difficult when slippage is permitted. Richard Posner, too, would keep the "physical" distinction in place when defining torture.[34] But current law already does define torture to include "mental pain or suffering": both the CAT and U.S. domestic law use those terms. A mock execution, for example, would clearly violate both the CAT and U.S. law prohibitions on torture. On the other hand, some of the conduct of U.S. military personnel at Abu Ghraib recorded on film—such as sexual humiliation—would not constitute torture under the legal definitions just cited.[35] It is reprehensible, to be sure, but it does not meet the existing legal definition of torture (the mock electrocutions that were also photographed, by contrast, would meet that definition). So it appears that limiting "torture" to mean "physical violence only" would actually require a *narrowing* of existing law.

In contrast to those who define torture by focusing on the infliction of severe pain, Parry suggests viewing it on a "continuum" of state violence. Presumably, his conceptualization would require us to look at use of threats, use of lesser pain, and use of fear and aversion. In addition to more iconic manifestations, then, for Parry torture includes "also the infliction of potentially escalating pain for purposes that include dominating the victim and ascribing responsibility to the victim for the pain incurred." With this modification, Parry hopes to avoid "exoticizing" torture, which can happen when the term is reserved for the most extreme and shocking events—events that happen in secret or happen in faraway places.[36] Instead, the "continuum" approach reminds us of the state violence that happens around us, here in the United States, in the varied contexts visited by the documents reproduced in following chapters of this book. Techniques used at Abu Ghraib that did not produce severe pain and techniques such as "walling" (chapter 5) that are intended to suggest greater violence than what is actually happening are more easily addressed using Parry's approach. The virtue of his approach is that it shows "a kinship between torture and forms of domination that rely on discipline instead of pain. If there is such a kinship, then torture is not exceptional conduct that belongs in a separate category, and the torture/not-torture distinction can no longer be used to legitimate lesser forms of state violence"[37]

Where does this leave us as we try to regulate state violence? We can address practices that are objectionable but fall short of severe pain; we can punish acts that we find reprehensible, even if they are not the worst that can be done to a person. Sanford Levinson reminds us that drawing any line to mark off torture from other practices necessarily means that one "must be willing to defend quite awful conduct that comes right up to the line."[38] The line drawn by the continuum approach is a line that can be adjusted to prohibit an increasing range of actions as we discover and understand them.

Beyond Definitions

While it is necessary to discuss legal definitions of torture before undertaking an analysis of specific torture incidents, one hesitates to settle on a fixed definition in view of the interpretive parsing engaged in by U.S. policy makers over the past twenty-five years. Philosopher Jeremy Waldron has suggested that "there is something wrong with trying to pin down the prohibition on torture with a precise legal definition." The reason that a "precise legal definition" was so important to the Bush administration, of course, was that it needed to green-light certain interrogation practices by calling them something short of torture. "Insisting on exact definitions may sound very lawyerly," Waldron cautions, "but there is something disturbing about it when the quest for precision is put to work in the service of a mentality that says, 'Give us a definition so we have something to work around, something to game, a determinate envelope to push.'"[39] Waldron suggests that inquiries into what constitutes torture, or what forms of state violence are out of bounds, should be guided by what he calls a "legal archetype" rather than a definitional exercise. The anti-torture archetype draws on a range of beliefs about the way individuals are to be respected in their personhood and about the limits of state intrusion on people's bodily integrity. Viewed this way, the question of whether to torture, or what the term *torture* means, goes deeper than positive (statutory) law and asks about the role of law in society and about what sort of people and what sort of community to be. It is not merely a matter of drawing a line between torture and "mere" cruelty, as the Bush administration would have it, but rather of determining what kinds of cruelty have been possible (and actualized) in our world, now and in the past, and what they suggest about a state that decides to employ them.

Outline of the Work

I will excerpt and annotate public, government documents that address torture in some way. Each set of documents is grouped according to historical period:

Colonial North America and the early republic
Slavery and the frontier
Imperialism, Jim Crow, and world war
Vietnam, the Cold War, and police abuse
The post-9/11 war on terror

The documents all originate from government sources, such as formal attorney general opinions, internal executive branch policy memos, and military reports and orders. The common feature of all the documents collected is that they represent the stance of someone in government vis-à-vis torture as a tool of state power. The authors of the documents may be opposed to torture or supportive of it; they may focus on legal constraints or on negative public opinion; they may define torture differently. In any event, I am interested in the development of official attitudes toward torture and the continuities and discontinuities of that development. In one sense, limiting the study to government documents is a challenge, for governments do not always acknowledge torture and other violent practices. At the same time, though, state documents provide a solid ground for study of torture and state violence because when they do exist, they provide a record that is not in doubt. The documents themselves will be reproduced in excerpt or in their entirety in the work, and each chapter presents the documents in their historical context through brief annotations. I follow the example of Richard Hofstadter's study, *American Violence: A Documentary History*, in my presentation style here. The format of my study—primary source documents preceded by annotations—will be similar to that of *American Violence*.

The Potential for Conflict between Human Rights and Democracy

Through the documents included and their annotations, this documentary history will encompass two concepts that are central to modern political philosophy: popular sovereignty and human rights. These concepts figure prominently in the legal history of state violence. Popular sovereignty generates, through positive (statutory) law, binding legal mandates for government conduct, and state actors are constrained by them. On the other hand, popular sovereignty can license the government to act in ways previously thought illegal. The PATRIOT Act, passed a month after the September 11 attacks, is an example of legislative action expanding the space for lawful exercise of state force. It is familiar, now, to observers of U.S. government activity after 9/11 that the PATRIOT Act raised questions about constitutional rights by expanding government search authority, limiting the right to freedom of association, and compromising due process by limiting grand jury secrecy, to take a few examples.[40] Thus, congressional action in passing the PATRIOT Act conflicted with settled understandings of individual rights.

Another example is the Military Commissions Act, which was passed in response to the Supreme Court's decision outlawing the Bush administration's military commissions. The administration had been struggling with the Court over the use of military commissions, and the 2006 *Hamdan* case outlawed the commissions established by President Bush's 2001 military order because they violated the Uniform Code of Military Justice, the Law of War, and the Geneva Conventions. But the *Hamdan* ruling left open the possibility that Congress could, in the future, authorize commissions that operated as the president wanted them to; they were simply illegal under then-existing law. In October 2006, Congress authorized by statute what the Supreme Court had found illegal based on previously existing law. Thus, popular sovereignty once again trumped human rights and allowed the administration to exercise its will through the procedures of majoritarian democratic law making, even if the result was to alter the prior boundary of an individual right.

The concept of popular sovereignty lies at the core of democratic government, and it dictates that the will of the majority expressed through legitimate voting procedures determines political outcomes. The concept of human rights, relying as it does on the Enlightenment view of the importance of protecting the autonomy of the individual reasoning subject, is necessarily antecedent to any particular legislative outcome. The idea that human rights ought to be protected, too, is a central tenet of modern liberalism. Tension results when a legislative enactment conflicts with the principle of inviolable individual right, and the need arises to adjudicate between the two. While this tension has been explored in works of political philosophy generally, it has not been examined in the context of torture. The documents that follow will generate questions about the relationship between popular sovereignty and human rights when the state utilizes torture or other state violence in particular situations. What do the officially expressed attitudes toward torture mean for American political development? How might critics of torture respond to those official statements? In what ways might the rights-sovereignty tension be productive of some of the excessive force and brutality seen in contemporary torture practices?

Aims of This Work

In the end, I hope that this study will provide two things. First, I want to correct the view that the current U.S. torture practices have recent origins. They did not start with the military personnel who used them, or even with the Bush administration, which authorized them. Rather, they continue trends in modern state practices that permit extreme uses of force against some subjects in some circumstances. Extreme force is condemned in theory but employed and accepted in practice. In view of the documented history of state brutality that follows, one could easily conclude that a "permanent state of exception" exists within the law-bounded regime of American government.[41]

Second, further exploration of torture in modern political theory could contribute to a necessary rethinking of the place of torture (and state force generally) in anti-terror policy. Many experts say that torture is not an effective means to obtaining useful intelligence; therefore, the results of torture belie its purported justifications. These practical arguments are important responses to Alan Dershowitz and others who advocate torture on utilitarian grounds: that torture is warranted when it could save many lives by revealing, for example, the location of a ticking time bomb.[42] But if such a scenario is not plausible, or if torture would not in fact "save the day," then the consequentialist case based in efficacy falls apart. In addition to practical arguments, though, we need a fuller response to the exigency-based justifications for torture that often sound tempting to a fearful public. In other words, if a choice is posed between mass casualties on the one hand and torture-interrogation of a terrorist that saves innocent lives on the other, there needs to be a clear understanding of what the state surrenders when it resorts to torture in such a case. Otherwise, it is all too easy for the observer to say, perhaps with regret, that torture is necessary and even unavoidable. Here, it is important to show how a ban on torture is symbolic of a commitment to a whole set of ideas about how human beings may be treated, and how transgression of that ban places the larger commitment in jeopardy, threatening to replace a "liberal culture" with a "torture culture."[43]

Notes

1. Judith Shklar, "The Liberalism of Fear," in Nancy Rosenblum, ed., *Liberalism and the Moral Life* (Cambridge, MA: Harvard University Press, 1989), p. 21.

2. Nancy Rosenblum, introduction to Rosenblum, *Liberalism and the Moral Life*, p. 2.

3. Shklar, "The Liberalism of Fear," p. 21.

4. Ibid., p. 27.

5. Ibid., p. 37.

6. Darius Rejali, *Torture and Democracy* (Princeton: Princeton University Press, 2007).

7. Daniel Rothenberg, "Commentary: 'What We Have Seen Has Been Terrible': Public Presentational Torture and the Communicative Logic of State Terror," 67 *Albany Law Review* 477 (2003).

8. Ibid., p. 481.

9. Modern political leaders are careful to condemn torture regardless of what is actually occurring. President Bush condemned torture publicly; so did Teddy Roosevelt in document 3.15. Kate Millett points out that even Stalin operated under a public ban on capital punishment while torture and executions took place in secret. Millett, *The Politics of Cruelty* (New York: Norton, 1994), p. 30.

10. Thomas P. Crocker, "Overcoming Necessity: Torture and the State of Constitutional Culture," 61 *Southern Methodist Law Review* 221, 230 (2008).

11. Article I, Section 9, Paragraph 2 states, "The Privilege of the Writ of Habeas Corpus shall not be suspended, unless when in Cases of Rebellion or Invasion the public Safety may require it."

12. *Boumediene v. Bush*, 128 S.Ct. 2229, 2259 (2008).

13. Crocker, "Overcoming Necessity," p. 244.

14. John T. Parry, "What Is Torture, Are We Doing It, and What If We Are?" 64 *University of Pittsburgh Law Review* 237, 251 (Winter 2003).

15. John T. Parry, "Fighting Terrorism with Torture: Where to Draw the Line?" 1 *Journal of National Security Law and Policy* 253, 276 (2005).

16. Gunter Frankenberg, "Torture and Taboo: An Essay Comparing Paradigms of Organized Cruelty," 56 *American Journal of Comparative Law* 403, 407 (2008).

17. *Rochin v. California*, 342 U.S. 165, 172 (1952).

18. Frankenberg, "Torture and Taboo," p. 414.

19. Alfred McCoy, *A Question of Torture* (New York: Henry Holt, 2006).

20. Paul Gilroy, *The Black Atlantic: Modernity and the Double Consciousness* (Cambridge, MA: Harvard University Press, 1993), p. 118.

21. David Svaldi, *Sand Creek and the Rhetoric of Extermination: A Case Study in Indian-White Relations* (Lanham, MD: University Press of America, 1989).

22. David Luban, "Liberalism, Torture and the Ticking Bomb," 91 *Virginia Law Review* 1425, 1432 (2005).

23. Indeed, the military personnel charged with offenses at Abu Ghraib explained that their actions were taken "just for fun." Parry, "Fighting Terrorism with Torture: Where to Draw the Line?" p. 253.

24. The photographs can be viewed at www.withoutsanctuary.org (accessed January 8, 2010).

25. Richard Posner, "Torture, Terrorism and Interrogation," in Sanford Levinson, ed., *Torture: A Collection* (Oxford: Oxford University Press, 2004), p. 295. Judge Posner is not the only one to take this view.

26. Memo of Jay Bybee to Alberto Gonzales, available at www.washingtonpost.com/wp-srv/politics/documents/cheney/torture_memo_aug2002.pdf (accessed January 2, 2008).

27. Harold Hongju Koh, "A World without Torture," 43 *Columbia Journal of Transnational Law* 641, 647 (2005). Among its failings, according to Koh, the memo defines torture in a way that conflicts with the "plain meaning" of the term, it misstates the nature of the commander in chief power, and it ignores the "landmark" Supreme Court precedent on congressional limitation on presidential power, *Youngstown Sheet and Tube v. Sawyer.*

28. See discussion of the Bybee memo, document 5.2 in chapter 5.

29. Omer Ze'ev Bekerman, "Torture: The Absolute Prohibition of a Relative Term; Does Everyone Know What Is in Room 101?" 53 *American Journal of Comparative Law* 743, 774 (2005).

30. Colin Dayan, *The Story of Cruel and Unusual* (Cambridge, MA: Boston Review, 2007).

31. The Convention against Torture, available at www.un.org (accessed December 30, 2007).

32. Bekerman, "Torture: The Absolute Prohibition of a Relative Term; Does Everyone Know What Is in Room 101?" p. 751.

33. Rejali, *Torture and Democracy*, p. 382.

34. Posner, "Torture, Terrorism and Interrogation," p. 292.

35. Sanford Levinson makes this point in "Fighting Terrorism with Torture: Where to Draw the Line?" 1 *Journal of National Security Law and Policy* 231, 234 (2005).

36. Parry, "Fighting Terrorism with Torture," pp. 257–59.

37. Ibid. p. 275.

38. Levinson, introduction to *Torture: A Collection*, p. 39.

39. Jeremy Waldron, "Torture and Positive Law: Jurisprudence for the White House," 105 *Columbia Law Review* 1681, 1687 (2005).

40. For a discussion of the effect of the PATRIOT Act and other post-9/11 legislation on the contours of constitutional rights, see chapter 4 of Robert Pallitto, and William Weaver, *Presidential Secrecy and the Law* (Baltimore: Johns Hopkins University Press, 2007).

41. See Mark Salter, "The Global Visa Regime and the Political Technologies of the International Self: Borders, Bodies, Biopolitics," *Alternatives: Global, Local Political*, 3, no. 2 (2006): 167–89.

42. Alan Dershowitz, *Shouting Fire: Civil Liberties in a Turbulent Age* (New York: Little Brown, 2002).

43. Waldron's notion of a "legal archetype" captures this point extremely well. The "liberal culture" and "torture culture" formulations come from Luban, "Liberalism, Torture and the Ticking Bomb," p. 1461, at n. 21.

The documents in this chapter include colonial statutes, records of the War of Independence, constitutional debates, and judicial proceedings in the early republic. The word *torture* is usually used with condemnation, but other violent actions not referred to as "torture" (e.g., lynching) are carried out. In correspondence, Benjamin Franklin, John Adams, and George Washington hint at "retaliation" for what we would now call British "war crimes," but they do not specify what that retaliation would be. Notwithstanding the vagueness and ambivalence of statements by Franklin et al., the Continental Congress resolved to respond in kind to British treatment of prisoners of war and noncombatants.

1.1 Massachusetts Body of Liberties, 1641

Considered an important document in the development of individual rights, the Massachusetts Body of Liberties specifies the rights of the accused, procedural and substantive, in significant detail. It is noteworthy, however, that even in this enumeration of rights, torture is explicitly permitted in certain cases, as long as such torture is not "barbarous or cruel."

"Then he may be tortured"

40. No Conveyance, Deede, or promise whatsoever shall be of validitie, If it be gotten by Illegal violence, imprisonment, threatening, or any kinde of forcible compulsion called Dures.

41. Everie man that is to Answere for any criminall cause, whether he be in prison or under bayle, his cause shall be heard and determined at the next Court that hath proper Cognizance thereof, And may be done without prejudice of Justice.

42. No man shall be twise sentenced by Civill Justice for one and the same Crime, offence, or Trespasse.

43. No man shall be beaten with above 40 stripes, nor shall any true gentleman, nor any man equall to a gentleman be punished with whipping, unles his crime be very shamefull, and his course of life vitious and profligate.

44. No man condemned to dye shall be put to death within fower dayes next after his condemnation, unles the Court see spetiall cause to the contrary, or in case of martiall law, nor shall the body of any man so put to death be unburied 12 howers unlesse it be in case of Anatomie.

45. No man shall be forced by Torture to confesse any Crime against himselfe nor any other unlesse it be in some Capitall case, where he is first fullie convicted by cleare and suffitient evidence to be guilty, After which if the cause be of that nature, That it is very apparent there be other conspiratours, or confederates with him, Then he may be tortured, yet not with such Tortures as be Barbarous and inhumane.

46. For bodilie punishments we allow amongst us none that are inhumane Barbarous or cruel.

47. No man shall be put to death without the testimony of two or three witnesses or that which is equivalent thereunto.

Source: Massachusetts Library, http://history.hanover.edu/texts/masslib.htm

1.2 Laws of the Maryland Colony, 1642

The Assembly of the Colony of Maryland passed a law providing for corporal punishment by dismemberment in cases of assault, forgery, and perjury. Public drunkenness was also punishable by corporal punishment, though less severely.

"To any other corporall shame or correction"

An Act for Punishmt of Some Offences not Capitall

Any person striking an Officer, Juror, or Witness in Presence of the Court, or striking any other person with a drawn weapon in the presence of the Court, or striking any Magistrate of highe Sheriff of a county in or for the doing of his office, or counterfeiting the hand or signe manuall, or any of the Seales of the Lord Proprietary within his Lopps. Iurisdiction to the preiudice of another, or willfully falsifying corrupting or embesilling of a record or giving false witness upon oath in Court, or perswading or hiring another to give such false witness; may be judged to lose his, or her right hand, or to be burned in the hand, or to any other corporall shame or correction (not extending to life) or be fined as the Court shall see fitt. This Act to endure for three yeares from this present day.

An Act for the punishment of drunkennesse

Every one convicted of being drunk (to be determined by the Judge) by or before any sworne Judge by view of the judge, confession of the partie or testimony of two sworne witnesses, shall forfeite one hundred weight of tobacco toward the building of a prison or such pulique use as the Lord Proprietary or his Liuetent Generall shall think good. Or if the offender be a servant and have not wherewith to satisfie the fine, he shalbe imprisoned, or sett in the stocks, or bilboes fasting for four & twenty houres. This Act to endure for three yeares from the present day.

Source: Maryland archives, http://aomol.net/megafile/msa/speccol/sc2900/sc2908/000001/000001/html/am1-193.html

---

1.3 Death Warrant of Bridget Bishop, 1692

Bridget Bishop was the first known North American to be executed for the crime of witchcraft. Her alleged crime was that she afflicted the bodies of her fellow townspeople with spells, at various unspecified times. She was hanged at Salem in 1692. After her death, Bishop's body was examined for signs that she was, indeed, a witch.

"Their bodyes were hurt afflicted pined, consumed Wasted and tormented"

To George Corwin Gent^m high Sheriffe of the County of Essex. Greeting.

Whereas Bridgett Bishop als Oliver the wife of Edward Bishop of Salem in the County of Essex, Sawyer, at a speciall court of Oyer and Terminer held at Salem the second Day of this instant month of June for the Countyes of Essex' Middlesex' and Suffolk before William Stoughton Esqr and his Associate Justices of the said Court was Indicted and arraigned upon five severall Indictments for useing practiceing and exercising on the nyneteenth day of April last past and divers other dayes and time before and after certain acts of Witchcraft in and upon the bodyes of Abigail Williams Ann puttnam Junr Mercy Lewis Mary Walcott and Elizabeth Hubbard of Salem Village Single-women whereby their bodyes were hurt afflicted pined, consumed Wasted and tormented contrary to the forme of the Statute in that Case made and provided.

To which Indictm^ss the said Bridgett Bishop pleaded not guilty and for tryall thereof put herselfe upon God and her Country whereupon she was found guilty of the felonys and witchcrafts whereof she stood Indicted and sentence of Death accordingly passed ag^t her as the Law, directs.

Execution where of yet remains to be done.

These are therefore in the name of their Maj^{ties} William and Mary now King and Queen over England &c to will and Comand you That upon Fryday next being the Tenth day of this instant month of June betweene the hours of Eight and twelve in the aforenoon of the same day you safely conduct the sd Bridget Bishop als Oliver from their Maj^{ties} Goal in Salem aforesd to the place of Execution and there cause her to be hanged by the neck untill she be dead. and of your doings herein make returne to the Clerke of the sd Court and p^{s}cept.

And hereof you are not to faile at your peril.

And this shall be your sufficient Warrant. Given under my hand and seal at Boston the Eighth day of June in the fourth yeer of the Reigne of our Sovereigne Lord and Lady William and Mary now King and Queen over England &c Annoq Dom 1692.

Wm. Stoughton

June 10th ==1692

According to the within Written precept I have taken the body of the within named Brigett Bishop out of theire Majesties Goale in Salem and Safely Conveighed her to the place provided for her Execution and caused y^e sd Brigett to be hanged by the neck until shee was dead all which was according to the time within Required and So I make Returne by me

George Corwin Sheriff.

Source: University of Virginia archives, http://etext.lib.virginia.edu/salem/witchcraft/ archives/ (Courtesy of the Boston Public Library/Rare Books)

1.4 Articles of War, 1775

The Continental Congress enacted the Articles of War in 1775, a precursor of the Uniform Code of Military Justice, which continues in force to the present day. Its importance as a body of law governing the conduct of U.S. military forces would be seen repeatedly, from the Civil War through the prosecution of the Nazi saboteurs in 1942 and 1944 and in the detainees' rights cases following 9/11. The 1775 version of the statute expressly provided for corporal punishment of soldiers, in the form of whipping.

"Whipping not exceeding thirty-nine lashes"

FRIDAY, JUNE 30, 1775

The Congress met according to adjournment.

The consideration of the articles of war being resumed, Congress agreed to the same:

Rules and Regulations

Whereas his Majesty's most faithful subjects in these Colonies are reduced to a dangerous and critical situation, by the attempts of the British Ministry, to carry into execution, by force of arms, several unconstitutional and oppressive acts of the British parliament for laying taxes in America, to enforce the collection of these taxes, and for altering and changing the constitution and internal police of some of these Colonies, in violation of the natural and civil rights of the Colonies.

And whereas hostilities have been actually commenced in Massachusetts Bay, by the British troops, under the command of General Gage, and the lives of a number of the inhabitants of that Colony destroyed; the town of Boston not only having been long occupied as a garrisoned town in an enemy's country, but the inhabitants thereof treated with a severity and cruelty not to be justified even towards declared enemies.

And whereas large reinforcements have been ordered, and are soon expected, for the declared purpose of compelling these Colonies to submit to the operation of the said acts, which hath rendered it necessary, and an indispensable duty, for the express purpose of securing and defending these Colonies, and preserving them in safety against all attempts to carry the said acts into execution; that an armed force be raised sufficient to defeat such hostile designs, and preserve and defend the lives, liberties and immunities of the Colonists: for the due regulating and well ordering of which;-

Resolved, That the following Rules and Orders be attended to, and observed by such forces as are or may hereafter be raised for the purposes aforesaid. . . .

Art. XXXVII. The commissioned officers of every regiment may, by the appointment of their Colonel or commanding officer, hold regimental courts-martial for the enquiring into such disputes or criminal mutters as may come before them, and for the inflicting corporal punishment, for small offences, and shall give judgment by the majority of voices; but no sentence shall be executed till the commanding officer (not being a member of the court-martial) shall have confirmed the same. . . .

Art. LI. That no persons shall be sentenced by a court-martial to suffer death, except in the cases expressly mentioned in the foregoing articles; nor shall any punishment be inflicted at the discretion of a court-martial, other than degrading, cashiering, drumming out of the army, whipping not exceeding thirty-nine lashes, fine not exceeding two months pay of the offender, imprisonment not exceeding one month.

Source: Avalon Project, http://avalon.law.yale.edu/18th_century/contcong_06-30-75 .asp

---

1.5 Letter from George Washington to the Continental Congress, 1776

In a report to the Continental Congress on an incident in which British troops killed surrendering members of the Continental army, General George Washington seeks action from the Congress but also warns that he will retaliate if such conduct by the British continues. Like many of the documents in this collection, Washington's letter expresses a distaste for the future extralegal violence, even as he suggests that it may be necessary.

"However abhorrent and disagreeable to our natures in cases of Torture and Capital Punishments"

The Cedars

I was this morning honoured with yours of the 13th. instant, with its important and necessary Inclosures, and in Obedience to the Commands of Congress have transmitted General Howe, the Resolves intended for him. Those for General Burgoyne I Inclosed and sent to General Schuyler with directions immediately to forward to him. The Inhuman Treatment to the whole, and Murder of part of our People after their Surrender and Capitulation, was certainly a flagrant violation of that Faith which ought to be held sacred by all civilized nations, and founded in the most Savage barbarity. It highly deserved the severest reprobation, and I trust the Spirited Measures Congress have adopted upon the Occasion, will prevent the like in future: But if they should not, and the claims of humanity are disregarded, Justice and Policy will require recourse to be had to the Law of retaliation, however abhorrent and disagreeable to our natures in cases of Torture and Capital Punishments. I have &ca.

Source: American Memory, Library of Congress, http://memory.loc.gov/ammem/ gwhtml/gwhome.html

1.6 Letter from John Adams, Benjamin Franklin, and Arthur Lee to Vergennes, January 1, 1779

Adams, Franklin, and Lee appeal to the French for intervention after the British government announced "a change in the whole nature and conduct of the war." The writers express concern that the British have already committed acts of brutality during a professed period of "benevolence," so that the proposed change could only mean more extreme acts of brutality. Once again, the writers warn that the Continental army will "retaliate," though no specifics are given.

"All the horrors of the barbarous ages may be introduced and justified"

Sir: Some late proceedings of the enemy have induced us to submit a few observations to your excellency's superior light and judgment.

His Britannic Majesty's commissioners, in their manifesto of the 3d of October, have denounced "a change in the whole nature and future conduct of the war;" they have declared "that the policy as well as the benevolence of Great Britain has thus far checked the extremes of war," when they tended "to distress the people and desolate the country"; that the whole contest is changed; that the laws of self-preservation must now direct the conduct of Great Britain; that these laws will direct her to render the United States of as little avail as possible to France if they are to become an accession to her, and by every means in her power to destroy the new connection contrived for her ruin. Motions have been made and supported by the wisest men in both Houses of Parliament to address the king to disavow these clauses; but these motions have been rejected by majorities in both Houses, so that the manifesto stands avowed by the three branches of the legislature.

Ministers of state made in Parliament a question concerning the meaning of this manifesto, but no man who reads it and knows the history of their past conduct in this war can doubt its import. There is to be a "change in the nature and conduct of the war." A change for the worse must be horrible indeed! They have already burned the beautiful towns of Charlestown, Falmouth, Norfolk, Kingston, Bedford, Egg Harbor, and German Flats, besides innumerable single buildings and smaller clusters of houses wherever their armies have marched. It is true they left Boston and Philadelphia unhurt; but in all probability it was merely the dread of a superior army that in these cases restrained their hands, not to mention that burning these towns would have been the ruin of the few secret friends they have still left, of whom there are more in those towns than in all America besides. They have not, indeed, murdered upon the spot every woman and child that fell in their way, nor have they in all cases refused quarter to the soldiers that at times have fallen into their power, though they have in many. They have also done their utmost in seducing negroes and Indians to commit inhuman barbarities upon the inhabitants, sparing neither age, sex, nor character. Although they have not in all cases refused quarter to soldiers and sailors, they have done what is worse than refusing quarter—they have thrust their prisoners into such dungeons, loaded them with such irons, and exposed them to such lingering torments of cold, hunger, and disease, as have destroyed greater numbers than they could have had an opportunity of murdering if they had made it a rule to give no quarter. Many others they have compelled by force to serve and fight on board their ships against fathers, brothers, friends, and countrymen—a destiny to every sensible mind more terrible than death itself.

It is therefore difficult to apprehend what they mean by a change in the conduct of the war; yet there seems to be no room to doubt that they mean to threaten something more cruel, greater extremes of war, measures that shall distress the people and lay waste the country more than anything they have yet done. The object of the war is now entirely changed. Heretofore their massacres and conflagrations were to divide us and reclaim us to Great Britain. Now, despairing of that end, and perceiving that we shall be faithful to our treaties, their principle is by destroying us to make us useless to France. This principle ought to be held in abhorrence not only by all Christians, but by all civilized nations. If it is once admitted that powers at war have a right to do whatever will weaken or terrify an enemy, it is not possible to foresee where it will end. It would be possible to burn the great cities of Europe. The savages who torture their prisoners do it to make themselves terrible. In fine, all the horrors of the barbarous ages may be introduced and justified.

The cruelties of our enemies have heretofore more than once exasperated the minds of the people so much as to excite apprehensions that they would proceed to retaliation, which, if once commenced, might be carried to extremities; to prevent which the Congress issued an address exhorting to forbearance and a further trial by examples of generosity and lenity to recall their enemies to the practice of humanity amidst the calamities of war. In consequence of which neither the Congress nor any of the States apart have ever exercised or authorized the exercise of the right of retaliation. But now that commissioners, vested with the authority of the nation, have avowed such principles and published such threats, the Congress have, by a resolution of the 30th of October, solemnly and unanimously declared that they will retaliate. Whatever may be the pretenses of the enemy, it is the manifest drift of their policy to disgust the people of America with their new alliance, by attempting to convince them that, instead of shielding them from distress, it has accumulated additional calamities upon them.

Nothing, certainly, can more become a great and amiable character than to disappoint their purpose, stop the progress of their cruelties, and vindicate the rights of humanity, which are so much injured by this manifesto. We therefore beg leave to suggest to your excellency's consideration whether it would not be advisable for his majesty to interfere, by some declaration to the court of London and to the world, bearing the royal testimony against this barbarous mode of war, and giving assurances that he will join the United States in retaliation, if Great Britain, by putting her threats in execution, should make it necessary. There is another measure, however, more effectual to control their designs and to bring the war to a speedy conclusion; that of sending a powerful fleet, sufficient to secure a naval superiority over them in the American seas. Such a naval force, acting in concert with the armies of the United States, would, in all human probability, take and destroy the whole British power in that part of the world.

We are the more earnest in representing these things to your excellency, as all our correspondence from England for some time has uniformly represented that the intention of the cabinet is conformable to the spirit of the manifesto; that all parties grow more and more out of temper with the Americans; that it has become fashionable with the minority as well as the majority and administration to reproach us both in and out of Parliament; that all parties join in speaking of us in the bitterest terms and in heartily wishing our destruction; that great clamors are raised about our alliance with France as an unnatural combination to ruin them; that the cry is for a speedy and powerful reenforcement of their army and for the activity of their fleet in making descents on the seacoast, while murdering and desolating parties are let loose upon the frontiers of the Carolinas, Virginia, Pennsylvania, New Jersey, New York, and New England, and that very early in the year they will carry all these projects into execution. The whole system may, as we conceive, be defeated and the power of Great Britain now in America totally subdued (and if their power is subdued there, it is reduced everywhere) by the measure we have the honor to propose.

We submit the whole merely as our opinion to your excellency's superior wisdom.

And have the honor to be, etc.,

B. Franklin

Arthur Lee

John Adams

Source: American Memory, Library of Congress, http://memory.loc.gov/ammem/
amlaw/lawhome.html

1.7 Bill for Proportioning Crimes and Punishments, 1779

*That Thomas Jefferson produced volume upon volume of writings cover-
ing subjects ranging from descriptions of Virginia's waterways to model
statutes is well known. His "Bill for Proportioning Crimes and Punishments" represents, in Jefferson's words, an attempt to coordinate crimes
with appropriate punishments so that rehabilitation of offenders might be
possible. This progressive goal is strikingly at odds with some of the actual
punishments prescribed in the model legislation: castration, mutilation of
a woman's nose, and death by poison, for example.*

"By cutting through the cartilage of her nose"

Whereas, it frequently happens that wicked and dissolute men, resigning
themselves to the dominion of inordinate passions, commit violations on
the lives, liberties and property of others, and, the secure enjoyment of these
having principally induced men to enter into society, government would be
defective in its principal purpose, were it not to restrain such criminal acts, by
inflicting due punishments on those who perpetrate them; but it appears, at
the same time, equally deducible from the purposes of society, that a member
thereof, committing an inferior injury, does not wholly forfeit the protection
of his fellow citizens, but, after suffering a punishment in proportion to his
offence, is entitled to their protection from all greater pain, so that it becomes
a duty in the legislature to arrange, in a proper scale, the crimes which it may
be necessary for them to repress, and to adjust thereto a corresponding gra-
dation of punishments.

And whereas, the reformation of offenders, though an object worthy the
attention of the laws, is not effected at all by capital punishments, which ex-
terminate instead of reforming, and should be the last melancholy resource
against those whose existence is become inconsistent with the safety of their
fellow citizens, which also weaken the State, by cutting off so many who, if
reformed, might be restored sound members to society, who, even under a
course of correction, might be rendered useful in various labors for the public, and would be living and long-continued spectacles to deter others from
committing the like offences.

And forasmuch as the experience of all ages and countries hath shown
that cruel and sanguinary laws defeat their own purpose, by engaging the be-

nevolence of mankind to withhold prosecutions, to smother testimony, or to listen to it with bias, when, if the punishment were only proportioned to the injury, men would feel it their inclination, as well as their duty, to see the laws observed.

For rendering crimes and punishments, therefore, more proportionate to each other:

Be it enacted by the General Assembly, that no crime shall be henceforth punished by the deprivation of life or limb, except those hereinafter ordained to be so punished.

If a man do levy war against the Commonwealth [in the same], or is adherent to the enemies of the Commonwealth [within the same], giving to them aid or comfort in the commonwealth, or elsewhere, and thereof be convicted of open deed, by the evidence of two sufficient witnesses, or his own voluntary confession, the said cases, and no other, shall be adjudged treasons which extend to the Commonwealth, and the person so convicted shall suffer death, by hanging, and shall forfeit his lands and goods to the Commonwealth.

If any person commits petty treason, or a husband murder his wife, a parent his child, or a child his parent, he shall suffer death by hanging, and his body be delivered to anatomists to be dissected.

Whosoever committeth murder by poisoning shall suffer death by poison.

Whosoever committeth murder by way of duel shall suffer death by hanging; and if he were the challenger, his body, after death, shall be gibbeted. He who removeth it from the gibbet shall be guilty of a misdemeanor; and the officer shall see that it be replaced.

Whosoever shall commit murder in any other way shall suffer death by hanging. . . .

Whosoever shall be guilty of rape, polygamy, or sodomy with man or woman, shall be punished, if a man, by castration, if a woman, by cutting through the cartilage of her nose a hole of one half inch diameter at the least.

But no one shall be punished for polygamy, who shall have married after probable information of the death of his or her husband or wife, or after his or her husband or wife, hath absented him or herself, so that no notice of his or her being alive hath reached such person for seven years together, or hath suffered the punishments before prescribed for rape, polygamy or sodomy.

Whosoever on purpose, and of malice aforethought, shall maim another, or shall disfigure him, by cutting out or disabling the tongue, slitting or cutting off a nose, lip or ear, branding or otherwise, shall be maimed, or disfigured in like sort: or if that cannot be, for want of the same part, then as nearly as may be, in some other part of at least equal value and estimation, in the opinion of a jury, and moreover, shall forfeit one half of his lands and goods to the sufferer.

Source: Thomas Jefferson, *Basic Writings of Thomas Jefferson*, ed. Philip Foner
(Garden City: Halcyon House, 1944), pp. 29–34

1.8 Bill concerning Slaves, 1779

*Thomas Jefferson drafted a companion statute to the Bill for Proportioning
Crimes and Punishments applicable to slaves. He makes a point to note
several times the circumstances in which slaves will be considered to be
"out of the protection of the laws." This phrase is strikingly reminiscent of
Dayan's discussion, in* The Story of Cruel and Unusual, *of those persons
who are "dead to the law." In Jefferson's model statute, slaves can receive
corporal punishment simply for traveling "without a pass."*

"Out of the protection of the laws"

Section I. Be it enacted in the General Assembly, that no persons shall,
henceforth, be slaves within this commonwealth, except as such were so on
the first day of this present session of the Assembly, and the descendants of
the females of them.

Section II. Negroes and mulattoes who shall hereafter be brought into this
commonwealth and kept therein one whole year, together, or so long at different times as shall amount to one year, shall be free. But if they shall not
depart the commonwealth within one year thereafter they shall be out of the
protection of the laws.

Section III. Those which shall come into this commonwealth of their own
accord shall be out of the protection of the laws; save only such as being sea-
faring persons and navigating vessels hither, shall not leave the same while
here more than twenty four hours together. . . .

Section V. If any white woman shall have a child by a Negro or mulatto,
she and her child shall depart the commonwealth within one year thereafter.
If they shall fail to do so, the woman shall be out of the protection of the laws,
and the child shall be bound out by the Aldermen of the county, in like manner as poor orphans are by law directed to be, and within one year after its
terms of service expired shall depart the commonwealth, or on failure to do
so, shall be out of the protection of the laws. . . .

Section VIII. No slave shall go from the tenements of his master, or other
person with whom he lives, without a pass, or some letter or token whereby
it may appear that he is proceeding by authority of his master, employer, or
overseer: If he does, it shall be lawful for any person to apprehend and carry

him before a Justice of the Peace, to be by his order punished with stripes, or not in his direction. . . .

Section X. Riots, routs, unlawful assemblies, trespasses and seditious speeches by Negro or mulatto shall be punished with stripes at the discretion of a Justice of the Peace; and he who will may apprehend and carry him before such a Justice.

Source: Thomas Jefferson, *Basic Writings of Thomas Jefferson*, ed. Philip Foner (Garden City: Halcyon House, 1944), pp. 28–29

1.9 Proclamation of the Continental Congress, April 7, 1781

In stating how prisoners were to be treated on the high seas, the Continental Congress specifically forbade not only torture but also "cruel" and "inhuman" treatment. This pairing of torture with cruel and inhuman treatment persists today, where it creates various legal-definitional quandaries. For example, the 1984 Convention against Torture, which is covered in chapter 4, prohibits torture and cruel, inhuman, and degrading treatment. However, it defines only torture, while leaving the other categories undefined. In adopting the treaty language into U.S. law, Congress similarly failed to define those terms. This omission makes it difficult for a victim to make out a claim for CAT violation short of torture.

"The practice of civilized nations in war"

Be it ordained, and it is hereby ordained, by the United States in Congress assembled, that the following instructions be observed by the captains or commanders of private armed vessels commissioned by letters of marque or general reprisals, or otherwise, by the authority of the United States in Congress assembled:

» I. You may by force of arms attack, subdue, and seize all ships, vessels and goods, belonging to the King or Crown of Great Britain, or to his subjects, or others inhabiting within any of the territories or possessions of the aforesaid King of Great Britain, on the high seas, or between high-water and low-water marks. And you may also annoy the enemy by all means in your power, by land as well as by water, taking care not to infringe or violate the laws of nations, or laws of neutrality. . . .

» VI. You shall send the master or pilot and one or more principal person or persons of the company of every ship or vessel by you taken, in such ship or vessel, as soon after the capture as may be, to be by the judge or judges of such court as aforesaid examined upon oath, and make answer to such interrogatories as may be propounded, touching the interest or property of the ship or vessel and her lading; and at the same time you shall deliver or cause to be delivered to the judge or judges, all passes, sea briefs, charter parties, bills of lading, cockers, letters, and other documents and writings found on board, proving the said papers by the affidavit of yourself, or of some other person present at the capture, to be produced as they were received, without fraud, addition, subduction or embezzlement.

» VII. You shall keep and preserve every ship or vessel and cargo by you taken, until they shall, by sentence of a court properly authorized, be adjudged lawful prize, or acquitted; not selling, spoiling, wasting or diminishing the same, or breaking the bulk thereof, nor suffering any such thing to be done.

» VIII. If you or any of your officers or crew shall, in cold blood, kill or maim, or by torture or otherwise, cruelly, inhumanly, and contrary to common usage, and the practice of civilized nations in war, treat any person or persons surprized in the ship or vessel you shall take, the offender shall be severely punished.

» IX. You shall, by all convenient opportunities, send to the Board of Admiralty, or Secretary of Marine, written accounts of the captures you shall make, with the number and names of the captives, and intelligence of what may occur, or be discovered, concerning the designs of the enemy, and the destinations, motions and operations of their fleets and armies.

Source: American Memory, Library of Congress, http://memory.loc.gov/ammem/

1.10 Letter from Judge Aedanus Burke to South Carolina Governor Ben Guerard, Charleston, December 14, 1784

Circuit Judge Aedanus Burke reports to the South Carolina governor on the extrajudicial execution, by hanging, of a man who formerly served with the British army. The hanging victim, a Mr. Love, had been accused of taking part in killing Continental army troops after those troops had disarmed and surrendered. Judge Burke's letter was written one week after the hanging. While it is unclear what knowledge or involvement the judge had with the executioners, he conveys their sentiments with sympathy.

"The injustice of killing a man without tryal"

Sir,

I arrived from my circuit this evening and take the earliest opportunity to communicate to your Excell'y a very extraordinary affair which happened in the town of Ninety Six on the 7th instant. I suppose your Excell'y has heard of an excursion made by the noted Will Cunningham in the winter of 1781 into the interior settlements at the head of about 150 white men and negroes, under orders from the British Colo. Balfour, Cunningham having killed in his rout every person he met with (it is said to the number of 50) whom he suspected to be friends to this country & burnt their habitations, came at length to a house in which were an armed party of 35 men, commanded by Colo. Hayes. Those refusing to surrender at discretion, an attack commenced of a hot fire kept up, with some loss on both sides, for about three hours; the British party possessed themselves of the outbuildings, & at last set fire to the house in which Colo. Hays was posted. In this distressful situation they refused to surrender at discretion; reasonable terms were offered; that they should march out, lay down their arms & be treated as prisoners of war until exchanged; & a capitulation was formally signed & interchanged.

The Americans had no sooner marched out & laid down their arms, but the British seized Colo. Hays & with the capitulation in his hand, pleading the terms of it & begging for mercy, they hanged him to the limb of a tree and then fired a bullet thro' him. Captn. Williams the second in command was treated in the same manner, after which Cunningham with his own hands slew some of the prisoners and ordered his men to follow his example. A most cruel slaughter of the prisoners ensued; nineteen of them were butchered & the rest escaped their fate by means too tedious now to mention.

A man by the name of Love, who had dwelt in the district before and since the war & had married there, was one of Cunningham's party & a principal actor in this tragical business. Love traversed over the ground where lay the dead & the dying, his former neighbors & old acquaintances, & if he saw signs of life in any one of them, he ran his sword thro' & dispatched him. Those already dead he stabbed again: & when others seemingly without life, pierced by the point of his sword were involuntarily convulsed with pain, to those he gave new wounds; lest any in so dreadful a calamity might sham death to avoid it. Many other circumstances of barbarous insult to the dead bodies of Colo. Hays, Captn. Williams & others are related by Major Downs, Major Mulvee, Captn. Saxon & sundry other gentlemen of great worth and honor, who were witnesses of this massacre, but fortunately escaped it; some through the good will of a neighbor, & others by the intercession of their own slaves.

Love was thenceforth held in universal execration, yet he some time ago ventured to return into the vicinity of Ninety Six. He was taken up, & a justice of the peace committed him to gaol, thinking that such barbarity did not come under the Treaty of Peace, so as to shelter him from prosecution. The State's attorney laid the affair before the Court of Sessions, who overruled the prosecution, I being of the opinion that under the Treaty, his conscience of his feelings alone stood responsible for what was alleged; & on motion of his Council he was discharged. I then observed that there was no appearance, no look of disapprobation directed against a man so generally detested: all seemed to be reconciled. The determination on Love's affair closed the business of the Sessions, & the Court immediately adjourned to the 26th of April next.

A party of men as respectable for services & good character as any in the district, composed of the fathers, sons, & brothers and friends of the slain prisoners, had attended Court, & waited until the Judge had left the Court House, & arrived at his lodgings. And then without tumult or noise made Love a prisoner & put him on horseback. They proceeded on, & tho' the house where they supposed the Judge had entered, led directly to the place where they intended to convey him, yet they took a circuit another way to the skirts of a wood, where they arrived under the limb of a tree, to which they tyed one end of a rope, with the other round his neck, & bid him prepare to die; he urging in vain the injustice of killing a man without tryal, & they reminding him, that he should have thought of that, when he was slaughtering their kinsman. The horse drawn from under him left him suspended til he expired.

Thus I have related this unhappy affair as I have heard it, & if I can assure your Excell'y, that whatever appearance this transaction may have to the country, the people of Ninety Six wish ardently to forget the injuries of the war, provided that those do not return among them, that have committed wanton acts of barbarity. Many plunderers and other mischievous people now set down among them without molestation, nor can I learn that there exists resentment against any man who acted like a soldier & fought them in fair & open action. But it is to be lamented that such men as Love is described to have been, will be so infatuated as to return among the citizens, & thus prevent the restoration of the publick tranquility.

Your Excellency's most obedient humble Servt.
(Signed) Aedanus Burke

Source: South Carolina Department of Archives and History, http://www.scdah.gov

1.11 Letter from South Carolina Governor Ben Guerard to the Legislature, 1785

In response to Judge Burke's letter reproduced in document 1.10, Governor Guerard makes a referral of the matter to the legislature.

"Desirous therefore are the people, to throw a veil over it"

Mr. Speaker and Gentlemen:
However just might be the melancholy and to be lamented catastrophe related in the letter from the Honorable Judge Burke accompanying this message, and desirous therefore are the people, to throw a veil over it, still the energy of government and national faith and honor require some inquiry into the matter.

The unfortunate person, subject of the letter, it seems returned to this state from Florida, through the back parts of Georgia, by which route (illegible) arrived in our back country a number of other equally infamous characters who instead of seeking and securing the protection of government as British subjects to settle their affairs, stipulated for them on the Treaty of Peace, are a terror to travelers, in as much as, that a company must be raised for apprehending or dispersing them, or the one-half of Captain Rumpf's useful company for the purpose ordered on ——, wherever they shall counsel any robberies.

Ben Guerard
    24 July 1785

Source: South Carolina Department of Archives and History, http://www.scdah.gov

1.12 Ratification Debates in Virginia, 1788

In June 1788, the various participants in the Virginia constitutional ratifying convention debated the necessity of a specific enumeration of rights in the federal constitution. The participants all agree that state use of torture should be prohibited, but they differ on the best means to that end. Is a specific prohibition needed, or is a general reservation of rights sufficient? The legal quandary consists in the following. If specific guarantees of rights are required in order to safeguard the people from government action, then a problem of infinite regression arises: every possible future

*abuse must be named by constitutional provision. Moreover, the specific
enumeration of rights negates the existence of natural rights. If a right
derives from the laws of nature or from the human condition itself, why is
it necessary to grant it in a Bill of Rights? On the other hand, the utility of
a specific prohibition is obvious: one can clearly and unambiguously claim
the protection of a specific limitation on state power.*

*Patrick Henry underscores the importance of this question by noting
that abstention from "tortures" has "distinguished our ancestors."*

"They would not admit of tortures, or cruel and barbarous punishment"

Mr. HENRY. Mr. Chairman, the necessity of a bill of rights appears to me to
be greater in this government than ever it was in any government before. I
have observed already, that the sense of the European nations, and particularly Great Britain, is against the construction of rights being retained which
are not expressly relinquished. I repeat, that all nations have adopted this
construction—that all rights not expressly and unequivocally reserved to the
people are impliedly and incidentally relinquished to rulers, as necessarily
inseparable from the delegated powers. . . . If the people do not think it necessary to reserve them, they will be supposed to be given up. How were the
congressional rights defined when the people of America united by a con-
federacy to defend their liberties and rights against the tyrannical attempts
of Great Britain? The states were not then contented with implied reservation. No, Mr. Chairman. It was expressly declared in our Confederation that
every right was retained by the states, respectively, which was not given up
to the government of the United States. But there is no such thing here. You,
therefore, by a natural and unavoidable implication, give up your rights to the
general government. . . .

In this business of legislation, your members of Congress will loose the
restriction of not imposing excessive fines, demanding excessive bail, and inflicting cruel and unusual punishments. These are prohibited by your declaration of rights. What has distinguished our ancestors?—That they would
not admit of tortures, or cruel and barbarous punishment. But Congress may
introduce the practice of the civil law, in preference to that of the common
law. They may introduce the practice of France, Spain, and Germany—of torturing, to extort a confession of the crime. They will say that they might as
well draw examples from those countries as from Great Britain, and they will
tell you that there is such a necessity of strengthening the arm of government,
that they must have a criminal equity, and extort confession by torture, in order to punish with still more relentless severity. We are then lost and undone.
And can any man think it troublesome, when we can, by a small interference,

prevent our rights from being lost? If you will, like the Virginian government, give them knowledge of the extent of the rights retained by the people, and the powers of themselves, they will, if they be honest men, thank you for it. Will they not wish to go on sure grounds? But if you leave them otherwise, they will not know how to proceed; and, being in a state of uncertainty, they will assume rather than give up powers by implication.

A bill of rights may be summed up in a few words. What do they tell us?— That our rights are reserved. Why not say so? Is it because it will consume too much paper?

Mr. GEORGE NICHOLAS, in answer to the two gentlemen last up, observed that, though there was a declaration of rights in the government of Virginia, it was no conclusive reason that there should be one in this Constitution; for, if it was unnecessary in the former, its omission in the latter could be no defect. They ought, therefore, to prove that it was essentially necessary to be inserted in the Constitution of Virginia. There were five or six states in the Union which had no bill of rights, separately and distinctly as such; but they annexed the substance of a bill of rights to their respective constitutions. These states, he further observed, were as free as this state, and their liberties as secure as ours. If so, gentlemen's arguments from the precedent were not good. In Virginia, all powers were given to the government without any exception. It was different in the general government, to which certain special powers were delegated for certain purposes. He asked which was the more safe. Was it safer to grant general powers than certain limited powers? This much as to the theory, continued he. What is the practice of this invaluable government? Have your citizens been bound by it? They have not, sir. You have violated that maxim, "that no man shall be condemned without a fair trial." That man who was killed, not secundum artem, was deprived of his life without the benefit of law, and in express violation of this declaration of rights, which they confide in so much. But, sir, this bill of rights was no security. It is but a paper check. It has been violated in many other instances. Therefore, from theory and practice, it may be concluded that this government, with special powers, without any express exceptions, is better than a government with general powers and special exceptions. But the practice of England is against us. The rights there reserved to the people are to limit and check the king's prerogative. It is easier to enumerate the exceptions to his prerogative, than to mention all the cases to which it extends. Besides, these reservations, being only formed in acts of the legislature, may be altered by the representatives of the people when they think proper. No comparison can be made of this with the other governments he mentioned. There is no stipulation between the king and people. The former is possessed of absolute, unlimited authority.

But, sir, this Constitution is defective because the common law is not declared to be in force! What would have been the consequence if it had? It would be immutable. But now it can be changed or modified as the legislative body may find necessary for the community. But the common law is not excluded. There is nothing in that paper to warrant the assertion. As to the exclusion of a jury from the vicinage, he has mistaken the fact. The legislature may direct a jury to come from the vicinage. But the gentleman says that, by this Constitution, they have power to make laws to define crimes and prescribe punishments; and that, consequently, we are not free from torture. Treason against the United States is defined in the Constitution, and the forfeiture limited to the life of the person attainted. Congress have power to define and punish piracies and felonies committed on the high seas, and offences against the laws of nations; but they cannot define or prescribe the punishment of any other crime whatever, without violating the Constitution. If we had no security against torture but our declaration of rights, we might be tortured to-morrow; for it has been repeatedly infringed and disregarded. A bill of rights is only an acknowledgment of the preëxisting claim to rights in the people. They belong to us as much as if they had been inserted in the Constitution. But it is said that, if it be doubtful, the possibility of dispute ought to be precluded. Admitting it was proper for the Convention to have inserted a bill of rights, it is not proper here to propose it as the condition of our accession to the Union. Would you reject this government for its omission, dissolve the Union, and bring miseries on yourselves and posterity? I hope the gentleman does not oppose it on this ground solely. Is there another reason? He said that it is not only the general wish of this state, but all the states, to have a bill of rights. If it be so, where is the difficulty of having this done by way of subsequent amendment? We shall find the other states willing to accord with their own favorite wish. The gentleman last up says that the power of legislation includes every thing. A general power of legislation does. But this is a special power of legislation. Therefore, it does not contain that plenitude of power which he imagines. They cannot legislate in any case but those particularly enumerated. No gentleman, who is a friend to the government, ought to withhold his assent from it for this reason.

Mr. GEORGE MASON replied that the worthy gentleman was mistaken in his assertion that the bill of rights did not prohibit torture; for that one clause expressly provided that no man can give evidence against himself; and that the worthy gentleman must know that, in those countries where torture is used, evidence was extorted from the criminal himself. Another clause of the bill of rights provided that no cruel and unusual punishments shall be inflicted; therefore, torture was included in the prohibition.

Mr. NICHOLAS acknowledged the bill of rights to contain that prohibition, and that the gentleman was right with respect to the practice of extorting confession from the criminal in those countries where torture is used; but still he saw no security arising from the bill of rights as separate from the Constitution, for that it had been frequently violated with impunity.

June 16, 1788

Source: American Memory, Library of Congress, http://memory.loc.gov/ammem/

1.13 Eighth Amendment to the United States Constitution, 1791

The Eighth Amendment to the Constitution contains a specific prohibition against cruel and unusual punishment. As such, it represents one of a number of specifically enumerated rights in the Bill of Rights. Subsequent history contains much debate about the interpretation of the Eighth Amendment with regard to when and how it should mark a limit to state power over bodies once they are committed to the state's custody.

"Nor cruel and unusual punishments inflicted"

Excessive bail shall not be required, nor excessive fines imposed, nor cruel and unusual punishments inflicted.

Source: Eighth Amendment to the United States Constitution

1.14 Fifth Amendment to the United States Constitution, 1791

The Fifth Amendment, like the Eighth, was adopted in response to the concerns of the Antifederalists, including Patrick Henry, who feared an abusive central government. The Fifth Amendment is included here because it prohibits "judicial torture," whereby suspects are forced to confess.

"No person . . . shall be compelled in any criminal case to be a witness against himself"

No person shall be held to answer for a capital, or otherwise infamous crime, unless on a presentment or indictment of a Grand Jury, except in cases arising in the land or naval forces, or in the Militia, when in actual service in time of War or public danger; nor shall any person be subject for the same offence to be twice put in jeopardy of life or limb; nor shall be compelled in any criminal case to be a witness against himself, nor be deprived of life, liberty, or property, without due process of law; nor shall private property be taken for public use, without just compensation.

Source: Fifth Amendment to the United States Constitution

1.15 Orders of Andrew Jackson, 1818

General Andrew Jackson captured, tried, and executed two British subjects, Alexander Arbuthnot and Robert Ambrister, in Florida in 1818. The charges were "aiding and abetting the enemy," "acting as a spy," and "exciting the Indians to murder." As Christopher Waldrep points out in Lynching in America, *the illegality of the proceedings against Arbuthnot and Ambrister was compound: the tribunal that tried them was not properly constituted, and then Jackson disregarded the sentence in Ambrister's case.*

Upon reconsideration, the court had sentenced Ambrister to whipping rather than death, but Jackson ordered him shot anyway. Jackson bluntly proclaimed that the executions were to serve as "an awful example to the world."

"To suffer death by being shot"

The court, on examination of evidence, and on mature deliberation, find the prisoner, Robert Ambrister, guilty of the first and second charges, and do therefore sentence him to suffer death by being shot. The members requesting a reconsideration of the vote on this sentence, and it being had, they sentence the prisoner to receive fifty stripes on his bare back, and he being confined with a ball and chain to hard labor for twelve calendar months.

The Commanding General approves the finding and sentence of the court in the case of A. Arbuthnot, and approves the finding and first sentence of the court in the case of Robert C. Ambrister, and disapproves the reconsideration of the honorable court in this case. It appears from the evidence and pleading of the prisoner that he did lead and command, within the territory of Spain (being a subject of Great Britain) the Indians in war against the United States, those nations being at peace. It is an established principle of the law of nations that any individual of a nation making war against the citizens of another nation, they being at peace, forfeits his allegiance, and becomes an outlaw and a pirate; this is the case of Robert C. Ambrister, clearly shown by the evidence adduced.

The Commanding General orders that Brevet Major A. C. W. Fanning, of the corps of artillery, will have, between the hours of eight and nine o'clock, A.M., A. Arbuthnot suspended by the neck, with a rope, until he is dead, and Robert C. Ambrister to be shot to death, agreeably to the sentence of the court.

Source: *American State Papers, 1789–1838: Military Affairs,* vol. 1, 15th Cong., 2nd sess., pub. no. 164

1.16 Letter from Georgia Governor William Rabun to Secretary of War John Calhoun, June 1, 1818

Georgia's governor ordered troops into military service against the Creek nation, and one detachment of those troops attacked a friendly town and killed some of its inhabitants. This incident was problematic, among other things, in terms of federal-state relations. Under Article I of the Constitution, only Congress may regulate relations with tribal governments, yet a Georgia detachment made an unprovoked attack on a friendly town. The delicacy of the situation can be seen in Governor Rabun's statement that he sought guidance from the U.S. military but received none. Moreover, he implores the War Department to try the offending officer in federal court.

"A production as inflammatory and indecorous, as it is unbecoming a gentleman and a soldier"

Sir,

You will no doubt have been informed by General Jackson, ere this reaches you, of an unfortunate attack recently made by a detachment of Georgia militia, under the command of Captain Obed Wright, on a village in the Creek nation of Indians, situated on the west side of the Flint River, generally known by the name of Chehaw. In order to bring the circumstances of this transaction fully before you, I must beg leave to refer you to a copy of a letter written by myself to General Jackson (herewith enclosed), by which you will perceive, that soon after the army entered the nation, and passed Fort Early, the Indians in that neighborhood, especially from two towns situated on the east side of the Flint river, generally denominated Hopaunees, and Philemmes, from chiefs of that name, had recommenced the depredations on our frontier. After having waited a considerable time in expectation of receiving an answer from the general, but in vain; and being repeatedly and earnestly requested by the distressed inhabitants of that frontier to afford them protection against the inroads of the savages; and being fully satisfied by the letters from respectable citizens from that quarter, that the murders and depredations committed were by Indians from the above-named towns, I took upon myself the responsibility of ordering a detachment into service for the special purpose of destroying them, having been convinced, by experience, that small detachments, stationed on the frontiers, were not sufficient to ensure protection of the inhabitants, as the Indians, acquainted with their situation, watched favorable opportunities for coming in on some unguarded point, committing murders, and returning with impunity. . . .

The only reason I have to offer for calling on the troops in service of the United States is, the danger to which the frontier was exposed, and the necessity for putting a stop to the incursions of the savages, which could only be done by the destruction of their towns, in order that the inhabitants might return to their homes, and prepare their farms for cultivation, the season for doing so having then commenced. The party, on their march learning that Hopaunee had left his village, and had taken up his residence in the Chehaw town, took on themselves the responsibility of pursuing him there; and having reached the town, commenced an attack on it; the result of which was, that several of the friendly Indians were killed. As the detachment was ordered into service by the state's authority, and as they had violated their orders by destroying a friendly town, I had ordered an investigation of the conduct of the commanding officer before a military tribunal; but I have since determined to stay all further proceedings until the pleasure of the President of the United States should be known on the subject. Captain Wright was arrested by order of General Jackson, but was released by the civil authority. I have the honor to transmit a copy of General Jackson's letter to me, demanding forthwith the delivery of Captain Wright to the officers sent by him to arrest and confine him. It is a production as inflammatory and indecorous, as it is unbecoming a gentleman and a soldier. Enclosed you will also receive a copy of my letter to the general in reply.

Should it meet the approbation of the President, I would prefer that the case of Captain Wright be referred to the Circuit Court of the United States, which will be held in Savannah, in December next.

With great respect, I have the honor to be, your most obedient servant,
William Rabun

Source: *American State Papers, 1789–1838: Military Affairs*, vol. 1, 15th Cong., 2nd sess., pub. no. 167

2

SLAVERY AND THE FRONTIER

The documents contained in this chapter cover a time span from the colonial era through the Civil War, so there is some overlap with chapter 1. However, the focus here is on slavery and conflicts with Native American tribes. Laws and other official discourses of the period were explicit in singling out slaves, "Indians," and persons of color for punishment and for disparate treatment generally. For example, document 2.14, an 1836 criminal statute from Tennessee, provides a defense to homicide in cases where a slaveholder kills a slave using "moderate correction." Dayan notes this developing doctrine of moderate correction, which licenses and excuses brutal treatment by classifying it as "moderate"—a subjective test of *degree* rather than a categorical test of *kind* of punishment. In chapter 5, we see a return of this development in the Bush administration's attempt to define "severe" pain when interpreting torture law.

2.1 Legislature of Connecticut, 1675

In June 1669 rumor spread of an impending attack on the English settlers by certain tribes of the Connecticut and Long Island area. Some settlers wanted to act preemptively, believing, as one put it, "'Tis good to kill such birds in the egg." A group of settlers set out to confront one of the chiefs, Ninigret, with weapons, but others "protested against any such eleagall or unlawful proceedings." In the end, this particular plot did not materialize. Six years later, however, the colony passed a law that kept one tribe, the Pequots, in a state of subservience to the colony. Among other provisions, the 1675 act prescribed corporal punishment specifically against Indians for such offenses as working on the Sabbath.

"Whosoever shall oppose or speake against the onely living & true God"

Laws for the Pequots
Laws for the Sayd Indians to Observe
    1. That whosoever shall oppose or speake against the onely living & true God, the creator & ruler of all things, shall be brought to some English court to be punished as the nature of the offence may require.

2. That whosoever shall powau or use witchcraft or any worship to the divill or any fals god shall be convented &. punished.

3. That whosoever shall prophane the holy Saboth day by servill worke or play, such as chopping or fetching home of wood, fishing, fowleing, hunting &c. shall pay as a fine tenn shillings, halfe to the cheife officers & the other halfe to the constable & informer, or be sharply whipt for every such offence.

4. Whosoever shall committ murder or manslaughter shall be brought to Hartford goale & be tryed by this Government, according to the English law, which punisheth by death.

5. Whosoever shall committ Adultery by lying with another man's wife, or to have or keep her from her husband, shall be imprisoned & tryed & punished with a fine of forty shillings for every offence. So in the case of the Adulteresse. The sayd fine to be distributed, as before.

6. Whosoever shall steale shall restore double to his neighboure for what he hath taken, when convict before theire officer & councill, and pay the constable two shillings sixpence for his paynes about executing the law.

7. Whosoever shall appeare and be proved to be drunck amongst them, shall pay tenn shillings or be whipt, as the officers shall see meete; and the fine divided as before, in the law about Sabboth breakeing. In like manner shall it be done to such Indians as doe bring the liquors or strong drinke amongst them.

8. It is ordered that a ready & comely attendance be given to heare the word of God preached by Mr. Fitch, or any other minister sent amongst them. The cheife officers & constables are to gather the people as they may. And if any be refractory & refuse, or doe misbehave themselve undecently, such shall be punished with a fine of five shillings, or be corporally punished, as the officers shall see most meet.

9. If the officers shall neglect in any of the premises, to doe their duty, they shall receive double punishment when convict thereof in any of our English Courts.

10. But whosoever shall either affront the principall officer, or refuse to assist the constable in the due execution of his office, shall pay for each affront so given ten shillings, and for such refuseall to assist the constable five shillings.

Source: Connecticut Archives, www.archive.org/stream/publicrecords02conn/
publicrecords02conn_djvu.txt

2.2 Act of the Province of New Jersey, 1704

A colonial-era statute from New Jersey specifies particularly harsh punishments for slaves, including branding and castration. The proffered justification in the preamble to the act is that slaves "do frequently steal from their masters, Mistresses or others." By providing payment to private citizens and state officials who apprehend or whip slaves, the law creates a financial incentive for finding violations.

"Burnt with a hot Iron . . . with the Letter (T)"

Whereas it is found by daily Experience, that Negro, Indian and Malatto-Slaves, under pretense of Trade, or liberty of Traffick, do frequently steal from their masters, Mistresses or others, . . . *Be it therefore enacted by the Governour, Council and Assembly now met and assembled, and by the Authority of the same,* . . .

That all and every person or persons within this Province who shall find or take up any Negro, Indian or Malatto slaves ten miles from his or her Master or mistresses Habitation, who hath not leave in writing from his or her said Master or Mistress, he, she, or they so taken up shall be or may be whipt, by the party that takes them up, on the bare back, not exceeding twenty Lashes; and the taker up shall have for his Reward the Sum of *Five Shillings* for every one so taken up, with reasonable charges of carrying home, paid him by the Master or Mistress of the said Slave; and if further, then *six Pence per Mile* for every Mile over and above the said ten Miles; to be recovered by Action of Debt of *Forty Shillings* or under, before any Justice of the Peace; if above 40s, then before the Court of Common Pleas of the County where the fact shall arise.

And be it further Enacted by the Authority aforesaid, That when any Negro, Indian or Malatto Slaves of or belonging to any other Province, without License under the hand of his or her Master or Mistress, shall be taken up by any person within this Province, he, she or they so taken up shall be whipt at the Publick Whipping-post belonging to the place where the said Negro, Indian or Malatto Slaves shall be taken up, not exceeding twenty lashes on the bare back, and to be committed by a Warrant from a Justice of the Peace, where the Fact shall arise, to the Goal of that County; and the person so taking them up, and carrying them to be whipt, shall have for his Reward the sum of *Ten Shillings* for each Slave, paid by the Mr. or Mrs. Of said Slaves, and to remain in Prison till it be paid, with all other Charges that shall accrew thereby.

And be it further Enacted by the Authority aforesaid, That when any Negro, Indian or Malatto Slaves shall be taken into custody for Fellony or Murder, or suspicion of Fellony or Murder, that three of the Justices of the Peace (one being of the Quorum) shall with all conveniency meet and try the said Negro, Indian or Malatto Slaves, and upon conviction by a jury of twelve lawful Men of the Neighborhood, Pronounce Sentence for such Crimes, and sign the Execution.

And be it further Enacted by the Authority aforesaid, That if any Negro, Indian or Malatto Slave shall steal to the value of *six Pence,* or above, and under the sum of *Five Shillings,* and be thereof convicted before two Justices of the Peace, one whereof to be a Quorum, upon the Oath or solemn Affirmation of one or more Witnesses, such Negro, Indian or Malatto Slave shall be whipt on the bare Back, at the publick Whipping-place, with Forty Lashes by the Constable of such Township or place where the Offence was committed, or such Person as he shall appoint. And that if any Negro, Indian or Malatto Slave shall steal to the value of *Five Shillings,* or above, and under the sum of *Forty Shillings,* and be thereof convicted in manner aforesaid, such Negro, Indian or Malatto Slave shall be whipt on the bare Back with Forty Stripes, as aforesaid, and be likewise burnt with a hot Iron on the most visible part of the left Cheek near the Nose, with the Letter (T) by the Constable, as aforesaid; the which Constable shall receive for the whipping of each Negro, Indian or Malatto Slave *five Shillings,* and for burning each Negro, Indian or Malatto Slave *Ten Shillings,* to be paid by the Master or Mistress of said Slave; and in default of payment to be levied by Warrant from any Justice of the Peace out of the goods of said Master or Mistress; and that every Constable that shall neglect or refuse to do his Duty herein shall forfeit the sum of *Forty Shillings,* to be levied by Warrant from any Justice of the Peace, directed to who he shall appoint, out of the Goods and Chattels of said Constable.

And if any Negro, Indian or Malatto Slave shall attempt by force or perswasion to Ravish or have carnal Knowledge of any White Woman, Maid or Child, and be thereof convicted by the Verdict of twelve Men of the Neighborhood before two Justices of the Peace, one whereof to be a Quorum, such Indian, Negro or Malatto shall be Castrated at the care and Charge of his Master or Mistress, and the Negro to continue in Goal at the charge of his Mr. or Mrs. Till Execution be performed.

And whereas the Baptizing of Slaves is thought by some to be a sufficient Reason to set them at Liberty; which being a groundless Opinion, and prejudicial to the Inhabitants of this Province, *Be it further Enacted by the Authority aforesaid,* That the baptizing of any Negro, Indian or Malatto Slave, shall not be any reason or cause for setting them, or any of them at Liberty; nor shall they nor any of them have or procure their or any of their Liberty by virtue thereof.

Source: New Jersey Division of Archives and Records Management, http://www.state .nj.us/state/darm/ (copy of law on file with editor)

2.3 Petition of David Kain, South Carolina, 1794

David Kain was convicted of killing a slave owned by a man named John Deas. His sentence was a fine of fifty pounds, payable to the state. He was ordered confined until he could pay the amount, and he petitioned the state legislature to remit the fine. Although this is in one sense a private action, that is, an act of violence committed by a private individual rather than by the state, it is included here because the state regulates use of violence against slaves and determines the extent to which such violence is lawful, thereby licensing certain actions. The court's sentence treats the matter more like a destruction of property than harm to a person.

"In an unguarded moment, & in the heat of passion"

To the Honorable the President and Members of the Senate of the State of South Carolina
The Petition of David Kain humbly herewith
  That your Petitioner in an unguarded moment, & in the heat of passion had the misfortune to wound a Negro man of the Estate of John Deas Esquire and in such a manner as to prove mortal, & which he sincerely laments & is truly penitent for—
  For which unfortunate action your petitioner was tried in January Sessions AD 1793 and sentenced to pay a fine of Fifty Pounds Sterling to the State, & to be confined in the common gaol untill it should be discharged—In pursuance of which Sentence your Petitioner was arrested & has remained a prisoner in Charleston Gaol since the 18th day of March last & not being entitled to the Benefit of the Act for the relief of insolvent debtors & being possessed of no property wherewith to pay said Fine, he has the melancholy prospect before him of ending his days in confinement, unless your honorable House can be prevailed upon to extend the arm of mercy & remit the aforesaid Fine & costs & afford him an opportunity of evincing by his future conduct, that it has not been extended in vain, & that he will add once again to the number of useful citizens—Your Petitioner therefore humbly craves the humane intervention of your honorable House by a remission of the aforesaid Fine & costs—and

as in Duty bound he will pray—Charleston Gaol 17 November 1794—David Kain

Source: South Carolina Department of Archives and History, http://www.scdah.gov

2.4 Committee's Response to Petition of David Kain, South Carolina, 1794

In December 1794 a three-person legislative committee declined to grant the relief Kain requested.

The Committee to whom was referred the petition of David Kain—Report
That they have inquired into the circumstances attending the killing of the Negroe mentioned in the petition & are of the opinion the prayer of the petitioner should not be granted.

Source: South Carolina Department of Archives and History, http://www.scdah.gov

2.5 Act of the General Assembly of the State of Georgia, 1810

A Georgia statute establishing a town allows corporal punishment to be used against people of color only.

"Except to people of color"

BE it enacted by the Senate and House of Representatives of the State of Georgia in General Assembly met, and by the authority aforesaid, That David Bush, George Cotton, Chappel Heath, Jeremiah Butt, and Hamilton Goss, be Commissioners of said town, and they and their successors in office shall have full power and authority to pass all bye-laws and regulations which may be necessary for the improvement and repairing of the streets of said town, and the preservation of the public good; *Provided nevertheless,* That such bye-laws and regulations shall not be repugnant to the Constitution and laws of this State, and that no penalty thereby imposed shall extend to corporal punishment, except to people of color. . . .

Source: Georgia Archives, http://content.sos.state.ga.us/cdm4/legdocs.php

2.6 Act of the General Assembly of the State of Georgia, 1811

An act of the Georgia legislature sets forth procedures for administering criminal laws against slaves. While allowing corporal punishment, the law forbids sentences of death or dismemberment in noncapital cases. Slaveholders would presumably object to corporal punishment that would render slaves unfit for work.

"Not extending to the taking away life or member" (1811)

§ 1. *Be it enacted by the Senate and House of Representatives of the State of Georgia in General Assembly met, and it is hereby enacted by the authority of the same,* That from and immediately after the passing of this act, upon complaint being made to, or information received upon oath by any Justice of the Peace of any crime having been committed by any slave or slaves within the county where such Justice is empowered to act, such Justice shall by warrant from under his hand cause such slave or slaves to be brought before him, and give notice thereof in writing to any two or more of the nearest Justices of the Peace of said county, to associate with him on a particular day in said notice, to be specified not exceeding three days from the date of said notice, for the trial of such slave or slaves. And the Justices so assembled, shall forthwith proceed to the examination of a witness or witnesses and other evidence, and in case the offender or offenders shall be convicted of any crime not capital, the said Justices or a majority of them shall give judgment for the inflicting any corporal punishment, not extending to the taking away life or member as in their discretion may seem reasonable and just, and shall award and cause execution to be done accordingly. And in case it should appear to them after investigation, that the crime or crimes wherewith such slave or slaves stand charged, is a crime or crimes for which he, she or they ought to suffer death, such slave or slaves shall immediately be committed to the public jail of said county, if any, provided, it should be sufficient, or to the custody of the sheriff of said county, or to the nearest sufficient jail thereto.

Source: Georgia Archives, http://content.sos.state.ga.us/cdm4/legdocs.php

2.7 Act of the General Assembly of the State of Georgia, 1811

An act creating a Georgia municipality provides for disparate treatment of convicted offenders—this time based on race rather than slave status.

"Nothing herein contained shall . . . authorise . . . corporal punishment on any white person"

§ 1. *BE it enacted by the Senate and House of Representatives in General Assembly met, and it is hereby enacted by the authority of the same,* That the town of Warrenton shall extend four hundred yards in every direction from the court-house, and that all citizens who have resided six months in the said town, and are qualified to vote for members of the Legislature, shall be entitled to vote for commissioners.

§ 2. *And be it further enacted,* That the said commissioners or a majority of them, are hereby authorised and empowered to pass such bye-laws and ordinances as they shall deem necessary for preserving the public property within the limits of the corporation, and improving the streets and public square, and also the lot containing the Meeting-house and burying ground, removing nuisances, and preventing damages by fire, and for promoting order and morality; *provided,* such bye laws and ordinances shall not be repugnant to the constitution and laws of this state; *Provided nevertheless,* that nothing herein contained shall be so construed as to authorise said commissioners to inflict corporal punishment on any white person, or to deprive any slave or free person of color of life, limb or member.

Source: Georgia Archives, http://content.sos.state.ga.us/cdm4/legdocs.php

---

2.8 Act of the General Assembly of the State of Georgia, 1815

In a racialized provision, a Georgia statute sets a limit on the number of lashes to be given as punishment.

"Whose punishment . . . shall not exceed thirty-nine lashes"

§ 1. *BE it enacted by the Senate and House of Representatives of the State of Georgia, in General Assembly met, and it is hereby enacted by the authority of the same,* That Thomas P. Carnes, John Brown, Augustin S. Clayton, Samuel Brown and Francis Farrar be, and they are hereby appointed commissioners of said town, and they and their successors in office, are hereby vested with full power and authority, to pass all bye laws and regulations which may be necessary for the improvement and keeping in good repair all the streets of the said town and the public roads leading from the same in every direction, and to the extent of one mile from the College Chapel and no further, and to have kept in repair, the public Spring, and to pass any other bye laws for the better Government of said town, as may not be repugnant to, or inconsistent with, the constitution and laws of this state. *Provided,* nothing herein contained shall be so construed as to extend the powers of said commissioners to the north east side of the Oconee river.

§ 2. *And be it further enacted by the authority aforesaid,* That the said commissioners and their successors in office shall be, and they are hereby authorised, to impose any tax upon the citizens resident within the bounds aforesaid, for public purposes, which shall not exceed one dollar on each poll within the term of any one year.

§ 3. *And be it further enacted,* That the said commissioners and their successors in office, may impose any fines or penalties not incompatible with the constitution or laws of this state—*Provided,* that no penalty thereby imposed shall extend to corporal punishment (except to people of color) whose punishment for any one violation of the bye laws of the corporation, shall not exceed thirty-nine lashes.

Source: Georgia Archives, http://content.sos.state.ga.us/cdm4/legdocs.php

---

2.9 Act of the General Assembly of the State of Georgia, 1817

A Georgia statute establishes "patroles," which are essentially vigilante organizations licensed by the state, and requires citizens to serve in the patrols or face fines.

"No punishment inflicted by such patrol . . . shall exceed moderate correction"

And be it further enacted, That the said Commissioners shall have full power and authority to appoint from among the persons residing within the limits of said corporation, a patrol or patroles for said corporation, at such times and on such occasions as they may deem proper—*Provided,* that one person at least, of those composing such patrol or patroles, shall be a slave holder, and that no punishment inflicted by such patrol or patroles on any slave or slaves, shall exceed moderate correction—*Provided also,* that all and every person or persons, who shall refuse to do patrol duty when required as aforesaid, shall, without good excuse to be rendered to said Commissioners, be liable to be fined by said Commissioners in any sum not exceeding five dollars, and the said delinquent shall have five days notice in writing, of the time and place for hearing said excuse.

Source: Georgia Archives, http://content.sos.state.ga.us/cdm4/legdocs.php

2.10 Address of President James Madison, 1813

President Madison's 1813 address criticizes the British alliance in the War of 1812 with Native American tribes. Madison attributes violence and brutality to the Creeks, casting them as "savages" and condemning their "usual practice of indiscriminate massacre on defenseless inhabitants." He blames the British for utilizing a fighting force that practices such habits and excuses the United States for doing the same—because the U.S. military's "retaliation has been mitigated as much as possible."

"All the laws of humanity and of honorable war"

The cruelty of the enemy, in enlisting the savages in a war with a nation desirous of mutual emulation in mitigating its calamities, has not been confined to any one quarter. Wherever they could be turned against us, no exertions to effect it have been spared. On our southwestern border, the Creek tribes, who, yielding to our persevering endeavors, were gradually acquiring more civilized habits, became the unfortunate victims of seduction. A war in that quarter has been the consequence, infuriated by a bloody fanaticism recently propagated among them.

It was necessary to crush such a war before it could spread among the contiguous tribes, and before it could favor enterprises of the enemy into that vicinity. With this in view a force was called into service of the United States from the states of Georgia and Tennessee, which, with the nearest regular troops, and other corps from the Mississippi Territory, might not only chastise the savages into present peace, but make a lasting impression on their fears.

The progress of the expedition, as far as is yet known, corresponds with the martial zeal with which it was espoused; and the best hopes of a satisfactory issue are authorized by the complete success with which a well-planned enterprise was executed against a body of hostile savages, by a detachment of the volunteer militia of Tennessee, under the gallant command of General Coffee; and by a still more important victory over a larger body of them, gained under the immediate command of Major General Jackson, an officer equally distinguished for his patriotism and his military talents.

The unfortunate perseverance of the enemy in courting the aid of the savages in all quarters, had the natural effect of kindling their ordinary propensity for war into a passion, which, even among those best disposed towards the United States, was ready, if not employed on our side, to be turned against us. A departure from our protracted forbearance to accept the services tendered by them, has thus been forced upon us. But in yielding to it, the retaliation has been mitigated as much as possible, both in its extent and in its character; stopping far short of the example of the enemy, who owe the advantages they have occasionally gained in battle, chiefly to the number of their savages associates, and who have not controlled them either from their usual practice of indiscriminate massacre on defenseless inhabitants, or from scenes of carnage without a parallel, or prisoners to British arms, guarded by all the laws of humanity and of honorable war.

For these enormities, the enemy are equally responsible, whether with the power to prevent them they want the will, or with a knowledge and a want of power, they still avail themselves of such instruments. In other respects, the enemy are pursuing a course which threatens consequences most afflicting to humanity.

Source: *American State Papers, 1789–1838: Foreign Relations*, vol. 1, 13th Cong., 2nd sess., pub. no. 36

2.11 Letter from Adjutant General Robert Parker to Inspector General Daniel Butler, 1818

At the same time General Andrew Jackson captured, tried and hanged Ambrister and Arbuthnot, as discussed in chapter 1, Jackson also captured two Native American chiefs. The chiefs did not receive a trial but were summarily hanged. Jackson faced criticism from government officials both within and outside the military—as much for the diplomatic and political ramifications of his expansion of the war as for his deviation even from the minimal procedural steps followed in Ambrister's and Arbuthnot's cases. One of the executed chiefs was a prophet, and that fact may have contributed to his death. "Spare them their prophets," Henry Clay would later say, in reference to this affair. Clay noted that through history, conquering powers did not typically destroy the religious institutions of the vanquished people. Whether or not Clay's reading of history is supported by the evidence, he does highlight an additional aspect of Jackson's destructive military campaign. The following communication by General Parker complains about Jackson's actions and tactics.

"They were hung without trial, and with little ceremony"

It appears that General Jackson advanced into Florida with a force of one thousand eight hundred men, composed of regulars, volunteers, and the

Georgia militia, and afterwards, on the 1st day of April, was joined by General McIntosh and his brigade of one thousand Indians, who had been previously organized by General Gaines; opposed to whom, it appears from the report of Captain Young, topographical engineer, and other evidence, the whole force of the fugitive Seminole Indians and runaway negroes, had they been embodied, could not have exceeded nine hundred or one thousand men, and at no time did half that number present themselves to oppose his march; of course, little or no resistance was made.

The Mikausky towns were first taken and destroyed; the army marched upon St. Marks, a feeble Spanish garrison, which was surrendered "without firing a gun," and then occupied as an American post; the Spanish commander having, first by humble entreaties and then by a timid protest, endeavored to avert the measure. Here Alexander Arbuthnot was found, taken prisoner, and put in confinement, for the purpose, as it was stated by General Jackson, "of collecting evidence to establish his guilt." And here also was taken two Indian chiefs, one of whom pretended to possess the spirit of prophecy; they were hung without trial, and with little ceremony. . . .

The tendency of these measures by the commanding general seems to have been to involve the nation in a war without her consent, and for reasons of his own, unconnected with his military functions. Your committee would be unwilling to attribute improper motives where those of a different character could possibly be inferred, more especially when it is to affect a character whose military fame is the pride and boast of the nation. But even such a character becomes more eminently dangerous when he exalts himself above the majesty of the laws, declares the public will, and becomes the arbiter between the United States and foreign nations. That these high and transcendent powers have been usurped, and exercised in the present case, is, it appears to the committee, incontrovertible from the facts adduced.

Source: *American State Papers, 1789–1838: Military Affairs,* vol. 1, 15th Cong., 2nd sess., pub. no. 164

2.12 Speech by Congressman Henry Clay, 1819, on the Seminole War

In an extended speech on the Seminole War, Congressman Henry Clay of Kentucky unequivocally condemns Jackson's extrajudicial killings of the chiefs, and he lays out an impassioned argument for respecting the rule of law and refraining from exercising the "right of retaliation" (here, killing captives). To be sure, he constructs the Native Americans as savage and primitive. He assumes that they will not recognize or respect the obligation to treat prisoners humanely. In fact, Clay says, they "care not about the execution of those of their warriors who are taken captive." However, he emphasizes that even prisoners who have committed atrocities themselves must be treated lawfully. It is the obligation to law, rather than the character of the prisoner, that should determine how prisoners are treated.

"What cares an Indian whether you hang or shoot him?"

The first circumstance which, in the course of his performing that duty, fixed our attention, had, Mr. C. said, filled him with regret. It was the execution of the Indian chiefs. How, he asked, did they come into our possession? Was it in the course of fair, and open, and honorable war? No; but by means of deception—by hoisting foreign colors on the staff from which the stars and stripes alone should have floated. Thus ensnared, the Indians were taken on shore, and without ceremony, without delay, were hung. Hang an Indian! We, sir, who are civilized, and can comprehend and feel the effect of moral causes and considerations, attach ignominy to that mode of death. And the gallant, and refined, and high-minded man, seeks by all possible means to avoid it. But, what cares an Indian whether you hang or shoot him? The moment he is captured, he is considered by his tribe as disgraced, if not lost. They, too, are indifferent to the manner in which he is despached. But, Mr. C. said, he regarded the occurrence with grief for other and higher considerations. It was the first instance that he knew of, in the annals of our country, in which retaliation, by executing Indian captives, had ever been deliberately practiced. There may have been exceptions, but if there were, they were met with contemporaneous condemnation and have been reprehended by the just pen of impartial history. The gentleman from Massachusetts may tell me, if he pleases, what he pleases about the tomahawk and scalping knife—about Indian enormities, and foreign miscreants and incendiaries. I, too, hate them; from my very soul I abominate them. But, I love my country, and its constitution; I love liberty and safety, and fear military despotism more even than I hate these monsters. The gentleman, in the course of his remarks, alluded to the state from which I have the honor to come. Little, sir, does he know of the high and magnanimous sentiments of the people of that state, if he supposes they will approve of the transaction to which he referred. Brave and generous, humanity and clemency towards a fallen foe constitute one of their noblest characteristics. Amidst all the struggles for that fair land between the natives and the present inhabitants, Mr. C. said he defied the gentleman to point out one instance in which a Kentuckian had stained his hand by—nothing but his high sense of the distinguished services and exalted merits of General Jackson prevented his using a different term—the execution of an unarmed and prostrate captive. Yes, said Mr. C. there was one solitary exception, in which a man, enraged at beholding an Indian prisoner, who had been celebrated for his enormities, and who had destroyed some of his kindred, plunged his sword into his bosom. The wicked deed was considered as an abominable outrage when it occurred, and the name of the man has been handed down to the execration of posterity. I deny your right thus to retaliate on the aboriginal proprietors of the country; and, unless I am utterly deceived, it may be shown that it does not exist. But, before I attempt this, said Mr. Callow, let me make the gentleman from Massachusetts a little better acquainted with those people, to whose feelings and sympathies he has appealed through their representative. During the late war with Great Britain, Col. Campbell, under the command of my honorable friend from Ohio, (Gen. Harrison) was placed at the head of a detachment consisting chiefly, he believed, of Kentucky volunteers, in order to destroy the Mississinaway towns. They proceeded and performed the duty, and took some prisoners. And here is evidence of the manner in which they treated them. (Here Mr. C. read the general orders issued on the return of the detachment.) I hope, sir, the honorable gentleman will be now able better to appreciate the character and conduct of my gallant countrymen than he appears hitherto to have done. But, sir, I have said that you have no right to practise, under color of retaliation, enormities on the Indians. I will advance, in support of this position, as applicable to the origin of all law, the principle, that whatever has been the custom, from the commencement of a subject, whatever has been the uniform usage co-eval and co-existent with the subject to which it relates, becomes its fixed law. Such was the foundation of all common law; and such, he believed, was the principal foundation of all public or international law. If, then, it could be shown that from the first settlement of the colonies, on this part of the American continent, to the present time, we have constantly abstained from retaliation upon the Indians the excesses practised by them towards us, we were morally bound by this invariable usage, and could not lawfully change it without the most cogent reasons. So far as his knowledge extended, he said, that, from the first settlement at Plymouth or at Jamestown, it had not been our practice to destroy Indian captives, combatants or noncombatants. He knew of but one deviation from the code which regulated the warfare between civilized communities, and that was the destruction of Indian towns, which was supposed to be authorised upon the ground that we could not bring the war to a termination but by destroying the means which nourished it. With this single exception, the other principles of the laws of civilized nations are extended to them, and are thus made law in regard to them. When did this humane custom, by which, in consideration of their ignorance, and of our enlightened condition, the rigours of war were mitigated, begin? At a time when we were weak, and they were comparatively strong—when they were the lords of the soil, and we were seeking, from the vices, from the corruptions, from the religious intolerance, and from the oppressions of Europe, to gain an asylum among them. And, when is it proposed to change this custom, to substitute for it the bloody maxims of barbarous ages, and to interpolate the Indian public law with revolting cruelties? At a time when the situation of the two parties is totally changed—when we are powerful and they are weak—at a time when, to use a figure drawn from their own sublime eloquence, the poor children of the forest have been driven by the great wave which has flowed in from the Atlantic ocean to almost the base of the Rocky Mountains, and, overwhelming them in its terrible progress, has left no other remains of hundreds of tribes, now extinct, than those which indicate the remote existence of their former companion, the Mammoth of the new world! Yes, sir, it is at this auspicious period of our country, when we hold a proud and lofty station, among the first nations of the world, that we are called upon to sanction a departure from the established laws and usages which have regulated our Indian hostilities. And does the honorable gentleman from Massachusetts expect, in this august body, this enlightened assembly of Christians and Americans, by glowing appeals to our passions, to make us forget our principles, our religion, our clemency, and our humanity? Why was it, Mr. C. asked, that we had not practiced towards the Indian tribes the right of retaliation, now for the first time asserted in regard to them? It was because it is a principle, proclaimed by reason, and enforced by every respectable writer on the law of nations, that retaliation is only justifiable as calculated to produce effect in the war. Vengeance was a new motive for resorting to it. If retaliation will produce no effect on the enemy, we are bound to abstain from it, by every consideration of humanity and of justice. Will it, then, produce effect on the Indian tribes? No; they care not about the execution of those of their warriors who are taken captive.

Source: *American State Papers, 1789–1838: Military Affairs*, vol. 6, 24th Cong., 1st sess., pub. no. 687

2.13 *State v. Mann* (excerpt), North Carolina, 1829

The court opinion in State v. Mann *(a criminal matter involving the crime of battery) overturns the trial court and disclaims any judicial authority over the master-slave relationship. First, the court says the nature of the master-slave relationship is a political question, about "things inherent in our political state," and therefore not a proper subject of judicial decision making. U.S. courts frequently cite the "political question" doctrine as a reason for refusing to rule on the merits of a case. Later, in the 1961 case of* Baker v. Carr, *a Tennessee court would cite the same grounds for refusing to decide an early voting rights case. Matters of legislative districting were the responsibility of the legislature, not the courts, the state court ruled. The Supreme Court reversed, and* Baker v. Carr *became the famous "one person, one vote" decision.*

Next, the court naturalizes the master-slave relationship. The court explains what the condition of slavery entails, how it differs from other human relationships, and why slave status is the negation of master status. This exposition relies not on legal principles but rather on abstract notions of the nature of freedom and bondage—all of which are functional for maintaining a slavery-based social order.

Finally, the court says that interfering in the master-slave relationship would be a "false and fanatical philanthropy . . . still more wicked and appalling" than the underlying battery itself.

In his classic study, Justice Accused, *Robert Cover writes of Judge Thomas Ruffin's opinion in* State v. Mann, *"So long as the continued existence of slavery was an unquestioned legislative policy, there could logically be no place for a principles preference for either liberty or kindness in the law's operation."[1]*

"The Power of the master must be absolute"

RUFFIN, Judge.— A Judge cannot but lament, when such cases as the present are brought into judgment. It is impossible that the reasons on which they go can be appreciated, but where institutions similar to our own, exist and are thoroughly understood. The struggle, too, in the Judge's own breast between the feelings of the man, and the duty of the magistrate is a severe one, presenting strong temptation to put aside such questions, if it be possible. It is useless however, to complain of things inherent in our political state. And it is criminal in a Court to avoid any responsibility which the laws impose. With whatever reluctance therefore it is done, the Court is compelled to express an opinion upon the extent of the dominion of the master over the slave in North-Carolina.

1. Robert Cover, *Justice Accused: Slavery and the Judicial Process* (New Haven: Yale University Press, 1984), p. 78.

The indictment charges a battery on *Lydia*, a slave of *Elizabeth Jones*. . . . The enquiry here is, whether a cruel and unreasonable battery on a slave, by the hirer, is indictable. The Judge below instructed the Jury, that it is. . . . The established habits and uniform practice of the country in this respect, is the best evidence of the portion of power, deemed by the whole community, requisite to the preservation of the master's dominion. If we thought differently, we could not set our notions in array against the judgment of every body else, and say that this, or that authority, may be safely lopped off. This has indeed been assimilated at the bar to the other domestic relations; and arguments drawn from the well established principles, which confer and restrain the authority of the parent over the child, the tutor over the pupil, the master over the apprentice, have been pressed on us. The Court does not recognize their application. There is no likeness between the cases. They are in opposition to each other, and there is an impassable gulf between them.—The difference is that which exists between freedom and slavery—and a greater cannot be imagined. In the one, the end in view is the happiness of the youth, born to equal rights with that governor, on whom the duty devolves of training the young to usefulness, in a station which he is afterwards to assume among freemen. To such an end, and with such a subject, moral and intellectual instruction seem the natural means; and for the most part, they are found to suffice. Moderate force is superadded, only to make the others effectual. If that fail, it is better to leave the party to his own headstrong passions, and the ultimate correction of the law, than to allow it to be immoderately inflicted by a private person. With slavery it is far otherwise. The end is the profit of the master, his security and the public safety; the subject, one doomed in his own person, and his posterity, to live without knowledge, and without the capacity to make any thing his own, and to toil that another may reap the fruits. What moral considerations shall be addressed to such a being, to convince him what, it is impossible but that the most stupid must feel and know can never be true—that he is thus to labour upon a principle of natural duty, or for the sake of his own personal happiness, such services can only be expected from one who has no will of his own; who surrenders his will in implicit obedience to that of another. Such obedience is the consequence only of uncontrolled authority over the body. There is nothing else which can operate to produce the effect. The power of the master must be absolute, to render the submission of the slave perfect. I most freely confess my sense of the harshness of this proposition, I feel it as deeply as any man can. And as a principle of moral right, every person in his retirement must repudiate it. But in the actual condition of things, it must be so. There is no remedy. This discipline belongs to the state of slavery. They cannot be disunited, without abrogating at once the rights of the master, and absolving the slave from his subjection. It constitutes the curse of slavery to both the bond and free portions of our population. But it is inherent in the relation of master and slave.

That there may be particular instances of cruelty and deliberate barbarity, where, in conscience the law might properly interfere, is most probable. The difficulty is to determine, where *a Court* may properly begin. Merely in the abstract it may well be asked, which power of the master accords with right. The answer will probably sweep away all of them. But we cannot look at the matter in that light. The truth is, that we are forbidden to enter upon a train of general reasoning on the subject. We cannot allow the right of the master to be brought into discussion in the Courts of Justice. The slave, to remain a slave, must be made sensible, that there is no appeal from his master; that his power is in no instance, usurped; but is conferred by the laws of man at least, if not by the law of God. The danger would be great indeed, if the tribunals of justice should be called on to graduate the punishment appropriate to every temper, and every dereliction of menial duty. No man can anticipate the many and aggravated provocations of the master, which the slave would be constantly stimulated by his own passions, or the instigation of others to give; or the consequent wrath of the master, prompting him to bloody vengeance, upon the turbulent traitor—a vengeance generally practised with impunity, by reason of its privacy. The Court therefore disclaims the power of changing the relation, in which these parts of our people stand to each other.

We are happy to see, that there is daily less and less occasion for the interposition of the Courts. The protection already afforded by several statutes, that all-powerful motive, the private interest of the owner, the benevolences towards each other, seated in the hearts of those who have been born and bred together, the frowns and deep execrations of the community upon the barbarian, who is guilty of excessive and brutal cruelty to his unprotected slave, all combined, have produced a mildness of treatment, and attention to the comforts of the unfortunate class of slaves, greatly mitigating the rigors of servitude, and ameliorating the condition of the slaves. The same causes are operating, and will continue to operate with increased action, until the disparity in numbers between the whites and blacks, shall have rendered the latter in no degree dangerous to the former, when the police now existing may be further relaxed. This result, greatly to be desired, may be much more rationally expected from the events above alluded to, and now in progress, than from any rash expositions of abstract truths, by a Judiciary tainted with a false and fanatical philanthropy, seeking to redress an acknowledged evil, by means still more wicked and appalling than even that evil.

I repeat, that I would gladly have avoided this ungrateful question. But being brought to it, the Court is compelled to declare, that while slavery exists amongst us in its present state, or until it shall seem fit to the Legislature to interpose express enactments to the contrary, it will be the imperative duty of the Judges to recognize the full dominion of the owner over the slave, except where the exercise of it is forbidden by statute. And this we do upon the ground, that this dominion is essential to the value of slaves as property, to the security of the master, and the public tranquillity, greatly dependent upon their subordination; and in fine, as most effectually securing the general protection and comfort of the slaves themselves.

PER CURIAM.—Let the judgment below be reversed, and judgment entered for the Defendant.

Source: *State v. Mann*, 13 N.C. 263 (1829)

2.14 Laws of Tennessee, 1836

The doctrine of "moderate correction," first seen in document 2.9, is fixed in statutory text as a defense to murder in cases where slaves are victims of homicide. Additionally, the statute excuses homicides arising from resisting one's lawful owner—a potential defense that is quite broad indeed.

"Any slave dying under moderate correction"

If any person shall willfully and maliciously kill any negro or mulatto slave, on due and legal conviction thereof and &c. shall be deemed guilty of murder, as if such person so killed had been a freeman, and shall suffer death without benefit of clergy.

Provided, this act shall not be extended to any person killing a slave in the act of resistance to his lawful owner or master, or any slave dying under moderate correction.

Source: George Stroud, *A Sketch of the Laws Relating to Slavery in the Several States of the United States* (Philadelphia: Henry Longstreth, 1856)

2.15 Letter from Georgia Governor William Schley to Secretary of War Lewis Cass, 1836

Georgia governor William Schley complains in a letter to Lewis Cass that further federal intervention with regard to the Creeks is necessary.

He characterizes the Creeks in strikingly negative terms and hints that residents will resort to the "laws of self-preservation" if President Andrew Jackson does not act. A week later, Schley wrote, "The Indians must now be conquered and sent to the west at the point of a bayonet."

"To relieve us from these troublesome, murdering neighbors"

The Indians must no longer be permitted to remain where they now are, to murder our people and destroy their property ad libitum. It is idle to talk of treaties and national faith with such savages. The proper course to adopt with them is to treat them as wards or as children, and make them do that which is for their benefit and our safety.

The Creeks are in a starving condition, and must be fed where they now are, by the United States, or they must be killed or driven out of the country. There can be no peace or quiet for the inhabitants of either side of the Chattahoochee while they remain; and the laws of self-preservation will force Georgia and Alabama to rid themselves of this population, "peaceably if they can, forcibly if they must." The United States ought no longer to delay the employment of some effectual means to relieve us from these troublesome, murdering neighbors, and I hope the President will be able to find a sufficient justification in the present attitude of the Creeks to induce him to take the responsibility of doing so.

Source: *American State Papers, 1789–1838: Military Affairs*, vol. 6, 24th Cong., 1st sess., pub. no. 687

2.16 Jury Charge by Judge Luke Lawless, 1836

Luke Lawless was the presiding judge over the grand jury investigating the public lynching of Francis McIntosh, a man accused of murdering a sheriff's deputy. Lawless's instruction to the grand jury suggested that if the act of lynching was performed by the "many," the grand jury should refuse to indict, as it was "beyond the reach of human law." The jury instruction also implicitly defended the practice of lynching in general, and this lynching in particular.

"Mysterious, metaphysical and almost electric phrenzy"

[W]hether the Grand Jury should act at all, depends upon the solution of the preliminary question, namely, whether the destruction of McIntosh was the act of the "few" or the act of the "many." . . .

If, on the other hand, the destruction of the murderer of Hammond was the act, as I have said, of the many—of the multitude, in the ordinary sense of those words— not the act of numerable and ascertainable malefactors, but of the congregated thousands, seized upon and impelled by that mysterious, metaphysical and almost electric phrenzy, which, in all ages and nations, has hurried on the infuriated multitude to deeds of death and destruction—then, I say, act not at all in the matter—the case then transcends your jurisdiction— it is beyond the reach of human law. . . .

When it is recollected that their respected and beloved fellow citizen, slain in the performance of his duty, lay dead before them . . . when they heard the shrieks of the widow and her desolate orphans, and added to all this, when their feelings and their understandings were assailed and outraged by the atrocious and savage demeanor of the murderer himself, . . . is it to be wondered at that the people should be moved? Is not something to be allowed for human sympathies in those appalling circumstances? Is there not some slight palliation of that deplorable disregard of Law and Constitution, which is now the subject of these deliberations?

. . . if you arrive at the ultimate conclusion, that the death of McIntosh was the act of the multitude, you will pursue the safest and wisest course, in declining all action with respect to it.

Source: Christopher Waldrep, *Lynching in America: A History in Documents* (New York: New York University Press, 2006), p. 55

2.17 Inaugural Address of Governor Charles Lynch of Mississippi, 1836

In his inaugural address, Mississippi governor Charles Lynch, a Democrat, references extrajudicial lynchings and criticized the abolitionist movement. Lynch served one term as Mississippi's governor, from 1836 to 1838, and then stepped down. In his defiant tone and his resentment of outside influence on the state, Lynch prefigures Alabama governor George Wallace's "segregation forever" inaugural speech a century later. In rhetorical terms, it is striking that Lynch insists, first, that it is wrong for northerners to criticize lynching before he undertakes an affirmative defense of the practice. This rhetorical structure will be seen again in twentieth-century debates over antilynching legislation, where southern legislators focus on the issue of "federal coercion" rather than the importance of preventing lynching.

"A Summary mode of trial and punishment unknown to law"

Occurrences of a highly exciting and offensive nature have recently taken place in some of the non-slave holding States calculated, if persisted in, to affect us in the most serious and vital manner. The subject is one of delicacy, and should be approached with courtesy and circumspection. The question of right involved admits of no parley, no intermeddling, no discussion from any quarter—nor can a proposition bearing on this point, either immediate or remotely, be listened to for a moment. . . .

Mississippi has given a practical demonstration of feeling on this exciting subject that may serve as an impressive admonition to offenders; and however we may regret the occasion, we are constrained to admit, that necessity will sometimes prompt a summary mode of trial and punishment unknown to the law. But no means should be spared to guard against and prevent similar occurrences. Nothing but the most manifest, imminent and unmediated peril can justify a repetition of such dangerous examples.

Source: Christopher Waldrep, *Lynching in America: A History in Documents* (New York: New York University Press, 2006), p. 67

2.18 Act of the General Assembly of the State of Georgia, 1857

Enacted just before the Civil War, this law allows for corporal punishment of free persons of color as well as slaves.

"Corporal punishment to slaves and free persons of color"

58. Sec. V. Be it further enacted, That said Commissioners be authorized to extend corporal punishment to slaves and free persons of color within the corporate limits of said Town to fifty stripes.

Source: Georgia Archives, http://content.sos.state.ga.us/cdm4/legdocs.php

2.19 Editorial Statement by Magistrate James Shackleford of Missouri, 1859

Following a lynching in Missouri, Magistrate Shackelford defends lynching in strident terms. He extols the character of the people in the county where it took place. He blames the criminality of African Americans in general, the abolitionists, and the legislature for the fact that lynching is necessary.

He relies on public opinion (presumably of the voters, who are all white)
to trump any rights-based objections to the practice of lynching, and he
makes clear the link between the lynchers themselves and the state actors,
like himself, who authorize and excuse them. Moreover, Shackleford cites
approvingly the actions of Andrew Jackson described in this chapter and
chapter 1.

"The people of Saline will so continue to act until the Legislature shall do their duty"

The summary punishment of four negroes, by the people of Saline County, on the 19th of this month, will excite a profound sensation throughout the country. It is due to the people of the State that they should know why the people of old Saline—distinguished, as they ever have been, for their devotion to law and order—should take law into their own hands.

Crime after crime has recently been perpetrated by the blacks. A most estimable young man had been murdered; another young man, in attempting to correct a slave whom he had forbidden to come to his place, had his arm cut with a deadly weapon, and has probably lost the use of his hand for life. . . .

. . . The people of Saline County will so continue to act until the Legislature shall do their duty, revise the criminal code, make the penalty adequate to the crime—satisfy the public opinion. Let the law harmonize with it. The law that is not based upon public opinion is but a rope of sand. An enlightened public opinion is the voice of God, and when brought into action it has a power and an energy that cannot be resisted. Abolitionists and negro sympathizers have had a great deal to do in creating a spirit of insubordination amongst our negro population. Every abolitionist ought to be driven out of the country; every free negro should be sold into slavery or go out of the state; no more emancipation without sending them off. These are the remedies I suggest. . . .

People may call it mob law. Well, it was mob law when Jackson drove the Legislature from their halls and closed the doors. It was mob law when he bombarded Pensacola, and hung Arbuthnot and Ambrister. It was mob law when the laboring men of Boston disguised themselves as Indians and threw the tea overboard. It was mob law when the people of France hurled the Bourbons from their throne, and crushed out the dominion of the priests and established a new order of things. Incapable of discriminating, they waded through oceans of blood of the innocent as well as the guilty, but they saved France. I know no reason why we should not have a little mob law in the state of Missouri, and the County of Saline, when the *occasion imperiously and of necessity demands it.*

Source: Christopher Waldrep, *Lynching in America: A History in Documents* (New York: New York University Press, 2006), p. 78

2.20 Telegraph from General Samuel Curtis to the Headquarters of the Army at Washington, D.C., 1865

On the morning of November 29, 1864, Colonel J. M. Chivington, commanding the Third Regiment of Colorado cavalry, attacked a Cheyenne and Arapaho encampment on Sand Creek in southeastern Colorado. The camp's residents were known to be seeking peace with military and territorial authorities and had even surrendered weapons to officers at nearby Fort Lyon. Nonetheless, Chivington ordered his force to make a surprise attack on the camp and stated repeatedly that no prisoners should be taken. Of the sixty-nine bodies recovered following the massacre, two-thirds were women and children. At a congressional hearing the following year, testimony described many atrocities committed by the soldiers, including soldiers using body parts as ornaments, "children shot at their mothers' breasts," a three year-old boy shot as he walked away from the scene, a prisoner executed after the fighting stopped, and scalping and other mutilation of victims. Chivington himself was relieved of his command shortly after the massacre, though he denied that any atrocities occurred and was defiant and unapologetic in the face of the congressional inquiry. Other civil and military authorities of the day wavered on the question of just treatment of Native Americans. They criticized Chivington's actions (as much for their consequences of greater native hostility toward whites as for anything else) but suggested, in various ways, that brutality by whites in the "Indian wars" was, at the least, unavoidable. General Samuel Curtis, whose telegraph message appears below, was Chivington's superior officer.

"I protest my desire to pursue the enemy everywhere"

I protest my desire to pursue the enemy everywhere, in his lodges especially; but I do not believe in killing women and children who can be taken, and if need be, camped east of the Mississippi, where they can be kept and cared for. I always did and do consider the Ash Hollow massacre a monstrous outrage, but the promotion and laudation that followed the transaction should excuse the indiscretion and cruelty of excited and outraged frontier soldiers, who have always heard Ash Hollow warfare extolled as the very brilliant point of glorious Indian warfare.

In my first movement last summer, when in pursuit of the Indians, I tried to restrain this plan of warfare, by issuing an order against the massacre of women and children, believing that taking such captive and bringing them away would just as effectually mortify and annoy the Indian robbers and warriors.

Source: *Report of the Committees of the Senate of the United States for the 38th Cong. 2nd sess. (1864–1865)* (Washington, DC: Government Printing Office, 1865), p. 77

2.21 Sworn Statement of James Cannon, 1865

James Cannon, a soldier who participated in the Sand Creek attack, provided a report to the 1865 congressional investigation of the massacre and was later called to testify before congress.

"He had cut a woman's private parts out"

I referred to the fact of there being a camp of friendly Indians in the immediate neighborhood, and remonstrated against simply attacking that camp, as I was aware that they were resting there in fancied security, under promises held out to them of safety. . . .

About daybreak on the morning of the 29th of November we came in sight of the camp of the friendly Indians aforementioned and was ordered by Colonel Chivington to attack the same, which was accordingly done. The command of Colonel Chivington was composed of about one thousand men. The village of the Indians consisted of from one hundred to one hundred and thirty lodges, and, as far as I am able to judge, of from five hundred to six hundred souls, the majority of whom were women and children.

In going over the battle-ground the next day, I did not see the body of a man, woman, or child but was scalped; and in many instances their bodies were mutilated in the most horrible manner, men, women and children—privates cut out &c. I heard one man say that he had cut a woman's private parts out, and had them for exhibition on a stick; I heard another man say that he had cut the fingers off an Indian to get the rings on his hand. According to the best of my knowledge and belief, those atrocities that were committed were with the knowledge of J. M. Chivington, and I do not know of his taking any measures to prevent them. I heard of one instance of a child a few months old being thrown in the feed-box of a wagon, and after being carried some distance, left on the ground to perish. I also heard of numerous instances in which men had cut out the private parts of females, and stretched them over the saddle-bows, and wore them over their hats, while riding in the ranks. All these matters were a subject of general conversation, and could not help being known by Colonel J. M. Chivington.

Source: *Report of the Committees of the Senate of the United States for the 38th Cong. 2nd sess., (1864–1865)* (Washington, DC: Government Printing Office, 1865), pp. 88–89

2.22 Congressional Testimony of John Smith, 1865

John Smith was also present during the attack. In addition to the atrocities he saw, he also described how his "half-breed" son, Jack, was executed after surrendering to U.S. troops.

"Worse mutilated than any I ever saw"

Question. Were the women and children slaughtered indiscriminately, or only so far as they were with the warriors?

Answer. Indiscriminately.

Question. Were there any acts of barbarity perpetrated there that came under your own observation?

Answer. Yes, sir; I saw the bodies of those lying there cut all to pieces, worse mutilated than any I ever saw before; the women cut all to pieces.

By Mr. Buckalew:

Question. How cut?

Answer. With knives; scalped; their brains knocked out; children two or three months old; all ages lying there, from sucking infants up to warriors.

By Mr. Gooch:

Question. Did you see it done?

Answer. Yes, sir; I saw them fall.

Question. Fall when they were killed?

Answer. Yes, sir.

Question. Did you see them when they were mutilated?

Answer. Yes, sir.

Question. By whom were they mutilated?

Answer. By the United States troops.

Question. Were there any other barbarities or atrocities committed there other than those you have mentioned, that you saw?

Answer. Yes, sir; I had a half-breed son there, who gave himself up. He started at the time the Indians fled; being a half-breed he had but little hope of being spared, and seeing them fire at me, he ran away with the Indians for the distance of about a mile. During the fight up there he walked back to my camp and went into the lodge. It was surrounded by soldiers at the time. He came in quietly and sat down; he remained there that day, that night, and the next day in the afternoon; about four o'clock in the evening, as I was sitting inside the camp, a soldier came up outside of the lodge and called me by name. I got up and went out; he took me by the arm and walked towards Colonel Chivington's camp, which was about sixty yards from my camp. Said he, "I am sorry to tell you, but they are going to kill your son Jack." I knew the feeling towards the whole camp of Indians, and that there was no use to make any resistance. I said, "I can't help it." I then walked on towards where Colonel Chivington was standing by his camp-fire; when I had got within a few feet of him I heard a gun fired, and saw a crowd run to my lodge, and they told me that Jack was dead.

Question. What action did Colonel Chivington take in regard to that matter?

Answer. Major Anthony, who was present, told Colonel Chivington that he had heard some remarks made, indicating that they were desirous of killing Jack; and that he (Colonel Chivington) had it in his power to save him, and that by saving him he might make him a very useful man, as he was well acquainted with all the Cheyenne and Arapahoe country, and he could be used as a guide or interpreter. Colonel Chivington replied to Major Anthony, as the Major himself told me, that he had no orders to receive and no advice to give. Major Anthony is now in this city.

Source: *Report of the Committees of the Senate of the United States for the 38th Cong., 2nd sess. (1864–1865)* (Washington, DC: Government Printing Office, 1865), pp. 9–10

2.23 Congressional Testimony of Colonel J. M. Chivington, 1865

Chivington himself was required to testify at the hearings, and his testimony differed dramatically from what other witnesses said. He denied any wrongdoing and claimed that there were few noncombatants in the camp. In this excerpt, he is openly scornful of Native Americans in general and of those in the vicinity of Fort Lyon in particular. He was relieved of his command following the incident. Chivington attributes claims of killing

noncombatants, mutilation, and the like to "the lying reports of interested
and malicious parties." However, his answer with regard to prisoners is in-
teresting. He claims that eight people surrendered and seven were brought
to Fort Lyon, but he also says that they cannot be taken prisoner without
endangering the troops. This appears to be a tacit admission that he did
not, as a rule, take prisoners.

"But few women or children had been slain"

7th question. What number of Indians were killed; and what number of
the killed were women, and what number were children?

Answer. From the best information I could obtain, I judge there were five
hundred or six hundred Indians killed; I cannot state positively the number
killed, nor can I state positively the number of women and children killed. Officers who passed over the field, by my orders, after the battle, for the purpose
of ascertaining the number of Indians killed, report that they saw but few
women or children dead, no more than would certainly fall in an attack upon
a camp in which they were. I myself passed over some portions of the field
after the fight, and I saw but one woman who had been killed, and one who
had hanged herself; I saw no dead children. From all I could learn, I arrived
at the conclusion that but few women or children had been slain. I am of the
opinion that when the attack was made on the Indian camp the greater number of squaws and children made their escape, while the warriors remained to
fight my troops.

8th question. State, as nearly as you can, the number of Indians that were
wounded, giving the number of women and the number of children among
the wounded.

Answer. I do not know that any Indians were wounded that were not killed;
if there were any wounded, I do not think they could have been made prisoners without endangering the lives of soldiers; Indians usually fight as long as
they have strength to resist. Eight Indians fell into the hands of the troops
alive, to my knowledge; these, with one exception, were sent to Fort Lyon and
properly cared for. . . .

10th question. What reason had you for making the attack? What reasons,
if any, had you to believe that Black Kettle or any other Indian or Indians in
the camp entertained feelings of hostility towards the whites? Give in detail
the names of all Indians so believed to be hostile, with the dates and places of
their hostile acts, so far as you may be able to do so.

Answer. My reason for making the attack on the Indian camp was, that I
believed the Indians in the camp were hostile to the whites. That they were of

the same tribes with those who had murdered many persons and destroyed much valuable property on the Platte and Arkansas rivers during the previous spring, summer and fall was beyond a doubt. When a tribe of Indians is at war with the whites it is impossible to determine what party or band of the tribe or the name of the Indian or Indians belonging to the tribe so at war are guilty of the acts of hostility. The most that can be ascertained is that Indians of the tribe have performed the acts. During the spring, summer and fall of the year 1864, the Arapaho and Cheyenne Indians, in some instances assisted or led on by Sioux, Kiowas, Comanches and Apaches, had committed many acts of hostility in the country lying between the Little Blue and the Rocky mountains and the Platte and Arkansas rivers. They had murdered many of the whites and taken others prisoners, and had destroyed valuable property, probably amounting to $200,000 or $300,000. Their rendezvous was on the headwaters of the Republican, probably one hundred miles from where the Indian camp was located. I had every reason to believe that these Indians were either directly or indirectly concerned in the outrages which had been committed upon the whites. I had no means of ascertaining what were the names of the Indians who had committed these outrages other than the declarations of the Indians themselves; and the character of Indians in the western country for truth and veracity, like their respect for the chastity of women who may become prisoners in their hands, is not of that order which is calculated to inspire confidence in what they may say. In this view I was supported by Major Anthony, lst Colorado cavalry, commanding at Fort Lyon, and Samuel G. Colby, United States Indian agent, who, as they had been in communication with these Indians, were more competent to judge of their disposition towards the whites than myself. Previous to the battle they expressed to me the opinion that the Indians should be punished. We found in the camp the scalps of nineteen (19) white persons. One of the surgeons informed me that one of these scalps had been taken from the victim's head not more than four days previously. I can furnish a child captured at the camp ornamented with six white women's scalps; these scalps must have been taken by these Indians or furnished to them for their gratification and amusement by some of their brethren, who, like themselves, were in amity with the whites . . . .

I questioned Major Anthony in regard to the whereabouts of hostile Indians. He said there was a camp of Cheyennes and Arapahoes about fifty miles distant; that he would have attacked before, but did not consider his force sufficient; that these Indians had threatened to attack the post, &c., and ought to be whipped, all of which was concurred in by Major Colley, Indian agent for the district of the Arkansas, which information, with the positive orders from

Major General Curtis, commanding the department, to punish these Indians, decided my course, and resulted in the battle of Sand Creek, which has created such a sensation in Congress through the lying reports of interested and malicious parties.

Source: *Report of the Committees of the Senate of the United States for the 38th Cong., 2nd sess. (1864–1865)* (Washington, DC: Government Printing Office, 1865), pp. 102–4

3

IMPERIALISM, JIM CROW, AND WORLD WAR

This chapter covers a range of contexts where torture and state violence occurred: the Civil War and Reconstruction, the Spanish-American War, U.S. military personnel policies, labor disputes, prison administration, "third degree" interrogation of criminal suspects, lynching, and world war. There are numerous connections, however. President Theodore Roosevelt refers to lynching in a 1902 speech on the war in the Philippines; the Wickersham Report finds police in the various states employing the same interrogation methods used against Filipino insurgents abroad; convicted prisoners are punished by the same means employed to produce confessions from criminal suspects.

Tensions are also evident between the impulse to condemn violent state practices and the recognition of the ends those practices serve. The police defend use of the "third degree," while military officials cite the need for strong counterinsurgency tactics and southern white politicians insist that lynching performs an important regulatory function. The rhetorical structure of these appeals is similar, and even the language usage moves from one context to another, as when American military officials refer to Filipinos as "niggers."

Violence, including torture, is essential to imperialistic ends in the Spanish-American War, but it is also functional for developing capitalism. The vagrancy law cited at the beginning of the chapter permits corporal punishment for the "offense" of being without work and also allows vagrants to be leased out as industrial laborers. In *Slavery by Another Name*, Douglas Blackmon documents this phenomenon in Alabama in the late nineteenth and early twentieth centuries. Local law enforcement benefited financially from convict leasing arrangements, as did southern industrialists operating foundries and the like. Convicts, on the other hand, were forced to work in dirty, unsafe conditions, without payment or means to complain about mistreatment.

I have included documents related to lynching here, even though lynchings themselves were carried out by private parties, because of the clear connections between state power and mob violence. In a number of cases, state officials licensed the lynchers to act and refused to prosecute them afterward. Moreover, the public spectacle aspect of the lynchings was so open and acknowledged that the event was sometimes advertised in the newspapers, as document 3.21 shows. The line between state actors torturing and state actors facilitating torture by others is a fine one indeed.

3.1 Lieber Code, 1863

The Lieber Code was drafted in 1863, at President Abraham Lincoln's direction, by Francis Lieber, a specialist in military law. The document represents an early attempt to codify the law of war. The author covers a range of issues, from assassination to prisoner treatment, and clearly states certain prohibitions, such as a prohibition on the use of torture to extract confessions (Article 80). In other places, however, the code shows a striking ambivalence about the use of violence, such as the use of retaliation (Article 27), starvation (Article 17), and "giving no quarter" (Article 60).

"Retaliation shall only be resorted to after careful inquiry into the real occurrence, and the character of the misdeeds that may demand retribution"

SECTION I
Martial Law—Military jurisdiction—Military necessity—Retaliation

Art. 1. A place, district, or country occupied by an enemy stands, in consequence of the occupation, under the Martial Law of the invading or occupying army, whether any proclamation declaring Martial Law, or any public warning to the inhabitants, has been issued or not. Martial Law is the immediate and direct effect and consequence of occupation or conquest.

The presence of a hostile army proclaims its Martial Law.

Art. 2. Martial Law does not cease during the hostile occupation, except by special proclamation, ordered by the commander in chief; or by special mention in the treaty of peace concluding the war, when the occupation of a place or territory continues beyond the conclusion of peace as one of the conditions of the same.

Art. 3. Martial Law in a hostile country consists in the suspension, by the occupying military authority, of the criminal and civil law, and of the domestic administration and government in the occupied place or territory, and in the substitution of military rule and force for the same, as well as in the dictation of general laws, as far as military necessity requires this suspension, substitution, or dictation.

The commander of the forces may proclaim that the administration of all civil and penal law shall continue either wholly or in part, as in times of peace, unless otherwise ordered by the military authority.

Art. 4. Martial Law is simply military authority exercised in accordance with the laws and usages of war. Military oppression is not Martial Law: it is the abuse of the power which that law confers. As Martial Law is executed by military force, it is incumbent upon those who administer it to be strictly guided by the principles of justice, honor, and humanity—virtues adorning a soldier even more than other men, for the very reason that he possesses the power of his arms against the unarmed.

Art. 5. Martial Law should be less stringent in places and countries fully occupied and fairly conquered. Much greater severity may be exercised in places or regions where actual hostilities exist, or are expected and must be prepared for. Its most complete sway is allowed—even in the commander's own country—when face to face with the enemy, because of the absolute necessities of the case, and of the paramount duty to defend the country against invasion.

To save the country is paramount to all other considerations.

Art. 6. All civil and penal law shall continue to take its usual course in the enemy's places and territories under Martial Law, unless interrupted or stopped by order of the occupying military power; but all the functions of the hostile government—legislative executive, or administrative—whether of a general, provincial, or local character, cease under Martial Law, or continue only with the sanction, or, if deemed necessary, the participation of the occupier or invader.

Art. 7. Martial Law extends to property, and to persons, whether they are subjects of the enemy or aliens to that government.

Art. 8. Consuls, among American and European nations, are not diplomatic agents. Nevertheless, their offices and persons will be subjected to Martial Law in cases of urgent necessity only: their property and business are not exempted. Any delinquency they commit against the established military rule may be punished as in the case of any other inhabitant, and such punishment furnishes no reasonable ground for international complaint.

Art. 9. The functions of Ambassadors, Ministers, or other diplomatic agents accredited by neutral powers to the hostile government, cease, so far as regards the displaced government; but the conquering or occupying power usually recognizes them as temporarily accredited to itself.

Art. 10. Martial Law affects chiefly the police and collection of public revenue and taxes, whether imposed by the expelled government or by the invader, and refers mainly to the support and efficiency of the army, its safety, and the safety of its operations.

Art. 11. The law of war does not only disclaim all cruelty and bad faith concerning engagements concluded with the enemy during the war, but also the breaking of stipulations solemnly contracted by the belligerents in time of peace, and avowedly intended to remain in force in case of war between the contracting powers.

It disclaims all extortions and other transactions for individual gain; all acts of private revenge, or connivance at such acts.

Offenses to the contrary shall be severely punished, and especially so if committed by officers.

Art. 12. Whenever feasible, Martial Law is carried out in cases of individual offenders by Military Courts; but sentences of death shall be executed only with the approval of the chief executive, provided the urgency of the case does not require a speedier execution, and then only with the approval of the chief commander.

Art. 13. Military jurisdiction is of two kinds: First, that which is conferred and defined by statute; second, that which is derived from the common law of war. Military offenses under the statute law must be tried in the manner therein directed; but military offenses which do not come within the statute must be tried and punished under the common law of war. The character of the courts which exercise these jurisdictions depends upon the local laws of each particular country.

In the armies of the United States the first is exercised by courts-martial, while cases which do not come within the "Rules and Articles of War," or the jurisdiction conferred by statute on courts-martial, are tried by military commissions.

Art. 14. Military necessity, as understood by modern civilized nations, consists in the necessity of those measures which are indispensable for securing the ends of the war, and which are lawful according to the modern law and usages of war.

Art. 15. Military necessity admits of all direct destruction of life or limb of armed enemies, and of other persons whose destruction is incidentally unavoidable in the armed contests of the war; it allows of the capturing of every armed enemy, and every enemy of importance to the hostile government, or of peculiar danger to the captor; it allows of all destruction of property, and obstruction of the ways and channels of traffic, travel, or communication, and of all withholding of sustenance or means of life from the enemy; of the appropriation of whatever an enemy's country affords necessary for the subsistence and safety of the army, and of such deception as does not involve the breaking of good faith either positively pledged, regarding agreements entered into during the war, or supposed by the modern law of war to exist. Men who take up arms against one another in public war do not cease on this account to be moral beings, responsible to one another and to God.

Art. 16. Military necessity does not admit of cruelty—that is, the infliction of suffering for the sake of suffering or for revenge, nor of maiming or wounding except in fight, nor of torture to extort confessions. It does not admit of the use of poison in any way, nor of the wanton devastation of a district. It admits of deception, but disclaims acts of perfidy; and, in general, military necessity does not include any act of hostility which makes the return to peace unnecessarily difficult.

Art. 17. War is not carried on by arms alone. It is lawful to starve the hostile belligerent, armed or unarmed, so that it leads to the speedier subjection of the enemy.

Art. 18. When a commander of a besieged place expels the noncombatants, in order to lessen the number of those who consume his stock of provisions, it is lawful, though an extreme measure, to drive them back, so as to hasten on the surrender.

Art. 19. Commanders, whenever admissible, inform the enemy of their intention to bombard a place, so that the noncombatants, and especially the women and children, may be removed before the bombardment commences. But it is no infraction of the common law of war to omit thus to inform the enemy. Surprise may be a necessity.

Art. 20. Public war is a state of armed hostility between sovereign nations or governments. It is a law and requisite of civilized existence that men live in political, continuous societies, forming organized units, called states or nations, whose constituents bear, enjoy, suffer, advance and retrograde together, in peace and in war.

Art. 21. The citizen or native of a hostile country is thus an enemy, as one of the constituents of the hostile state or nation, and as such is subjected to the hardships of the war.

Art. 22. Nevertheless, as civilization has advanced during the last centuries, so has likewise steadily advanced, especially in war on land, the distinction between the private individual belonging to a hostile country and the hostile country itself, with its men in arms. The principle has been more and more acknowledged that the unarmed citizen is to be spared in person, property, and honor as much as the exigencies of war will admit.

Art. 23. Private citizens are no longer murdered, enslaved, or carried off to distant parts, and the inoffensive individual is as little disturbed in his private relations as the commander of the hostile troops can afford to grant in the overruling demands of a vigorous war.

Art. 24. The almost universal rule in remote times was, and continues to be with barbarous armies, that the private individual of the hostile country is destined to suffer every privation of liberty and protection, and every disruption of family ties. Protection was, and still is with uncivilized people, the exception.

Art. 25. In modern regular wars of the Europeans, and their descendants in other portions of the globe, protection of the inoffensive citizen of the hostile country is the rule; privation and disturbance of private relations are the exceptions.

Art. 26. Commanding generals may cause the magistrates and civil officers of the hostile country to take the oath of temporary allegiance or an oath of fidelity to their own victorious government or rulers, and they may expel everyone who declines to do so. But whether they do so or not, the people and their civil officers owe strict obedience to them as long as they hold sway over the district or country, at the peril of their lives.

Art. 27. The law of war can no more wholly dispense with retaliation than can the law of nations, of which it is a branch. Yet civilized nations acknowledge retaliation as the sternest feature of war. A reckless enemy often leaves to his opponent no other means of securing himself against the repetition of barbarous outrage

Art. 28. Retaliation will, therefore, never be resorted to as a measure of mere revenge, but only as a means of protective retribution, and moreover, cautiously and unavoidably; that is to say, retaliation shall only be resorted to after careful inquiry into the real occurrence, and the character of the misdeeds that may demand retribution.

Unjust or inconsiderate retaliation removes the belligerents farther and farther from the mitigating rules of regular war, and by rapid steps leads them nearer to the internecine wars of savages.

Art. 29. Modern times are distinguished from earlier ages by the existence, at one and the same time, of many nations and great governments related to one another in close intercourse.

Peace is their normal condition; war is the exception. The ultimate object of all modern war is a renewed state of peace.

The more vigorously wars are pursued, the better it is for humanity. Sharp wars are brief.

Art. 30. Ever since the formation and coexistence of modern nations, and ever since wars have become great national wars, war has come to be acknowledged not to be its own end, but the means to obtain great ends of state, or to consist in defense against wrong; and no conventional restriction of the modes adopted to injure the enemy is any longer admitted; but the law of war imposes many limitations and restrictions on principles of justice, faith, and honor.

SECTION II

Public and private property of the enemy—Protection of persons, and especially of women, of religion, the arts and sciences—Punishment of crimes against the inhabitants of hostile countries. . . .

Art. 37. The United States acknowledge and protect, in hostile countries occupied by them, religion and morality; strictly private property; the persons of the inhabitants, especially those of women: and the sacredness of domestic relations. Offenses to the contrary shall be rigorously punished.

This rule does not interfere with the right of the victorious invader to tax the people or their property, to levy forced loans, to billet soldiers, or to appropriate property, especially houses, lands, boats or ships, and churches, for temporary and military uses. . . .

Art. 40. There exists no law or body of authoritative rules of action between hostile armies, except that branch of the law of nature and nations which is called the law and usages of war on land. . . .

Art. 42. Slavery, complicating and confounding the ideas of property, (that is of a thing,) and of personality, (that is of humanity,) exists according to municipal or local law only. The law of nature and nations has never acknowledged it. The digest of the Roman law enacts the early dictum of the pagan jurist, that "so far as the law of nature is concerned, all men are equal." Fugitives escaping from a country in which they were slaves, villains, or serfs, into another country, have, for centuries past, been held free and acknowledged free by judicial decisions of European countries, even though the municipal law of the country in which the slave had taken refuge acknowledged slavery within its own dominions.

Art. 43. Therefore, in a war between the United States and a belligerent which admits of slavery, if a person held in bondage by that belligerent be captured by or come as a fugitive under the protection of the military forces of the United States, such person is immediately entitled to the rights and privileges of a freeman. To return such person into slavery would amount to enslaving a free person, and neither the United States nor any officer under their authority can enslave any human being. Moreover, a person so made free by the law of war is under the shield of the law of nations, and the former owner or State can have, by the law of postliminy, no belligerent lien or claim of service.

Art. 44. All wanton violence committed against persons in the invaded country, all destruction of property not commanded by the authorized officer, all robbery, all pillage or sacking, even after taking a place by main force, all rape, wounding, maiming, or killing of such inhabitants, are prohibited under the penalty of death, or such other severe punishment as may seem adequate for the gravity of the offense.

A soldier, officer or private, in the act of committing such violence, and disobeying a superior ordering him to abstain from it, may be lawfully killed on the spot by such superior. . . .

Art. 47. Crimes punishable by all penal codes, such as arson, murder, maiming, assaults, highway robbery, theft, burglary, fraud, forgery, and rape, if committed by an American soldier in a hostile country against its inhabitants, are not only punishable as at home, but in all cases in which death is not inflicted, the severer punishment shall be preferred.

SECTION III

Deserters—Prisoners of war—Hostages—Booty on the battle-field.

Art. 56. A prisoner of war is subject to no punishment for being a public enemy, nor is any revenge wreaked upon him by the intentional infliction of any suffering, or disgrace, by cruel imprisonment, want of food, by mutilation, death, or any other barbarity. . . .

Art. 58. The law of nations knows of no distinction of color, and if an enemy of the United States should enslave and sell any captured persons of their army, it would be a case for the severest retaliation, if not redressed upon complaint.

The United States cannot retaliate by enslavement; therefore death must be the retaliation for this crime against the law of nations.

Art. 59. A prisoner of war remains answerable for his crimes committed against the captor's army or people, committed before he was captured, and for which he has not been punished by his own authorities.

All prisoners of war are liable to the infliction of retaliatory measures.

Art. 60. It is against the usage of modern war to resolve, in hatred and revenge, to give no quarter. No body of troops has the right to declare that it will not give, and therefore will not expect, quarter; but a commander is permitted to direct his troops to give no quarter, in great straits, when his own salvation makes it impossible to cumber himself with prisoners.

Art. 61. Troops that give no quarter have no right to kill enemies already disabled on the ground, or prisoners captured by other troops.

Art. 62. All troops of the enemy known or discovered to give no quarter in general, or to any portion of the army, receive none.

Art. 63. Troops who fight in the uniform of their enemies, without any plain, striking, and uniform mark of distinction of their own, can expect no quarter.

Art. 64. If American troops capture a train containing uniforms of the enemy, and the commander considers it advisable to distribute them for use among his men, some striking mark or sign must be adopted to distinguish the American soldier from the enemy.

Art. 65. The use of the enemy's national standard, flag, or other emblem of nationality, for the purpose of deceiving the enemy in battle, is an act of perfidy by which they lose all claim to the protection of the laws of war.

Art. 66. Quarter having been given to an enemy by American troops, under a misapprehension of his true character, he may, nevertheless, be ordered to suffer death if, within three days after the battle, it be discovered that he belongs to a corps which gives no quarter.

Art. 67. The law of nations allows every sovereign government to make war upon another sovereign state, and, therefore, admits of no rules or laws different from those of regular warfare, regarding the treatment of prisoners of war, although they may belong to the army of a government which the captor may consider as a wanton and unjust assailant.

Art. 68. Modern wars are not internecine wars, in which the killing of the enemy is the object. The destruction of the enemy in modern war, and, indeed, modern war itself, are means to obtain that object of the belligerent which lies beyond the war. Unnecessary or revengeful destruction of life is not lawful.

Art. 69. Outposts, sentinels, or pickets are not to be fired upon, except to drive them in, or when a positive order, special or general, has been issued to that effect.

Art. 70. The use of poison in any manner, be it to poison wells, or food, or arms, is wholly excluded from modern warfare. He that uses it puts himself out of the pale of the law and usages of war.

Art. 71. Whoever intentionally inflicts additional wounds on an enemy already wholly disabled, or kills such an enemy, or who orders or encourages soldiers to do so, shall suffer death, if duly convicted, whether he belongs to the Army of the United States, or is an enemy captured after having committed his misdeed. . . .

Art. 75. Prisoners of war are subject to confinement or imprisonment such as may be deemed necessary on account of safety, but they are to be subjected to no other intentional suffering or indignity. The confinement and mode of treating a prisoner may be varied during his captivity according to the demands of safety.

Art. 76. Prisoners of war shall be fed upon plain and wholesome food, whenever practicable, and treated with humanity.

They may be required to work for the benefit of the captor's government, according to their rank and condition.

Art. 77. A prisoner of war who escapes may be shot or otherwise killed in his flight; but neither death nor any other punishment shall be inflicted upon him simply for his attempt to escape, which the law of war does not consider a crime. Stricter means of security shall be used after an unsuccessful attempt at escape.

If, however, a conspiracy is discovered, the purpose of which is a united or general escape, the conspirators may be rigorously punished, even with death; and capital punishment may also be inflicted upon prisoners of war discovered to have plotted rebellion against the authorities of the captors, whether in union with fellow prisoners or other persons.

Art. 78. If prisoners of war, having given no pledge nor made any promise on their honor, forcibly or otherwise escape, and are captured again in battle after having rejoined their own army, they shall not be punished for their escape, but shall be treated as simple prisoners of war, although they will be subjected to stricter confinement.

Art. 79. Every captured wounded enemy shall be medically treated, according to the ability of the medical staff.

Art. 80. Honorable men, when captured, will abstain from giving to the enemy information concerning their own army, and the modern law of war permits no longer the use of any violence against prisoners in order to extort the desired information or to punish them for having given false information.

SECTION IV
Partisans—Armed enemies not belonging to the hostile army—Scouts—Armed prowlers—War-rebels

Art. 81. Partisans are soldiers armed and wearing the uniform of their army, but belonging to a corps which acts detached from the main body for the purpose of making inroads into the territory occupied by the enemy. If captured, they are entitled to all the privileges of the prisoner of war.

Art. 82. Men, or squads of men, who commit hostilities, whether by fighting, or inroads for destruction or plunder, or by raids of any kind, without commission, without being part and portion of the organized hostile army, and without sharing continuously in the war, but who do so with intermitting returns to their homes and avocations, or with the occasional assumption of the semblance of peaceful pursuits, divesting themselves of the character or appearance of soldiers - such men, or squads of men, are not public enemies, and, therefore, if captured, are not entitled to the privileges of prisoners of war, but shall be treated summarily as highway robbers or pirates.

Art. 83. Scouts, or single soldiers, if disguised in the dress of the country or in the uniform of the army hostile to their own, employed in obtaining information, if found within or lurking about the lines of the captor, are treated as spies, and suffer death.

Art. 84. Armed prowlers, by whatever names they may be called, or persons of the enemy's territory, who steal within the lines of the hostile army for the purpose of robbing, killing, or of destroying bridges, roads or canals, or of robbing or destroying the mail, or of cutting the telegraph wires, are not entitled to the privileges of the prisoner of war.

Art. 85. War-rebels are persons within an occupied territory who rise in arms against the occupying or conquering army, or against the authorities established by the same. If captured, they may suffer death, whether they rise singly, in small or large bands, and whether called upon to do so by their own, but expelled, government or not. They are not prisoners of war; nor are they if discovered and secured before their conspiracy has matured to an actual rising or armed violence.

SECTION IX
Assassination

Art. 148. The law of war does not allow proclaiming either an individual belonging to the hostile army, or a citizen, or a subject of the hostile government, an outlaw, who may be slain without trial by any captor, any more than the modern law of peace allows such intentional outlawry; on the contrary, it abhors such outrage. The sternest retaliation should follow the murder committed in consequence of such proclamation, made by whatever authority. Civilized nations look with horror upon offers of rewards for the assassination of enemies as relapses into barbarism.

Source: www.icrc.org

3.2 Congressional Testimony of Rev. William John Hamilton, 1869

The Confederate prison at Andersonville, Georgia, was notorious for its appalling conditions of overcrowding, disease, and brutality. After the war, the prison warden Henry Wirz was tried, condemned, and executed for his role in the deaths of Andersonville prisoners. While some argue that Wirz was scapegoated for the thousands of Union prisoners who died at Andersonville and at other Confederate prison camps, the trial record clearly establishes the extent of the prisoners' suffering and the shocking conditions of the prison, regardless of Wirz's legal culpability. The following testimony was reproduced in a congressional report published in 1869.

"They were not only covered with the ordinary vermin, but with maggots"

Q. Give the court some idea of the condition of the stockade.

A. I found the stockade extremely filthy; the men all huddled together, covered with vermin. The best idea I can give the court of the condition of the place is, perhaps, this: I went in there with a white linen coat on, and I had not been in there more than ten minutes or a quarter of an hour when a gentleman drew my attention to the condition of my coat. It was all covered over with vermin, and I had to take my coat off and leave it with one of the guards and perform my duties in short-sleeves, the place was so filthy.

Q. What did you observe with regard to shelter in the stockade and the suffering of the men from heat there?

A. When I visited the stockade there was no shelter at all, so far as I could see, except that some of the men who had their blankets there had put them up on little bits of roots that they had abstracted from the ground; but I could not see any tents or shelter of any other kind. I got the names of several prisoners who had relatives living in the south and wrote their friends when I returned to Macon, and I had some tents introduced there; they were sent down, and the men received them.

. . . There is a branch that runs right in the center of the stockade, and I tried to cross the branch, but was unable to do so as the men were crowding around there trying to get into the water to cool themselves, and wash themselves. I could not get over the branch . . . the heat there was intolerable; there was no air at all in the stockade. The logs of which the stockade was composed were so close together that I could not feel any fresh air inside; and with a strong sun beaming down on it and no shelter at all, of course the heat must have been insufferable; at least I felt it so.

. . . I have seen a person in the hospital in a nude condition, perfectly naked. They were not only covered with the ordinary vermin, but with maggots. They had involuntary evacuations, and there were no persons to look after them. The nurses did not seem to pay any attention whatever, and in consequence of being allowed to lie in their own filth for some hours, vermin of every description had got on them which they were unable to keep off them. . . . I have seen them making little places from a foot to a foot and a half deep, and stretching their blankets over them. I have crawled into such places frequently to hear the confession of the dying. They would hold from one to two; sometimes a prisoner would share his blanket with another and allow him to get under shelter.

Source: *U.S. House of Representatives Report on the Treatment of Prisoners of War by the Rebel Authorities* (Washington, DC: Government Printing Office, 1869), p. 87.

3.3 Statement of Sergeant Warren Lee Goss, Andersonville Prisoner, 1869

An Andersonville prisoner swore an affidavit in order to present his account to Congress. The excerpt is from the published account of his testimony. In it, he describes the use of a "dead-line," a marked (sometimes poorly marked) line within the prison stockade that prisoners were forbidden to cross, or even to approach.

"One of the great instruments of death in the prison was the dead-line"

One of the great instruments of death in the prison was the dead-line. This line consisted of a row of stakes driven into the ground, with narrow board strips nailed down upon the top, at the distance of about fifteen feet from the stockade, on the interior side. This line was closely guarded by sentinels, stationed above on the stockade, and any person who approached it, as many unconsciously did, and as in the crowd was often unavoidable, was shot dead, with no warning whatever to admonish him that death was near. An instance of this kind came to my notice the second day I was in prison. A poor one-legged cripple placed one hand on the dead line to support him while he got his crutch, which had fallen from his feeble grasp to the ground. In this position he was shot through the lungs, and laid near the dead-line writhing in torments during most of the forenoon, until at last death came to his relief. None dared approach him to relieve his sufferings through fear of the same fate. The guard loaded his musket after he had performed this dastardly act, and grinning with satisfaction, viewed the body of the dying, murdered man, for nearly an hour, with apparent pleasure, occasionally raising his gun to threaten any one who, from curiosity or pity, dared to approach the poor fellow. In a similar manner men were continually shot upon the smallest pretext, and that it was nothing but a pretext was apparent from the fact that one man approaching the dead line could have in no manner harmed the cumbersome stockade, even had he been inclined to do so, and a hundred men could not, with their united strength, have forced it. Frequently the guard fired indiscriminately into a crowd. On one occasion I saw a man wounded and another killed; one was lying under his blanket asleep, the other standing some distance from the dead-line.

Source: *U.S. House of Representatives Report on the Treatment of Prisoners of War by the Rebel Authorities* (Washington, DC: Government Printing Office, 1869), p. 56

3.4 Report of the House Special Committee on the Treatment of Prisoners of War and Union Citizens, 1869

The House Committee summarizes punishment methods used at Andersonville and other Confederate prisons.

"'Tying up by the thumbs' was . . . one of the most severe punishments inflicted"

The "stocks" were of two kinds. In one the prisoner was tied to a wooden frame, with arms extended, and his feet closely tied together, in which position, unable to move either hand or foot, he was compelled to stand or, as was sometimes the case, lie upon his back during the time of confinement. In the other, the prisoner's feet were fastened in a wooden frame, elevated so that it was usually impossible for him to sit up, and compelling him to lie upon his back. The stocks were without shelter of any kind. In them prisoners were confined for days, exposed to the scorching sun and rain.

Many of those confined in the stocks died while undergoing the fearful punishment. The stocks at Andersonville were between the headquarters of Wirz and the stockade. This punishment, which was adopted at other prison pens, was inflicted on recaptured prisoners, and for so-called insubordination.

The "chain gang" was composed usually of twelve or more prisoners placed in two ranks. Their feet were shackled so they could step but a few inches, and a heavy iron collar was placed around each man's neck. A heavy chain extended from collar to collar, and from shackle to shackle. Each man had a small iron ball attached to one of his legs, while a sixty-four pound ball was added to every four men, upon the inside of a square thus formed. If a prisoner died while in the chain-gang, as was sometimes the case, he was not immediately removed. His comrades were compelled to drag his dead body with them until the pleasure of the officer or guard relieved them. Prisoners were kept in the chain gangs as long as two weeks at a time, the shackle around the ankles in the meantime cutting or wearing through the flesh to the bones.

"Bucking and gagging" was frequently resorted to. The prisoner was seated on the ground, his wrists firmly tied together and placed over his knees, and a stick run under his knees and over his arms at the elbow joints. A stick or "gag" was then placed in his mouth and tied tightly by strings extending back of his head. In this position the sufferer (often a sick man) was kept several hours in the sun. This mode of punishment prevailed at all the prisons, and was inflicted for the most trivial (real or imaginary) offenses.

"Spread eagle" or the "sweating process" was inflicted as follows: The victim was placed upon his back on the ground and his arms and legs extended, in which position he was fastened and left without either food or water. Many who were subjected to this punishment died before the expiration of the sentence.

The "wooden horse" was a high trestle, upon which the prisoner was placed, his hands tied behind him, a gag placed in his mouth, and his legs drawn apart by ropes attached to his ankles and fastened to stakes in the ground. During the winter of 1863-'64, at Belle Isle, men were kept on the "wooden horse" until nearly frozen to death.

"Tying up by the thumbs" was, during its continuance, one of the most severe punishments inflicted. The prisoner's arms were elevated, his thumbs tied up by strings, and then he was raised up so that his heels would clear the ground, thus bringing a considerable portion of his weight upon his extended arms and thumbs. The victims usually fainted while undergoing this torture; in such cases they were let down until restored to consciousness, and then hung up again.

Source: *U.S. House of Representatives Report on the Treatment of Prisoners of War by the Rebel Authorities* (Washington, DC: Government Printing Office, 1869), p. 204

3.5 Alabama Black Codes, 1865

The Black Codes are familiar to observers of U.S. history as Reconstruction-era laws designed to maintain a racialized caste system in the South. They stipulated limits on the rights of African Americans and, in some cases, denied rights entirely. In this first example, the criminal offense of vagrancy is established. Appearing in public without work (or even, as Blackmon shows in Slavery by Another Name, *traveling on an errand), often led directly to arrest, sentencing, and captive, unpaid labor in nearby mines and foundries. The sheriff would receive lease payment, and the foundry would get free labor. This process was structured by legal rules such as the one that follows.*

It is also worth noting that the standard for permissible corporal punishment privatizes the matter of employee discipline, suggesting limits on the state's power to intervene.

"Such reasonable correction as a parent may inflict on a stubborn, refractory child"

An Act concerning vagrants and vagrancy

Be it enacted by the Senate and House of Representatives of the State of Alabama, in General Assembly convened, That the Commissioners' Court of any county in this State may purchase, rent or provide such lands, buildings and other property as may be necessary for a poor-house, or house of correction for any such county, and may appoint suitable officers for the management thereof, and make all necessary by-laws, rules and regulations or the government of the inmates thereof, and cause the same to be enforced; but in no case shall the punishment inflicted exceed hard labor, either in or out of said house; the use of chain-gangs, putting in stocks, if necessary, to prevent escapes; such reasonable correction as a parent may inflict upon a stubborn, refractory child; and solitary confinement for not longer than one week, on bread and water; and may cause to be hired out such as vagrants, to work in chain-gangs or otherwise, for the length of time for which they are sentenced; and the proceeds of such hiring must be paid into the county treasury, for the benefit of the helpless in said poor-house, or house of correction.

Sec. 2. *Be it further enacted,* That the following persons are vagrants in addition to those already declared to be vagrants by law, or that may be hereafter be so declared by law; a stubborn or refractory servant; a laborer or servant who loiters away his time, or refuses to comply with any contract for a term of service without just cause; any such person may be sent to the house of correction in the county in which such offense is committed; and for want of such house of correction the common jail of the county may be used for that purpose.

Sec. 3. *Be it further enacted,* That when a vagrant is found, any justice of the peace of the county, must upon complaint made upon oath, or on his own knowledge, issue his warrant to the sheriff or any constable of the county, to bring such a person to him; and if, upon examination and hearing of testimony, it appears to the justice, that such person is a vagrant, he shall assess a fine of fifty dollars and costs against such vagrant; and in default of payment, he must commit such vagrant to the house of correction; or if no such house to the common jail of the county for a term not exceeding six months; and until such fine, cost and charges are paid, or such party is otherwise discharged by law; Provided, That when committed to jail under this section, the commissioners' court may cause him to be hired out in like manner as in section one of this act.

Source: Transcription available at http://home.gwu.edu/~jjhawkin/BlackCodes/BlackCodes.htm

3.6 Alabama Black Codes, 1865

This second provision of the Alabama Black Codes describes procedures for the apprenticeship of minors in a feudal relationship with their "masters": they owe a personal obligation to the master, and the master must feed and clothe them in return. The former owner of a "freedman" minor's parent is entitled to claim that minor as servant, and corporal punishment is permitted, under a "moderate" standard such as the pre–Civil War laws specified.

"Such moderate corporeal chastisement as a father or guardian is allowed to inflict on his or her child"

AN ACT

To define the relative duties of master and apprentice.

Sec. 1. *Be it enacted by the Senate and House of Representatives of the State of Alabama in General Assembly convened,* That it shall be the duty of all sheriffs, justices of the peace, and other civil officers of the several counties in this State, to report to the probate courts of their respective counties, at any time, all minors under the age of eighteen years, within their respective counties, beats, or districts, who are orphans without visible means of support, or whose parent or parents have not the means, or who refuse to provide for and support said minors, and thereupon it shall be the duty of said probate court to apprentice said minor to some suitable and competent person, on such terms as the court may direct, having a particular case to the interest of said minor; Provided, If the said minor be the child of a freedman, the former owner of said minor shall have the preference, when proof shall be made that he or she shall be a suitable person for that purpose; and provided, that the judge of probate shall make a record of all the proceedings in such case, for which he shall be entitled to a compensation of one dollar, to be paid by the master or mistress.

Sec. 2. *Be it further enacted,* That when proof shall be fully made before such court, that the person or persons to whom said minor shall be apprenticed shall be a suitable person to have the charge and care of said minor, and fully to protect the interest of said minor, the said court shall require the said master or mistress to execute bond with security to the State of Alabama, conditioned that he or she shall furnish said minor with sufficient food and clothing, to treat said minor humanely, furnish medical attention in case of sickness, teach or cause to be taught him or her to read and write, if under fifteen years old, and will conform to any law that may be hereafter passed for the regulation of the duties and relation of the master and apprentice.

Sec. 3. *Be it further enacted,* That in the management and control of said apprentices, said master or mistress shall have power to inflict such moderate corporeal chastisement as a father or guardian is allowed to inflict on his or her child, or ward at common law; Provided, That in no case shall cruel or inhumane punishment be inflicted.

Source: Transcription available at http://home.gwu.edu/~jjhawkin/BlackCodes/ BlackCodes.htm

3.7 Act of Congress, 1872

As Rejali points out in Torture and Democracy, *punishment by branding in the U.S. military became illegal in 1872.*

"It shall be illegal to brand, mark, or tattoo"

That hereafter it shall be illegal to brand, mark, or tattoo on the body of any soldier by sentence of court-martial, and the word "corporeal" shall be stricken from the forty-fifth of the rules and articles for the government of the armies of the United States.

Source: 42nd Cong., 2nd sess., June 6, 1872, chap. 316, para. 668.

3.8 Opinion in *In re Debs,* 1895

Labor activist Eugene Debs was sentenced to confinement for contempt of court after he violated an injunction against striking. In re Debs *is an appeal of the denial of habeas corpus petition, by which Debs sought release from unlawful confinement. He was represented by Clarence Darrow before the Supreme Court, but his appeal was unsuccessful. The Court's sympathies clearly lay with management rather than labor, and the opinion counts Debs lucky that he was punished by confinement rather than by violence.*

"Enforcing that determination by the club of the policeman and the bayonet of the soldier"

So, in the case before us, the right to use force does not exclude the right of appeal to the courts for a judicial determination and for the exercise of all their powers of prevention. Indeed, it is more to the price [sic] than to the blame of the government, that, instead of determining for itself questions of right and wrong on the part of these petitioners and their associates and enforcing that determination by the club of the policeman and the bayonet of the soldier, it submitted all those questions to the peaceful determination of judicial tribunals, and invoked their consideration and judgment as to the measure of its rights and powers and the correlative obligations of those against whom it made complaint. And it is equally to the credit of the latter that the judgment of those tribunals was by the great body of them respected, and the troubles which threatened so much disaster terminated.

Source: *In re Debs*, 158 U.S. 564 (1895)

3.9 Statement of Sheriff James Martin on the "Lattimer Massacre," 1897

In what was later known as the "Lattimer Massacre," Luzerne County (Pennsylvania) sheriff James Martin and his deputies fired on unarmed striking mineworkers, killing twenty of them. This was one of the deadliest incidents of labor violence in U.S. history, made worse by the ethnic divisions involved. The victims were Italian, Polish, Slovak, and Lithuanian immigrants, and the sheriff's party represented the "English-speaking establishment," in the words of one historian. Undercurrents of nativist sentiment can be discerned in the remarks of Sheriff Martin immediately after the incident. Martin and his deputies were eventually acquitted of murder and felonious wounding in an 1898 criminal proceeding.

"Some big Italian came from the crowd"

We first met the mob at West Hazleton, and we saw by their actions that they were going to resume their marching. I went over to them and told them that they should not commit any lawless act and that they should disperse and cease any public demonstration. One of the leaders of the mob, who was an Italian, came out from the crowd and told me they had made up their minds to march to Lattimer and get the men out of the mine there. I again read the riot act to them and told them that they were violating the law of the Commonwealth by so doing and that if they attempted to interfere with any more of the workingmen it would be my duty as sheriff of the county, to prevent them from doing so.

At this the leader said in broken English, "The English miners have not treated us right since we have been here and we are going to have some rights of our own. We pay taxes here and we have as much right to march on the streets as any one else."

I again told the men that if they marched to Lattimer I would follow them with the deputies.

This ended the conversation for the time being and the men started out on their journey. I then went to Hazleton and summoned the deputies and told them to take their Winchesters with them. There were about seventy-five of them altogether. We boarded trolley cars and started for Lattimer.

When within a short distance of that place we saw the column advancing toward the mine and we stopped the car and got out in the road.

When the strikers reached us I ordered them to halt and they did so. For the third time I told them that I had warned them to disperse and that if they did not obey my warning there would be trouble. A few of the men came up from the head of the crowd and all shouted at once that they did not care for me or my deputies and they intended to go to Lattimer and stop the mine. While I was arguing with the men I saw them talking secretly and I knew that some sort of trouble was brewing. The [illegible] thing I knew some big Italian came from the crowd, one of the men who had been shouting at me, and grabbed me by the throat. He called me a vile name and said that I had no right to interfere in their business. The fellow pulled my head under his arms and struck me on the shoulder, and when I got a chance to look up I saw that I was surrounded by several fierce-looking men. I shouted to the men that they should arrest the person who had attacked me, but in the confusion the deputies evidently did not hear what I said.

Then I heard a shot and it was soon followed by another. This seemed a signal for a combined volley on the part of the deputies and before I could extricate myself from the crowd that had surrounded me there was one rifle crack after another. I do not know how many bullets were fired, but there was an awful din and I imagine that at least 150 bullets were sent on their deadly mission. . . .

Did you give the order to fire, sheriff? (reporter)

No sir, I did not. Those words never came from my lips. When the deputies saw that I was attacked, I suppose they thought it was their duty to protect me. One of the men fired, then another and then the firing became general. I suppose they thought the strikers were about to attack them and also followed the example of the first man who fired.

Do you think the deputies were justified in doing what they did? (reporter)

Concerning that I will say nothing.

Source: *Wilkes-Barre Record,* September 11, 1897 (courtesy of Bishop Library, Luzerne County Historical Society, Wilkes-Barre, PA)

3.10 Jury Charge of Judge Woodward at Trial of Sheriff Martin and Deputies, 1898

There were, of course, conflicting versions of the events immediately preceding the "Lattimer Massacre." Sheriff Martin himself gave a different version of the facts at trial from the one presented above. At trial, he said he was attacked by a man with a knife, while immediately after the event he said the man grabbed him with his hands. Some accounts state that Martin waved a pistol over his head just before the shooting began. In any case, trial judge Stanley Woodward gave final instructions to the jury that virtually guaranteed acquittal. Judge Woodward instructed the jury that if the order to disperse was lawful, then the shootings were lawful.

"In a time of great emergency, or in a crisis of unusual danger, the limits under which his discretion may be exercised have been held by the courts to be without fixed limits"

The office of sheriff is recognized in the earliest annals of the English law. It is much older than Magna Charta, and the exact time of its creation is involved in much obscurity. But the place and function of the sheriff is easily determined. He has been for all times the chief peace officer of his bailiwick. Under all the systems of government which have recognized the law as the supreme rule of action it has been found absolutely necessary to vest in some one person the ultimate power to preserve the peace, to quell disorder, and to suppress riot. And this person is the sheriff, and his power is largely a discretionary one. In a time of great emergency, or in a crisis of unusual danger, the limits under which his discretion may be exercised have been held by the courts to be without fixed limits. . . .

As the employer has no right to compel a man to work who does not wish to work, so also is it true that the employee has no right to compel his fellow workman to quit work if he wishes to work. The distinction between the right to strike and the right to compel others to strike is a natural and palpable one, and is approved by the instinctive law of right and wrong as well as by the statutes and the decisions of the courts, and the compulsion denounced by the law is not alone that which consists in actual physical force applied by one set of men upon another. It may consist in a course of action tending to overawe or frighten or stampede a body of men who are anxious to work, as well as in laying a violent hand upon the individual workmen and forcing them by main strength to abandon their employment and unite in a strike. . . .

Leaving out of view all the facts on this branch of the case which are controverted and in reference to which the witnesses differ, it is certainly true that both at West Hazleton and Lattimer the great body of the strikers failed to obey the sheriff when he ordered them to disperse and insisted in pushing on. Nor can it be doubted that the sheriff had the right in the exercise of the discretion vested in him by the law to issue the order. And if it was the right of the sheriff to command the crowd to disperse, then it was the duty of the crowd to obey his command. The right to give the order implies the duty of obedience to the order, and disobedience of it is evidence of a riotous purpose. If I push on when the sheriff orders me to stop, I do so at my own peril.

Of course this obligation of obedience to the authority of the peace officer of the county is not confined to laboring men. It extends to and embraces all the inhabitants of the county, rich and poor, high and low. A company composed of the most wealthy and most prominent men of a community, if marching upon a public highway at a time or under circumstances which, in the judgment and discretion of the sheriff, makes such a demonstration dangerous to the public peace, would be bound to disperse if ordered so to do. And compliance with the order should be prompt and complete.

If you are satisfied, gentlemen, from the evidence that the purpose of the sheriff and of the posse was to preserve order and prevent riot, then it would follow that their intent and object was not a criminal or unlawful one, and the rule of the law which makes the act of one the act of all has no application to the facts of the case. If on the contrary, you are convinced by the evidence that the sheriff was not actuated by desire and intention to preserve the peace, but that he summoned his posse with the idea of inflicting upon the body of men known in the case as strikers wanton and unnecessary outrage and injury without reference to their action and conduct; if, in short, his purpose was a base, malicious, and wicked one, then so far as he was concerned and so far as the deputies were concerned, if they understood his motive and acted with the same intent, the fact of a criminal and unlawful combination would be established, and then all the defendants might be convicted, altho [sic] the shot which took the life of the deceased was fired by a single one of the defendants. The act of any one would in that event be the act of all.

If under all the evidence in the case you are not satisfied beyond a reasonable doubt that the sheriff and his posse were impelled by a criminal and unlawful purpose, then the doctrine of the law which the Commonwealth invokes, that where there are many defendants the criminal act of one of them is under certain circumstances to be regarded as the criminal act of all, has, as we have already said, no place in this case.

Source: *Literary Digest*, March 19, 1898 (courtesy of Bishop Library, Luzerne County Historical Society, Wilkes-Barre, PA)

3.11 Act of the General Assembly of the State of Georgia, 1901

This corporal punishment statute allowed physical force to make a convict work.

"Corporal punishment sufficient to force said convict to so work"

Sec. 40. Be it further enacted, That said mayor and aldermen shall have full power and authority to prescribe, by ordinance, adequate penalties for all offenses against the ordinances of said city not hereinbefore provided for, and to punish offenses by imprisonment in the guard-house of said city, or work on the chain-gang of said city, for a term not exceeding fifty days, or a fine of not exceeding one hundred dollars; the officer trying said offender may, on conviction of said offender, impose any one or all of said penalties. If the offender sentenced to work in the chain gang of said city shall refuse to work, then the person having charge of said chain-gang may, under the direct supervision of the mayor, administer to such convict corporal punishment sufficient to force said convict to so work.

Source: Georgia Archives, http://content.sos.state.ga.us/cdm4/legdocs.php

---

3.12 Letter from Secretary of War Elihu Root to Henry Cabot Lodge, February 27, 1902

The campaign against Filipino insurgents as part of the Spanish-American War occasioned widespread acts of torture and killing by the U.S. forces. The use of the "water cure" interrogation technique was well known. In fact Paul Kramer includes a photograph of the "water cure" being administered in his book The Blood of Government. *"The very fact that a portrait of it was created," Kramer says, "—one that itself includes casual spectators— suggests both the status of atrocity as spectacle and the complacency with which this torture was conducted, despite vigorous denials of its practice" (p. 142). Secretary Elihu Root took pains to deny that torture was occurring, while at the same time explaining how U.S. troops might be excused for doing it, given the behavior of the insurgents themselves. However, as Moorfield Storey has shown, Root at the time of writing the following letter had received credible evidence that he does not address in the letter.*

"Either unfounded or grossly exaggerated"

You will perceive that in substantially every case the report has proved to be either unfounded or grossly exaggerated. The particular report which was called to the attention of the Senate last week—viz., that the "water cure " is the favorite torture of the American, and especially of the Macabebe, scouts, to force the natives to give information, and that a soldier who was with General Funston had stated that he helped to administer the water cure to one hundred and sixty natives, all but twenty-six of whom died—was already under investigation which is still in progress. . . .

The Filipino troops have frequently fired upon our men from under protection of flags of truce, tortured to death American prisoners who have fallen into their hands, buried alive both Americans and friendly natives, and horribly mutilated the bodies of the American dead. That the soldiers fighting against such an enemy, and with their own eyes witnessing such deeds, should occasionally be regardless of these orders and retaliate by unjustifiable severities, is not incredible. . . .

That such occurrences have been sanctioned or permitted is not true.

Source: Moorfield Storey and Julian Codman, *Marked Severities: Secretary Root's Record in Philippine Warfare* (Boston: George W. Ellis, 1902), pp. 44–45

3.13 Report by Civil Governor of Tayabas, Colonel Gardener, February 7, 1902

The American governor of Tayabas, Colonel Cornelius Gardener, frankly acknowledges the use of the "water cure" and other actions by U.S. troops and suggests that such actions "had best be done by native troops" because of the reaction that would follow. Colonel Gardener focuses on the consequences, rather than the legality, of torture. He also notes the use of the word "nigger" in reference to Filipinos.

"A deep hatred toward us engendered"

Of late, by reason of the conduct of the troops, such as the extensive burning of barrios in trying to lay waste the country so that the insurgents cannot occupy it, the torturing of natives by so-called "water cure," and other methods, in order to obtain information, the harsh treatment of natives generally, and the failure of inexperienced, lately appointed lieutenants commanding posts to distinguish between those who are friendly and those unfriendly, and treating every native as if he were, whether or no, an insurrecto at heart, this favorable sentiment above referred to is being fast destroyed and a deep hatred toward us engendered. If these things need be done, they had best be done by native troops, so that the people of the United States will not be credited therewith. Almost without exception, soldiers, and also many officers, refer to the natives in their presence as "niggers," and the natives are beginning to understand what the word " nigger" means.

The course now being pursued in this province, and in the provinces of Batangas, Laguna, and Samar, is, in my opinion, sowing the seeds for a perpetual revolution, or at least preparing the people of these provinces to rise up in revolution against us hereafter whenever a good opportunity offers.

Source: Moorfield Storey and Julian Codman, *Marked Severities: Secretary Root's Record in Philippine Warfare* (Boston: George W. Ellis, 1902), pp. 66–67

3.14 Testimony of Sergeant Charles Riley before Senate Committee, 1902

Here, a U.S. soldier testifies before the Senate, in detail, about administering the "water cure" in the Philippines. He states that an American physician is present at the scene.

"He was directly under the faucet, with his mouth held wide open"

[T]he presidente was tied and placed on his back under a water-tank holding probably one hundred gallons. The faucet was opened, and a stream of water was forced down or allowed to run down his throat. His throat was held so he could not prevent swallowing the water, so that he had to allow the water to run into his stomach. He was directly under the faucet, with his mouth held wide open. When he was filled with water, it was forced out of him by pressing a foot on his stomach or else with the hands. . . . A native interpreter stood directly over this man as he lay on the floor, and kept saying some one word which I should judge meant "confess" or "answer." When this unhappy man was taken down and asked more questions, he again refused to answer, and then was treated again. . . .

Q. In front?

A. Yes, on the stone walk. They started to take him inside the building, and Captain Glenn said, "Don't take him inside. Right here is good enough." One of the men of the Eighteenth Infantry went to his saddle and took a syringe from the saddlebag, and another man was sent for a can of water, what we call a kerosene can, holding about five gallons. He brought this can of water down from upstairs, and then a syringe was inserted one end in the water and the other end in his mouth. This time he was not bound, but he was held by four or five men and the water was forced into his mouth from the can, through the syringe.

By Senator Burrows:—

Q. Was this another party?

A. No, this was the same man. The syringe did not seem to have the desired effect, and the doctor ordered a second one. The man got a second syringe, and that was inserted in his nose. Then the doctor ordered some salt, and a handful of salt was procured and thrown into the water. Two syringes were then in operation. The interpreter stood over him in the meantime asking for this second information that was desired. Finally, he gave in and gave the information that they sought, and then he was allowed to rise.

Q. May I ask the name of the doctor?

A. Dr. Lyons, the contract surgeon.

Q. An American?

A. Yes, sir.

Source: Moorfield Storey and Julian Codman, *Marked Severities: Secretary Root's Record in Philippine Warfare* (Boston: George W. Ellis, 1902), p. 50

3.15 Speech by President Theodore Roosevelt, 1902

Theodore Roosevelt spoke at Arlington Cemetery on Memorial Day in 1902. He sought to connect the memory of the Civil War dead with the U.S. fighting forces in the Philippines. He displays a marked ambivalence about torture and unlawful killings by U.S. forces. He condemns those actions but quickly minimizes them and cites the difficulty and danger of warfare generally. He also references lynching in the United States. In an unusual rhetorical turn, Roosevelt uses the prevalence of lynching at home (a "beam" in the eye of the U.S., in his biblical allusion) to the "mote" of atrocities in the Philippines. He suggests that Americans are critical of torture in the war in the Philippines, while they remain silent about lynch-

ing. It is interesting that he does not call for an end to lynching, but rather for an end to criticism of the U.S. military. The president uses one atrocity to deflect criticism of the other, while leaving it unstated that he has the power to combat both.

"Our warfare in the Philippines has been carried on with a singular humanity"

Just at this moment the Army of the United States, led by men who served among you in the great war, is carrying to completion a small but peculiarly trying and difficult war in which is involved not only the honor of the flag but the triumph of civilization over forces which stand for the black chaos of savagery and barbarism. The task has not been as difficult or as important as yours, but, oh, my comrades, the men in uniform of the United States, who have for the last three years patiently and uncomplainingly championed the American cause in the Philippine Islands, are your brothers, your sons. They have shown themselves not unworthy of you, and they are entitled to the support of all men who are proud of what you did.

These younger comrades of yours have fought under terrible difficulties and have received terrible provocation from a very cruel and very treacherous enemy. Under strain of these provocations I deeply deplore to say that some of them have so far forgotten themselves as to counsel and commit, in retaliation, acts of cruelty. The fact that for every guilty act committed by one of our troops a hundred acts of far greater atrocity have been committed by the hostile natives upon our own troops, or upon the peaceable and law-abiding natives who are friendly to us, can not be held to excuse any wrongdoers on our side. Determined and unswerving effort must be made, and has been and is being made, to find out every instance of barbarity on the part of our troops, to punish those guilty of it, and to take, if possible, even stronger measures than have already been taken to minimize or prevent the occurrence of all such acts in the future.

Is it only in the army in the Philippines that Americans sometimes commit deeds that cause all other Americans to regret? No! From time to time there occur in our country, to the deep and lasting shame of our people, lynchings carried on under circumstances on inhuman cruelty and barbarity—cruelty infinitely worse than any that has ever been committed by our troops in the Philippines; worse to the victims, and far more brutalizing to those guilty of it. The men who fail to condemn these lynchings, and yet clamor about what has been done in the Philippines, are indeed guilty of neglecting the beam in their own eye while taunting their brother about the mote in his. Understand me. These lynchings afford us no excuse for failure to stop cruelty in the Philippines. But keep in mind that these cruelties in the Philippines have been wholly exceptional, and have been shamelessly exaggerated. We deeply and bitterly regret that they should have been committed, no matter how rarely, no matter under what provocation, by American troops. But they afford far less ground for a general condemnation of our army than these lynchings afford for the condemnation of the communities in which they occur. In each case it is well to condemn the deed, and it is well also to refrain from including both guilty and innocent in the same sweeping condemnation.

In every community there are people who commit acts of well-nigh inconceivable horror and baseness. If we fix our eyes only upon these individuals and upon their acts, if we forget the far more numerous citizens of upright and honest life and blind ourselves to their countless deeds of wisdom and justice and philanthropy, it is easy enough to condemn the community. There is not a city in this land which we could not condemn if we fixed out eyes solely upon its police record and refused to look at what it had accomplished for decency and justice and charity. Yet this is exactly the attitude which has been taken by too many men with reference to our army in the Philippines; and it is an attitude iniquitous in its absurdity and its injustice.

The rules of warfare which have been promulgated by the War Department and accepted as the basis of conduct by our troops in the field are the rules laid down by Abraham Lincoln when you, my hearers, were fighting for the Union. These rules provide, of course, for the just severity necessary in war. The most destructive of all forms of cruelty would be to show weakness where sternness is demanded by iron need. But all cruelty is forbidden, and all harshness beyond what is called for by need. Our enemies in the Philippines have not merely violated every rule of war, but have made of these violations their only method of carrying on the war. Think over that! It is not a rhetorical statement—it is a bald statement of contemporary history. They have been able to prolong the war at all only by recourse to acts each one of which would put them beyond the pale of civilized warfare. We would have been justified by Abraham Lincoln's rules of war in infinitely greater severity than has been shown.

The fact really is that our warfare in the Philippines has been carried on with a singular humanity. For every act of cruelty by our men there have been innumerable acts of forbearance, magnanimity, and generous kindness. These are the qualities which have characterized the war as a whole. The cruelties on our part have been wholly exceptional.

The guilty are to be punished; but in punishing them, let those who sit at ease at home, who walk delicately and live in the soft places of the earth, remember also to do them common justice. Let not the effortless and the untempted rail overmuch at strong men who with blood and sweat face years of toil and days of agony, and at need lay down their lives in remote tropic jungles to bring the light of civilization into the world's dark places. The warfare that has extended the boundaries of civilization at the expense of barbarism and savagery has been for centuries one of the most potent factors in the progress of humanity. Yet from its very nature it has always and everywhere been liable to dark abuses.

It behoves [sic] us to keep a vigilant watch to prevent these abuses and to punish those who commit them; but if because of them we flinch from finishing the task on which we have entered, we show ourselves cravens and weaklings, unworthy of the sires from whose loins we sprang. Oh, my comrades, how the men of the present tend to forget not merely what was done but what was spoken in the past! There were abuses and to spare in the Civil War; and slender enough, too, by each side against the other. . . .

Verily, those men who thus foully slandered you have their heirs to-day in those who traduce our armies in the Philippines, who fix their eyes on individual deeds of wrong so keenly that at last they become blind to the great work of peace and freedom that has already been accomplished.

Source: Alfred Henry Lewis, ed., *A Compilation of the Messages and Speeches of Theodore Roosevelt, 1901–1905* (New York: Bureau of National Literature and Art, 1906), pp. 28–34

3.16 Excerpts of California Assembly Report, 1903

The California Assembly produced a report detailing the use of torture at Folsom and San Quentin prisons.

"He cried for water, but the night guards laughed at him"

At Folsom we found Robert Smith had been permanently crippled in his right arm and hand. Morris Weiss, a tailor, sustained such injuries to his hands and arms as a result of the punishment that in all probability he will never be able to work at his trade again. . . .

Sometimes a small jacket or vest is placed on first. This is composed of hair, the straitjacket proper being placed over it. The man is now in a standing position, the jacket being laced as tight as possible.

The prisoner is then placed on his back, the guards kneeling on him so as to bring the edges of the jacket tighter across his back. Should they wish to extract a confession a short stick three feet long is used, it being inserted in the lacing and worked in the manner of a Spanish windlass. The lacing this becomes as taut as ingenuity can make it.

The first serious case was that of Robert Smith, serving twenty years. This man is big, stout and healthy and has lost the use of his right hand.

The next case was the killing of James Deare, the Coroner's office bringing in a verdict of death while undergoing punishment in a straitjacket. This man was insane, as any number of prisoners will testify. Turnkey Timothy Haggerty said: "We'll find out if he's crazy or not."

As the cries of the prisoners punished kept the convicts awake at night, they are placed in dungeons, where executions take place. Frank Howard was in there when James Deare was being punished. Deare during the night told Howard he was dying. When he was taken out the next day he was unable to walk, and Tim Haggerty kicked him in the side, as he was unable to wash himself. He cried for water, but the night guards laughed at him. He was unable to help himself. He was found dead in the morning.

Source: State Senator George H. Williams, quoted in the *New York Times*, February 14, 1903

3.17 Report of the Georgia Legislature, 1908

A report was prepared following an investigation by the Georgia legislature into allegations of illegal treatment of convicts. In one instance, a warden admitted shooting and killing a prisoner even though the warden's life was not in danger. He admits that he shot and killed a man in order to preserve his own disciplinary authority over the other prisoners. The grand jury convened in his case refused to indict. The report also suggests that the complaints of white prisoners are inherently more credible than those of African American prisoners.

"Charges of cruelty are well founded"

Charges of cruel and excessive punishment of convicts in quite a number of cases have been brought to our attention. We have investigated several of these cases. Many others have been mentioned to different members of the committee, but the committee has not had time to investigate every case, nor have we considered it necessary to do so. We have deemed it the duty of the committee to investigate such charges only as would indicate whether these cases were merely sporadic, or as liable to occur under the system, or as chargeable to the indifference of the State's officials or the lessees, to the common dictates of humanity. We believe from the evidence that charges of cruelty are well founded. We are unwilling to dismiss as unworthy of belief some of the evidence taken in regard thereto because given by ex-convicts, once convicted murderers, perjurers, or discharged employees and disgruntled contractors. In some cases we have given little weight to all or parts of such testimony, but it should be remembered that much of this evidence is from white ex-convicts, who have been recommended for pardons by the Prison Commission, after serving very small parts of their sentences; that it has related in a majority of instances to cruelties to others, and in exaggerating which they would have no interest; that in many instances their testimony has been corroborated certainly in important particulars, and frequently in whole, and in every instance as to the fact of punishment. It should be remembered that the one case, to-wit, that of the negro convict who was sweated to death in Flower's camp at Jakin, in which the chairman of the Commission and the State Warden acted as prosecutors, was brought to their attention a year after its occurrence through the public press because of revelations made by an ex-convict. The truth is, we deem it almost impossible to secure evidence of cruelties from convicts now in prison or from officers and guards who inflict or permit such while in the employ of the State and the lessees; it is hardly natural to expect evidence from these sources. The State now has two inspectors. One of them has sworn that he has never been, nor ever expects to go into a mine in which the State's convicts are worked, to see what they are doing therein, what is required of them, or what tasks are required of them. The deputy wardens by their own testimony and admissions, rarely inspect these mines, and yet they punish, frequently and severely, on the report of an employee of the lessee that some task has not been accomplished, without actual knowledge of the severity of the task, or of the conditions under which imposed. Under these conditions, about the only source of information as to what happens in these mines or as to the condition under which the convicts are worked, must come from ex-convicts, or ex-guards, or ex-employees.

A white boy, Abe Winn, afflicted with tuberculosis, accidently or purposely, it is immaterial which, pours hot coffee on a deputy warden's hog. The deputy warden and owner of the hog, decides that the scalding was purposely done. He proceeds to whip the boy until he is exhausted, and is compelled to go into the hospital, from which only eight weeks later he is brought out a corpse, never having left his bed after admission. The camp physician first reported his case as pneumonia, which he testified afterwards developed into consumption, and that this was the cause of his death. This is doubtless technically true. The boy's own brother, knowing his desperate condition, accepts this as true. These can all be real facts, consumption, let it be admitted, was the cause of the death. But the shocking, horrible truth is that an angry and cruel State officer, selfishly interested in punishing, whipped to the very door of the hospital, from which he was later brought a corpse, a boy within eight weeks of a consumptive's death. The whipping under such circumstances was the cruel fact, whether it was to the death or only to the hospital door.

The negro convict at Jakin, referred to above, is disobedient, unruly, or attempts to escape, it matters not. He doubtless deserves punishment, severe punishment. Let all this be granted; an inhuman State officer decides that he will sweat him, and gives orders accordingly. The convict is sweated, wrapped head and body and feet in blankets and enclosed in a box. He dies. A camp physician certifies that his death was caused by congestion of the lungs. Doubtless it was. The report is accepted without question or investigation. One year later a convict who has finished his term, tells the truth, and though inspectors had visited that camp time and again, no whisper of the truth seems to have reached them. Upon investigation it was found that an ex-convict can tell the truth, though while he is a convict he dare not open his mouth. The cruelty was in the form of punishment administered.

Another negro, Peter Harris by name, claiming to be sick, is whipped and put to work, till he falls exhausted, and two hours later is dead. Some of the witnesses testify that he was whipped to death, others, including the camp physician, that his death was due to congestion from the excessive drinking of cold water while overheated. Whether the whipping caused death or not, does not mitigate the fact that a sick convict, to whom the camp physician swears he had that morning given a purgative, is later whipped, put to work at admittedly the severest and hottest task, and in a few hours is dead. This constitutes cruelty.

A white man is confined at the Durham Coal Mines under a twenty-year sentence. He refuses to work. The warden decides to administer a whipping. He has the reputation of being a very desperate character. He doubtless needed severe punishment and should have received it. The warden calls him out and orders him to strip to receive a whipping. He refuses and resists all appeals and threats. Finally he draws a razor and starts toward the warden, though shackled. The warden insists he made three efforts to reach him (the warden) and that he finally told him he would shoot if he did not submit. The warden admits he could have kept out of his reach by retreating, and virtually admits his life was not in danger, but that he decided that if he did not shoot him, his authority would be lost, and guards and convicts would no longer respect it, and as he declares, he shot to kill him, aiming directly between his eyes. He hit him in the side of the neck and killed him almost instantly. Ex-guard Tatum swears that when the warden shot, the convict was standing still, had covered his eyes with his hands, and told the warden to shoot. The evidence shows that a coroner's jury investigated this homicide, and two grand juries returned "No Bill."

The committee condemns this homicide. It does not believe a warden has a right to kill a convict merely to assert his authority or for any salutary effect such a show of authority may have on guards or convicts. He could have only been justified when necessary to protect his own life or that of his guards. He could not have been in serious danger surrounded as he was at the time of the shooting by twenty-five guards, each with loaded shotguns. Any one of them, had the man started to cross the ten or fifteen feet intervening, could have stopped him with a shot. The warden might have been excusable had he shot merely to cripple. When he deliberately killed the man under the circumstances related by him, he committed an unlawful act and should have been punished therefor.

The monthly whipping reports to the Commission, examined by the committee, show an unusually large number of whippings at the Durham Coal Mines, the Lookout Mountain Mines, and the Chattahoochee Brick Company. A large percentage of the whippings at these two mining camps are for "shortage of tasks" and for "slate in coal." The hospital reports from the Durham Mines also show what seems to be a large percentage of cases in the hospital resulting from accidents in the mines, from falling slate and similar causes. The evidence before us shows that in these two mines the convicts are required to mine certain quantities of coal in a day, free from some unproven percentage of slate, and that when they fail to secure these tasks or have too much slate in the coal, on complaint of the mining bosses they are whipped by the State's officers. The evidence also shows that the reasonableness of these tasks depends largely on the size of the vein, on the conditions under which the mining is carried on, on the expertness of the particular operator, on the amount of "propping" to be done, and the fact as to whether properly prepared and sized propping material is supplied, on the "greenness" of the operator, etc.

The evidence further shows that the mining boss or foreman, an employee of the lessee, fixes the task, and decides if it has been obtained, or if there is too much slate in it.

The evidence shows that neither inspector Deadwyler, nor inspector Burke have ever been into either of these mines. Inspector Deadwyler is seventy-three years old, too old in our opinion for the arduous duties of an inspector—he declares that he never expects go into a mine to see what is required of these convicts, or under what conditions it is required, and frankly admits that he does not know what is a reasonable task. Inspector Burke testified that he started into the Durham mines once and went about a hundred yards, when the water and mud were so bad it would ruin the only suit of clothes he had with him, and he abandoned the inspection. He further testified that he could not enter the Lookout mine if he wanted to.

The evidence is that occasionally a deputy warden goes into the mine, but that others have never been.

Deputy warden Ivey was formerly in charge of about fifty convicts at the Palmer Brick Yard. His evidence, and his reports show, that he would go for weeks or months without a whipping, or only one or two. Some time since he and his squad were moved to the Lookout mine, and at once he began to frequently administer to this same squad twenty-five and upwards whippings a month, a large percentage of which were for "idleness" or "failure to get tasks."

The undersigned are satisfied from the evidence that the whippings at these two mines are excessive and too frequent. These official reports, we are satisfied from the evidence, are not always accurate, but ought to be investigated. Men, even convicts, are not going to "idle" or fail to get their tasks week after week, when they know a whipping is certain, if the tasks are fair, reasonable, and within their ability.

We have not found in our investigations, a single State official who has fairly investigated this task question, or the conditions under which they are required, and the possibilities of the cruel treatment of the convicts in regard thereto are limitless.

Source: Georgia Archives, http://content.sos.state.ga.us/cdm4/legdocs.php

---

3.18 Act of the Georgia Legislature, 1918

This Georgia statutory provision appears to be an attempt at measurement of penological techniques.

"A record of number of times a convict was whipped"

Sec. 74. Be it further enacted, That the whipping boss, superintendent or other person having the convicts in charge shall keep a book in which he shall record the names of all persons placed in his charge, giving their age, sex, color, time received, time worked, behavior while confined, offense with which they are charged, a record of number of times a convict was whipped and the number of licks given, time of discharge and such other information as may be required of him by the city authorities.

Source: Georgia Archives, http://content.sos.state.ga.us/cdm4/legdocs.php

3.19 Public Statement of Senator T. H. Caraway, 1922

Through the first half of the twentieth century, repeated efforts were made to pass a federal antilynching bill. Supporters of the bills wanted to create federal criminal penalties for those who engaged in lynching and for law enforcement officials who allowed it to happen to prisoners in their charge. Southern whites fiercely opposed these efforts, sometimes putting their opposition in terms of states' rights, and calling the proposed legislation "vicious" and "tyrannical." The 1922 bill failed after southern senators denounced it; the filibuster was used to block the legislation, even after the House had voted to pass it. As the Senate declared in its 2005 resolution (S. Res. 39) apologizing for Senate obstruction of antilynching measures in the past, "at least 4,742 people, predominantly African-Americans, were reported lynched in the United States between1882 and 1968." Senator T. H. Caraway of Arkansas made the following public statement on March 5, 1922.

"A man will have to stand over his family with his gun"

To start with, I take the position that the Congress has no power to enact legislation to deal with crimes within a State. Exclusive jurisdiction is given to the States to deal with crimes, except when they are committed on Government reservations. We all swear to uphold the Constitution, and it's clear we have no right to enact a law in violation of it.

Beyond that the psychology of the negro's mind is peculiar. He has a very great deal of respect for Federal authority, but very little for the State, since all he knows about government is that emancipation was proclaimed by the President. Therefore, as I say, he has great respect for the Federal government, but none for the local. If such legislation as this was passed, it will fix the belief in the negro's mind that a guarantee is given to him, and that he may execute his desires whether they are [illegible] legal, lawful [illegible] or not.

[illegible] a bill is put on the statute books, in my country, where the population is equally divided between two races, a man will have to stand over his family with his gun. It will be construed as an invitation to commit crime, and it is extended by the only authority that the negro concedes has the right to speak.

In my own State we have quite a goodly number of people born in States north of the Mason and Dixon line, reared to maturity there, who have come

to live among us. Some are Democrats and some are Republicans, but sentiment is 100 per cent, against enactment of this legislation, irrespective of
the places where the white man lived before he came to Arkansas. When the
people realize the conditions in the South and the peril they invite, they are
unalterably opposed to it.

There is a pretty general belief, since there is a provision in the bill for the
payment to the family of the one who may be lynched of $10,000 to be col-
lected from the county, that the opportunity to sell one's relative to have him
lynched, will inspire some people to organize the lynching party. That is by no
means a visionary objection.

Source: U.S. Senator T. H. Caraway of Arkansas, quoted in the *New York Times*,
March 5, 1922.

3.20 Dyer Antilynching Bill, 1920

*The Dyer Bill, portions of which are provided here, would have made
lynching a federal crime and facilitated punishment of lynch mobs as well
as individuals.*

"Every person participating in such mob or riotous assemblage"

Sec. 8. That the putting to death within any State of any person within the
jurisdiction of the State by a mob or riotous assemblage of three or more persons openly acting in concert, in violation of law and in default of protection
of such person by such State or the officers thereof, shall be deemed a denial
to such person by such State of the equal protection of the laws and a violation of the peace of the United States and an offense against the same.

Sec. 9. That every person participating in such mob or riotous assemblage
by which such person is put to death, as described in the section immediately
preceding, shall be guilty of murder and shall be liable to prosecution, and,
upon conviction, to punishment therefor, according to law, in any District
Court of the United States having jurisdiction in the place where such unlawful putting to death occurs shall be subject to a forfeiture of $10,000, which
may be recovered by an action therefore in the name of the United States
against such county for the use of the dependent family, if any, of the person
so put to death; and if no one, for the use of the United States, which action
shall be brought and prosecuted by the attorney of the United States for the
district in which such county is situated in any District Court of the United
States having jurisdiction therein.

Sec. 13. That every State or municipal officer having the custody within a State of any person charged with or held to answer for any crime or offense, who suffers such person to be taken from his custody by a mob or riotous assemblage of three or more persons openly acting in Concert, in violation of law, with the purpose of putting such person to death or inflicting bodily violence upon him in default of protection of such person by such State or the officers thereof, shall be deemed guilty of an offense against the United States and shall be liable to prosecution therefore in any district court of the United States having jurisdiction in the place where the same occurs, and upon conviction thereof shall be punished by imprisonment not exceeding five years, or by fine not exceeding $5,000, or by both such fine and imprisonment.

Source: Dyer Bill, H.R. 14097, 66th Cong., 2nd sess., May 17, 1920

3.21 Report on Dyer Antilynching Bill, 1920

A report submitted in support of the Dyer Bill includes statistics on the number of lynchings, broken down by race and allegations involved. Reasons for lynching included failure to move aside for a white motorist and complaining about another lynching.

"The newspapers of New Orleans and Jackson advertised in large red type one lynching that was to take place"

Lynching is a crime widespread throughout the country, which, in many States, the state authorities have almost wholly failed to prevent or punish. In a vast majority of the cases, it seems to have been induced by local prejudice against the race, color, nationality or religion of the person lynched.

It is a chief cause of unrest among Negroes. In the 30 years from 1889 to 1918, 3,224 persons were lynched, of whom 2,522 were negroes, and of those 50 were women. The North had 219, the West 156, Alaska and unknown localities 15, and the South 2,884, with Georgia leading with 386, and Mississippi following with 373. Yet in Georgia, Negroes paid taxes on 1,664,368 acres, and owned property assessed at $47,423,499. In the five years up to and including 1918, there were 21 persons lynched in the North and West, and 304 in the South. Of the colored victims 19 percent were accused of rape, and 9.4 per cent of attacks on women; the principal accusation was that of murder.

In the year 1919, 77 Negroes, 4 whites and 2 Mexicans were lynched. 10 of the negroes were ex-soldiers; one was a woman. The newspapers of New Orleans and Jackson advertised in large red type one lynching that was to take place. The governor of Mississippi announced himself powerless to prevent one lynching.

Source: Report on Dyer Bill, H.R. 14097, 66th Cong., 2nd sess., May 17, 1920

3.22 Wickersham Commission Report, 1931

The Wickersham Commission studied the U.S. criminal justice system in the 1920s and early 1930, searching for "lawlessness in law enforcement." They produce a voluminous and comprehensive 1931 report that documented police practices, including use of the "third degree" to induce confessions. The commission relied on court opinions, surveys, and interviews as well as scholarly works, and it documented a range of abuses that are striking for their kind, degree, and prevalence. Here, the commission introduces its extended discussion of the "third degree."

"The sweat box is a small cell completely dark and arranged to be heated"

The third degree is a secret and illegal practice. Those who employ it either will not talk, or else will make formal denial of its existence. The victims are likely either to present exaggerated or even fabricated accounts to further their ends or to decline to talk because of the fear of police retaliation. Police reporters know a great deal, but they are dependent upon the police for their information, and are often likewise reticent. . . .

To obtain confessions or admissions the officers (usually detectives) proceed to "work" the prisoner. "Work" is the term used to signify any form of what is commonly called the third degree, and may consist in nothing more than a severe cross-examination. Perhaps in most cases it is no more than that, but the prisoner knows that he is wholly at the mercy of his inquisitor and that the severe cross-examination may at any moment shift to a severe beating. This knowledge itself undoubtedly induces speedy confessions in many instances and makes unnecessary a resort to force. If the prisoner refuses to answer, he may be returned to his cell with notice that there he will stay till ready to "come clean." The cell may be especially chosen for the purpose—cold, dark, without bed or chair. The sweat box is a small cell completely dark and arranged to be heated till the prisoner, unable to endure the temperature, will promise to answer as desired. Or refusal to answer may be overcome by whipping, by beating, with rubber hose, clubs, or fists, or by kicking, or by threats, or promises.

Powerful lights turned full on the prisoner's face, or switched on and off, have been found effective. The electric chair is another device to extort confessions.

Source: 9 U.S. Wickersham Commission Reports. U.S. National Commission on Law Observance and Enforcement [i] 1931, pp. 21, 55

3.23 Appellate Opinion Reversing Conviction in *State v. Nagle*, 1930

The Missouri appellate court details the abuse and resulting injuries inflicted by the police that led to the defendant's forced confession.

"Kicked him, beat him with a rubber hose, struck him with a revolver, a chair, and a blackjack, and squeezed and twisted his testicles, and refused to let him sleep"

The defendant offered to testify that from about 8.30 in the evening of June 14, when he was arrested, until about noon on June 16, when he was taken to the prosecuting attorney's office, he was sweated almost continuously by various police officers and detectives, who kicked him, beat him with a rubber hose, struck him with a revolver, a chair, and a blackjack, and squeezed and twisted his testicles, and refused to let him sleep and to let him have anything to eat or drink, and threatened to kill him, in their efforts to force him to admit that he actually participated in the robbery and the killing of Officer Smith and to inform them as to others who participated in the perpetration of said crimes; that by means of such mistreatment, torture, threats, and coercion, he was forced, at police headquarters on June 15, to sign the first statement about 9 o'clock in the morning of June 15, and to sign the additional statement sometime in the afternoon of that day, without first having an opportunity to read said statements and without having said statements read to him; that, about noon on June 16, he was taken from police headquarters to the prosecuting attorney's office by two detectives, Thurman and Kellerstrauss, who had actively participated in the mistreatment, torture, threats, and coercion to which he had been subjected at police headquarters; that immediately before he was taken into the office of the prosecuting attorney he was told by Thurman that unless, when questioned by the prosecuting attorney, he confirmed the statements signed by him at police headquarters, they (the detectives) would take him back to police headquarters and "finish" him; that Thurman remained in the prosecuting attorney's office throughout his (the defendant's) conversation with the prosecuting attorney; that at the time of said conversation he was suffering from the lack of sleep and food and from 'the injuries inflicted upon him by said police officers and detectives; and that he confirmed the statements signed by him at police headquarters, when the same were read to him by the prosecuting attorney because he was afraid he would be subjected to further mistreatment and torture at the hands of said police, officers and detectives if he did not do so. And the defendant offered to show that on June 18, 1928, upon his motion a commission of physicians was appointed by one of the judges of the circuit court of Jackson County to make a physical examination of him. And he also offered to show by the testimony of two of said physicians that on June 21, 1928, they made a physical examination of him in the county jail and found him suffering from two deep scalp wounds, an echymosis of both lower eyelids, or "black eyes," a broken rib on his left side, and numerous bruises and abrasions on his left side and on his shins.

The prosecuting attorney, in his testimony concerning his conversation with the defendant, admitted that when officer Thurman brought the defendant into his office about noon on June 16 the defendant had "some blood on the left side of his coat," and "one eye had an abrasion over it"; that he did not ask the defendant what had happened; that he was present on June 18, representing the State, when one of the judges of the circuit court of Jackson County heard the defendant's motion for the appointment of a commission of physicians to make a physical examination of him; and that during the course of that proceeding he said: "Nobody denies that they (referring to the defendant and his codefendants) were beaten up." In answering the question as to whether or not he made that statement, he said "I think that is true—before they were brought to my office." And when asked if it was customary " to have them beaten up before they got there," he said: "Apparently someone had done something of that kind before he (the defendant) got there." A photograph of the defendant, taken in the prosecuting attorney's office on June 16 immediately before his conversation with the prosecuting attorney, shows that his face, under both eyes, was swollen and discolored, and that there were numerous dark spots or stains on the left side of his coat, on the left shoulder, and the left side of the collar. Other photographs of the defendant, taken in the county jail on June 20, show a deep scalp wound at or near the crown of his head and numerous bruises and abrasions on his left side and on both of his shins. This evidence furnishes ample support for the conclusion that the statements signed by the defendant at police headquarters on June 15 were not signed by him voluntarily, but as the result of fear and intimidation. Indeed, the record shows that such was the impression of the prosecuting attorney and the trial judge. The prosecuting attorney did not offer these statements as confessions made by the defendant at police headquarters on June 15, and the trial judge said he would exclude "statements taken at the police station" because they were "probably" involuntary.

Source: *State v. Nagle*, 32 S.W. 2d 596 (Mo. 1930) 3–19

3.24 Wickersham Commission Report, 1931

The Wickersham Report documents several cases where bizarre scenes were staged in efforts to secure confessions. The resulting convictions were overturned. A published record of the appellate proceedings was available for the commission to draw upon.

"She was taken into a cell lighted by candles where the skeleton of the victim had been strung up"

In Manistee, Mich., an illiterate Polish woman, who had been arrested for the murder of a nun, said that she was taken into a cell lighted by candles where the skeleton of the victim had been strung up so that it could be manipulated, and was forced to remain there for two hours. The evidence was conflicting as to some phases of her story, but the presence of the skeleton in the cell was not explained. . . .

In a case not included in our survey of appellate decisions, *Commonwealth v. Williams*, 275 Pa. 58, 67, 118 Atl. 617, 620 (1922), the court said in reversing the convictions of two Negroes, charged with murdering a watchman: "They were taken to the cemetery and separately locked in a vault with the corpse of the murdered watchman and there cross-examined; not only was this done in the daytime but again at 1 o'clock at night, amidst a severe electric storm, where for a long time they were separately locked again with the corpse and, among other stratagems, commanded, by a voice ostensibly from heaven, to disclose who killed George Mauer, an ordeal to which they never should have been subjected; and the resourceful district attorney ascribes their passing unflinching through it to their familiarity with scenes of death and horror acquired while serving on foreign battlefields in the World War. . . .

In another Texas murder case, in Reeves County, where the victim had been burned to death in a store, the defendant, a Mexican, was taken at night by the sheriff and five private citizens to the scene of the fire and seated in front of the charred remains of a body, which he was forced to view. There was strong evidence that men were gathering wood and threatening to burn him to death unless he confessed. The conviction was reversed.

Source: 9 U.S. Wickersham Commission Reports. U.S. National Commission on Law
Observance and Enforcement [i] 1931, pp. 69–71

3.25 Wickersham Commission Report, 1931

*In this section, the Wickersham Commission provides law enforcement's
arguments in support of coercive interrogation of criminal suspects.
Though a precise dividing line between permissible and impermissible
tactics is never drawn, police officers argue forcefully that rough tactics are
necessary in order to do their job effectively.*

"If an occasional slap on the face will mean sending a hardened criminal
to prison, why should it not be used?"

Thus representatives of a point of view common among the police say that the
criminals against whom the police are fighting are often tough and shrewd.
Some of them have excellent lawyers, and the detectives feel that they must
build up their case before the lawyer gets to the prisoner.

Questioning the suspect is the normal human method of getting at the
facts, and the advantages of this method ought not to be taken away by rules
requiring the questioning to stop part way toward success. The suggestion
that the police should be permitted to use all the force that is necessary, and
perhaps even more, in order to arrest a man and bring him to the station,
but that after that they should be forbidden to use force or fatiguing interrogation, is said to be futile. After all, relay questioning gets results. Then
it is natural, these persons argue, for the policemen to manhandle a person
who knows the facts and will not talk. The police point of view must be understood. Despite the occasional influences of politics and corruption, most
policemen are to be conceived as conscientious and hard working. They risk
their lives continually, and if an occasional slap on the face will mean sending
a hardened criminal to prison, why should it not be used even if by mistake
force is now and then applied to an innocent man?

Harshness ought on the whole to be reserved for old offenders, but the
officer must be governed by his discretion in the individual case and it is impossible to lay down strict general rules covering all situations. Unprovoked
brutality should not be condoned, but an occasional punch in the jaw helps
preserve respect for the police. "It is strange," said one official, the effect that
a slap on the jaw with the open hand has."

Similar arguments by the police officials in 1910 have already been quoted
in the Survey of Literature at the outset of the preceding chapter. The same

point of view is vigorously expressed by Captain Willemse, of New York, in *Behind the Green Lights:* "Against a hardened criminal I never hesitated. I've forced confessions—with fist, black-Jack, and hose—from men who would have continued to rob and to kill if I had not made them talk. The hardened criminal knows only one language and laughs at the detective who tries any other. Remember that this is war after all! I'm convinced my tactics saved many lives."

Source: 9 U.S. Wickersham Commission Reports. U.S. National Commission on Law Observance and Enforcement [i] 1931

3.26 Statement of Governor James Rolph, California, 1933

A San Jose mob broke into jail and lynched two men believed to have killed their kidnap victim, Brooke Hart. After the lynching occurred, California governor James Rolph made statements to the news media praising the lynching and promising to pardon anyone who was convicted of a crime arising out of it. Some members of the public praised his pro-lynching stance, but others criticized it, suggesting that he was irresponsible and in dereliction of his duty as the state's chief executive.

"They made a good job of it"

They made a good job of it and I hope this lesson will serve in every state of the Union. I don't think they will arrest anyone for the lynchings. If they do I'll pardon them.

It is about time the people should have comfort in their homes. This kidnapping business has become so bad that mothers and fathers are afraid to let their children out of their homes. Now they have taken to kidnapping men and women for the purpose of extracting money from their distracted relatives.

Source: *Montreal Gazette,* November 28, 1933

3.27 Opinion in *Brown v. Mississippi,* 1936

The defendants here were subjected to incredible tortures, including repeated hangings and whippings, after which they provided confessions to murder. One of the most striking aspects of this case is that the torture was readily and openly admitted by those involved. As a result, there was no question as to whether defendants had been tortured, and it was easy for the Supreme Court to cite uncontroverted facts from the record as it ruled that the convictions were invalid.

"The transcript reads more like pages torn from some medieval account"

MR. CHIEF JUSTICE HUGHES delivered the opinion of the Court. . . .

The crime with which these defendants, all ignorant negroes, are charged, was discovered about one o'clock p.m. on Friday, March 30, 1934. On that night one Dial, a deputy sheriff, accompanied by others, came to the home of Ellington, one of the defendants, and requested him to accompany them to the house of the deceased, and there a number of white men were gathered, who began to accuse the defendant of the crime. Upon his denial they seized him, and with the participation of the deputy they hanged him by a rope to the limb of a tree, and having let him down, they hung him again, and when he was let down the second time, and he still protested his innocence, he was tied to a tree and whipped, and still declining to accede to the demands that he confess, he was finally released and he returned with some difficulty to his home, suffering intense pain and agony. The record of the testimony shows that the signs of the rope on his neck were plainly visible during the so-called trial. A day or two thereafter the said deputy, accompanied by another, returned to the home of the said defendant and arrested him, and departed with the prisoner towards the jail in an adjoining county, but went by a route which led into the State of Alabama; and while on the way, in that State, the deputy stopped and again severely whipped the defendant, declaring that he would continue the whipping until he confessed, and the defendant then agreed to confess to such a statement as the deputy would dictate, and he did so, after which he was delivered to jail.

The other two defendants, Ed Brown and Henry Shields, were also arrested and taken to the same jail. On Sunday night, April 1, 1934, the same deputy, accompanied by a number of white men, one of whom was also an officer, and by the jailer, came to the jail, and the two last named defendants were made to strip and they were laid over chairs and their backs were cut to pieces with a leather strap with buckles on it, and they were likewise made by the said deputy definitely to understand that the whipping would be continued unless and until they confessed, and not only confessed, but confessed in every matter of detail as demanded by those present; and in this manner the defendants confessed the crime, and as the whippings progressed and were repeated, they changed or adjusted their confession in all particulars of detail so as to conform to the demands of their torturers. When the confessions had been obtained in the exact form and contents as desired by the mob, they left with the parting admonition and warning that, if the defendants changed their story at any time in any respect from that last stated, the perpetrators of the outrage would administer the same or equally effective treatment.

Further details of the brutal treatment to which these helpless prisoners were subjected need not be pursued. It is sufficient to say that in pertinent respects the transcript reads more like pages torn from some medieval account, than a record made within the confines of a modern civilization which aspires to an enlightened constitutional government.

All this having been accomplished, on the next day, that is, on Monday, April 2, when the defendants had been given time to recuperate somewhat from the tortures to which they had been subjected, the two sheriffs, one of the county where the crime was committed, and the other of the county of the jail in which the prisoners were confined, came to the jail, accompanied by eight other persons, some of them deputies, there to hear the free and voluntary confession of these miserable and abject defendants. The sheriff of the county of the crime admitted that he had heard of the whipping, but averred that he had no personal knowledge of it. He admitted that one of the defendants, when brought before him to confess, was limping and did not sit down, and that this particular defendant then and there stated that he had been strapped so severely that he could not sit down, and as already stated, the signs of the rope on the neck of another of the defendants were plainly visible to all. Nevertheless the solemn farce of hearing the free and voluntary confessions was gone through with, and these two sheriffs and one other person then present were the three witnesses used in court to establish the so-called confessions, which were received by the court and admitted in evidence over the objections of the defendants duly entered of record as each of the said three witnesses delivered their alleged testimony. There was thus enough before the court when these confessions were first offered to make known to the court that they were not, beyond all reasonable doubt, free and voluntary; and the failure of the court then to exclude the confessions is sufficient to reverse the judgment, under every rule of procedure that has heretofore been prescribed, and hence it was not necessary subsequently to renew the objections by motion or otherwise.

The spurious confessions having been obtained—and the farce last mentioned having been gone through with on Monday, April 2d—the court, then in session, on the following day, Tuesday, April 3, 1934, ordered the grand jury to reassemble on the succeeding day, April 4, 1934, at nine o'clock, and on the morning of the day last mentioned the grand jury returned an indictment against the defendants for murder. Late that afternoon the defendants were brought from the jail in the adjoining county and arraigned, when one or more of them offered to plead guilty, which the court declined to accept, and, upon inquiry whether they had or desired counsel, they stated that they had none, and did not suppose that counsel could be of any assistance to them. The court thereupon appointed counsel, and set the case for trial for the following morning at nine o'clock, and the defendants were returned to the jail in the adjoining county about thirty miles away.

The defendants were brought to the courthouse of the county on the following morning, April 5th, and the so-called trial was opened, and was concluded on the next day, April 6, 1934, and resulted in a pretended conviction with death sentences. The evidence upon which the conviction was obtained was the so-called confessions. Without this evidence a peremptory instruction to find for the defendants would have been inescapable. The defendants were put on the stand, and by their testimony the facts and the details thereof as to the manner by which the confessions were extorted from them were fully developed, and it is further disclosed by the record that the same deputy, Dial, under whose guiding hand and active participation the tortures to coerce the confessions were administered, was actively in the performance of the supposed duties of a court deputy in the courthouse and in the presence of the prisoners during what is denominated, in complimentary terms, the trial of these defendants. This deputy was put on the stand by the state in rebuttal, and admitted the whippings. It is interesting to note that in his testimony with reference to the whipping of the defendant Ellington, and in response to the inquiry as to how severely he was whipped, the deputy stated, "Not too much for a negro; not as much as I would have done if it were left to me." Two others who had participated in these whippings were introduced and admitted it—not a single witness was introduced who denied it. The facts are not only undisputed, they are admitted, and admitted to have been done by officers of the state, in conjunction with other participants, and all this was definitely well known to everybody connected with the trial, and during the trial, including the state's prosecuting attorney and the trial judge presiding.

. . .

The State is free to regulate the procedure of its courts in accordance with its own conceptions of policy, unless in so doing it "offends some principle of justice so rooted in the traditions and conscience of our people as to be ranked as fundamental." The State may abolish trial by jury. It may dispense with indictment by a grand jury and substitute complaint or information. But the freedom of the State in establishing its policy is the freedom of constitutional government and is limited by the requirement of due process of law. Because a State may dispense with a jury trial, it does not follow that it may substitute trial by ordeal. The rack and torture chamber may not be substituted for the witness stand. The State may not permit an accused to be hurried to conviction under mob domination—where the whole proceeding is but a mask—without supplying corrective process. The State may not deny to the accused the aid of counsel. Nor may a State, through the action of its officers, contrive a conviction through the pretense of a trial which in truth is "but used as a means of depriving a defendant of liberty through a deliberate deception of court and jury by the presentation of testimony known to be perjured." And the trial equally is a mere pretense where the state authorities have contrived a conviction resting solely upon confessions obtained by violence. The due process clause requires "that state action, whether through one agency or another, shall be consistent with the fundamental principles of liberty and justice which lie at the base of all our civil and political institutions." It would be difficult to conceive of methods more revolting to the sense of justice than those taken to procure the confessions of these petitioners, and the use of the confessions thus obtained as the basis for conviction and sentence was a clear denial of due process. . . . [Petitioners'] complaint is not of the commission of mere error, but of a wrong so fundamental that it made the whole proceeding a mere pretense of a trial and rendered the conviction and sentence wholly void. We are not concerned with a mere question of state practice, or whether counsel assigned to petitioners were competent or mistakenly assumed that their first objections were sufficient. In an earlier case the Supreme Court of the State had recognized the duty of the court to supply corrective process where due process of law had been denied. In *Fisher v. State*, the court said: "Coercing the supposed state's criminals into confessions and using such confessions so coerced from them against them in trials has been the curse of all countries. It was the chief inequity, the crowning infamy of the Star Chamber, and the Inquisition, and other similar institutions. The constitution recognized the evils that lay behind these practices and prohibited them in this country. . . . The duty of maintaining constitutional rights of a person on trial for his life rises above mere rules of procedure and wherever the court is clearly satisfied that such violations exist, it will refuse to sanction such violations and will apply the corrective."

In the instant case, the trial court was fully advised by the undisputed evidence of the way in which the confessions had been procured. The trial court knew that there was no other evidence upon which conviction and sentence could be based. Yet it proceeded to permit conviction and to pronounce sentence. The conviction and sentence were void for want of the essential elements of due process, and the proceeding thus vitiated could be challenged in any appropriate manner. It was challenged before the Supreme Court of the

State by the express invocation of the Fourteenth Amendment. That court entertained the challenge, considered the federal question thus presented, but declined to enforce petitioners' constitutional right. The court thus denied a federal right fully established and specially set up and claimed and the judgment must be

Reversed.

Source: *Brown v. Mississippi,* 297 U.S. 278 (1936)

3.28 Opinion in *Chambers v. Florida,* 1940

Following the murder of an elderly white man, Broward County (Florida) police rounded up thirty to forty African American men in the area for questioning. Four of those detained, who were tenant farmers, were interrogated continuously for five days, after which three of them confessed. The fourth man went to trial, and the confessions elicited from the others were used to convict him. All four were sentenced to death. Justice Hugo Black wrote for a unanimous Court, overturning the verdict because the confessions were coerced.

Chambers v. Florida was decided four years after Brown v. Mississippi, and although the means of coercion were less shocking than those employed in Brown, the case provided an opportunity for Justice Black to discuss at greater length the history of judicial torture and the bearing of that history on modern civil liberties jurisprudence.

"Confessions thus obtained would make of the constitutional requirement of due process of law a meaningless symbol"

The scope and operation of the Fourteenth Amendment have been fruitful sources of controversy in our constitutional history. However, in view of its historical setting and the wrongs which called it into being, the due process provision of the Fourteenth Amendment—just as that in the Fifth—has led few to doubt that it was intended to guarantee procedural standards adequate and appropriate, then and thereafter, to protect, at all times, people charged with or suspected of crime by those holding positions of power and authority. Tyrannical governments had immemorially utilized dictatorial criminal procedure and punishment to make scapegoats of the weak, or of helpless political, religious, or racial minorities and those who differed, who would not conform and who resisted tyranny. The instruments of such governments were, in the main, two. Conduct, innocent when engaged in, was subsequently made by fiat criminally punishable without legislation. And a liberty loving people won the principle that criminal punishments could not be inflicted save for that which proper legislative action had already by "the law of the land" forbidden when done. But even more was needed. From the popular hatred and abhorrence of illegal confinement, torture and extortion of confessions of violations of the "law of the land" evolved the fundamental idea that no man's life, liberty or property be forfeited as criminal punishment for violation of that law until there had been a charge fairly made and fairly tried in a public tribunal free of prejudice, passion, excitement, and tyrannical power. Thus, as assurance against ancient evils, our country, in order to preserve "the blessings of liberty," wrote into its basic law the requirement, among others, that the forfeiture of the lives, liberties or property of people accused of crime can only follow if procedural safeguards of due process have been obeyed.

The determination to preserve an accused's right to procedural due process sprang in large part from knowledge of the historical truth that the rights and liberties of people accused of crime could not be safely entrusted to secret inquisitorial processes. The testimony of centuries, in governments of varying kinds over populations of different races and beliefs, stood as proof that physical and mental torture and coercion had brought about the tragically unjust sacrifices of some who were the noblest and most useful of their generations. The rack, the thumbscrew, the wheel, solitary confinement, protracted questioning and cross questioning, and other ingenious forms of entrapment of the helpless or unpopular had left their wake of mutilated bodies and shattered minds along the way to the cross, the guillotine, the stake and the hangman's noose. And they who have suffered most from secret and dictatorial proceedings have almost always been the poor, the ignorant, the numerically weak, the friendless, and the powerless. . .

Here, the record develops a sharp conflict upon the issue of physical violence and mistreatment, but shows, without conflict, the dragnet methods of arrest on suspicion without warrant, and the protracted questioning and cross questioning of these ignorant young colored tenant farmers by state officers and other white citizens, in a fourth floor jail room, where as prisoners they were without friends, advisers or counselors, and under circumstances calculated to break the strongest nerves and the stoutest resistance. Just as our decision in *Brown v. Mississippi* was based upon the fact that the confessions were the result of compulsion, so in the present case, the admitted practices were such as to justify the statement that "The undisputed facts showed that compulsion was applied."

For five days petitioners were subjected to interrogations culminating in Saturday's (May 20th) all night examination. Over a period of five days they steadily refused to confess and disclaimed any guilt. The very circumstances surrounding their confinement and their questioning without any formal charges having been brought, were such as to fill petitioners with terror and frightful misgivings. Some were practical strangers in the community; three were arrested in a one-room farm tenant house which was their home; the haunting fear of mob violence was around them in an atmosphere charged with excitement and public indignation. From virtually the moment of their arrest until their eventual confessions, they never knew just when any one would be called back to the fourth floor room, and there, surrounded by his accusers and others, interrogated by men who held their very lives—so far as these ignorant petitioners could know—in the balance. The rejection of petitioner Woodward's first "confession," given in the early hours of Sunday morning, because it was found wanting, demonstrates the relentless tenacity which "broke" petitioners' will and rendered them helpless to resist their accusers further. To permit human lives to be forfeited upon confessions thus obtained would make of the constitutional requirement of due process of law a meaningless symbol.

We are not impressed by the argument that law enforcement methods such as those under review are necessary to uphold our laws. The Constitution proscribes such lawless means irrespective of the end. And this argument flouts the basic principle that all people must stand on an equality before the bar of justice in every American court. Today, as in ages past, we are not without tragic proof that the exalted power of some governments to punish manufactured crime dictatorially is the handmaid of tyranny. Under our constitutional system, courts stand against any winds that blow as havens of refuge for those who might otherwise suffer because they are helpless, weak, outnumbered, or because they are non-conforming victims of prejudice and public excitement. Due process of law, preserved for all by our Constitution, commands that no such practice as that disclosed by this record shall send any accused to his death. No higher duty, no more solemn responsibility, rests upon this Court, than that of translating into living law and maintaining this constitutional shield deliberately planned and inscribed for the benefit of every human being subject to our Constitution—of whatever race, creed or persuasion.

Source: *Chambers v. Florida*, 309 U.S. 227 (1940)

3.29 Closing Argument of Justice Jackson at Nuremburg, 1946

Supreme Court Justice Robert H. Jackson was head prosecutor at the Nuremberg trials following World War II. Before and afterward, he served as an associate justice on the U.S. Supreme Court. In his closing argument, Jackson noted the singular place of the twentieth century in human history, distinguished as it was by the deaths and cruelties that occurred. A major part of his closing was spent outlining the nature of the defendants' crimes and the evidence produced to prove them. Jackson had a difficult task in trying to put the enormous human tragedy and evil of the events of the Holocaust and the war in Europe into legal terms.

"No half-century ever witnessed slaughter on such a scale"

It is common to think of our own time as standing at the apex of civilization, from which the deficiencies of preceding ages may patronizingly be viewed in the light of what is assumed to be "progress." The reality is that in the long perspective of history the present century will not hold an admirable position, unless its second half is to redeem its first. These two-score years in this Twentieth Century will be recorded in the book of years as one of the most bloody in all annals. Two World Wars have left a legacy of dead which number more than all the armies engaged in any war that made ancient or medieval history. No half-century ever witnessed slaughter on such a scale, such cruelties and inhumanities, such wholesale deportations of peoples into slavery, such annihilations of minorities. The Terror of Torquemada pales before the Nazi Inquisition. These deeds are the overshadowing historical facts by which generations to come will remember this decade. If we cannot eliminate the causes and prevent the repetition of these barbaric events, it is not an irresponsible prophecy to say that this Twentieth Century may yet succeed in bringing the doom of civilization. Goaded by these facts, we have moved to redress the blight on the record of our era. The defendants complain that our pace is too fast. In drawing the Charter of this Tribunal, we thought we were recording an accomplished advance in International Law. But they say that we have outrun our times, that we have anticipated an advance that should be, but has not yet been made. The Agreement of London, whether it originates or merely records, at all events marks a transition in International Law which roughly corresponds to that in the evolution of local law when men ceased to punish local crime by "hue and cry" and began to let reason and inquiry govern punishment. The society of nations has emerged from the primitive "hue and cry," the law of "catch and kill." It seeks to apply sanctions to enforce

International Law, but to guide their application by evidence, law, and reason, instead of outcry. The defendants denounce the law under which their accounting is asked. Their dislike for the law which condemns them is not original. It has been remarked before that

"No thief ere felt the halter draw
With good opinion of the law."

. . . Of one thing we may be sure. The future will never have to ask, with misgiving, what could the Nazis have said in their favor. History will know that whatever could be said, they were allowed to say. They have been given the kind of a trial which they, in the days of their pomp and power, never gave to any man. . . .

It is unnecessary to labor this point on the facts. Goering asserts that the Rules of Land Warfare were obsolete, that no nation could fight a total war within their limits. He testified that the Nazis would have denounced the Conventions to which Germany was a party, but that General Jodl wanted captured German soldiers to continue to benefit from their observance by the Allies. It was, however, against the Soviet people and Soviet prisoners that Teutonic fury knew no bounds, in spite of a warning by Admiral Canaris that the treatment was in violation of International Law. We need not, therefore, for purposes of the Conspiracy count, recite the revolting details of starving, beating, murdering, freezing, and mass extermination admittedly used against the eastern soldiery. Also, we may take as established or admitted that lawless conduct such as shooting British and American airmen, mistreatment of Western prisoners of war, forcing French prisoners of war into German war work, and other deliberate violations of the Hague and Geneva Conventions, did occur, and in obedience to highest levels of authority.

4. Enslavement and Plunder of Populations in Occupied Countries

The defendant Sauckel, Plenipotentiary General for the Utilization of Labor, is authority for the statement that "out of five million foreign workers who arrived in Germany, not even 200,000 came voluntarily." It was officially reported to defendant Rosenberg that in his territory "recruiting methods were used which probably have their origin in the blackest period of the slave trade." Sauckel himself reported that male and female agents went hunting for men, got them drunk, and "shanghaied" them to Germany. These captives were shipped in trains without heat, food, or sanitary facilities. The dead were thrown out at stations, and the newborn were thrown out of the windows of moving trains. Sauckel ordered that "all the men must be fed, sheltered and treated in such a way as to exploit them to the highest possible extent at the lowest conceivable degree of expenditure." About two million of these were employed directly in the manufacture of armaments and munitions. The director of the Krupp Locomotive factory in Essen complained to the company that Russian forced laborers were so underfed that they were too weakened to do their work, and the Krupp doctor confirmed their pitiable condition. Soviet workers were put in camps under Gestapo guards, who were allowed to punish disobedience by confinement in a concentration camp or by hanging on the spot. Populations of occupied countries were otherwise exploited and oppressed unmercifully. Terrorism was the order of the day. Civilians were arrested without charges, committed without counsel, executed without hearing. Villages were destroyed, the male inhabitants shot or sent to concentration camps, the women sent to forced labor, and the children scattered abroad. The extent of the slaughter in Poland alone was indicated by Frank, who reported : "If I wanted to have a poster put up for every seven Poles who were shot, the forests of Poland would not suffice for producing the paper for such posters." . . .

Persecution and Extermination of Jews and Christians

The Nazi movement will be of evil memory in history because of its persecution of the Jews, the most far-flung and terrible racial persecution of time. Although the Nazi party neither invented nor monopolized anti-Semitism, its leaders from the very beginning embraced it, incited it, and exploited it. They used it as "the psychological spark that ignites the mob." After the seizure of power, it became an official state policy, The persecution began in a series of discriminatory laws eliminating the Jews from the civil service, the professions, and economic life. As it became more intense it included segregation of Jews in ghettos and exile. Riots were organized by party leaders to loot Jewish business places and to burn synagogues. Jewish property was confiscated and a collective fine of a billion marks was imposed upon German Jewry. The program progressed in fury and irresponsibility to the "final solution." This consisted of sending all Jews who were fit to work to concentration camps as slave laborers, and all who were not fit, which included children under 12 and people over 50, as well as any other judged unfit by an SS doctor, to concentration camps for extermination.

Adolf Eichmann, the sinister figure who had charge of the extermination program, has estimated that the anti-Jewish activities resulted in the killing of six million Jews. Of these, four million were killed in extermination institutions, and two million were killed by *Einsatzgruppen,* mobile units of the Security Police and SD which pursued Jews in the ghettos and in their homes and slaughtered them by gas wagons, by mass shooting in anti-tank ditches, and by every device which Nazi ingenuity could conceive. So thorough and uncompromising was this program that the Jews of Europe as a race no longer exist, thus fulfilling the diabolic "prophecy" of Adolf Hitler at the beginning of the war.

Source: Justice Robert Jackson Archive, http://archive.roberthjackson.org/items/show/62

3.30 Act of the Georgia Legislature, 1946

This Georgia statute outlaws corporal punishment in prisons.

"All shackles, manacles, picks, leg-irons, and chains shall be barred from use"

Sec. 12. Whipping of inmates and all forms of corporal punishment shall be prohibited. All shackles, manacles, picks, leg-irons, and chains shall be barred from use by any correctional institution, public work camp, highway camp, or other institution of confinement operated under authority of the State Board of Corrections.

In transferring prisoners from one locality to another, manacles may be used where necessary to restrain or prevent the prisoner's escape. The wearing of stripes shall not be required, but may be used as punishment for violation of prison rules and regulations for such time as the State Board of Corrections, or the Director of Corrections may direct.

Source: Georgia Archives, http://content.sos.state.ga.us/cdm4/legdocs.php

---

3.31 United Nations Declaration of Human Rights, 1948

The United Nations Declaration of Human Rights and the subsequent Geneva Conventions of 1949 represent attempts to codify rules of humane treatment in the wake of World War II.

"Barbarous acts which have outraged the conscience of mankind"

PREAMBLE

Whereas recognition of the inherent dignity and of the equal and inalienable rights of all members of the human family is the foundation of freedom, justice and peace in the world,

Whereas disregard and contempt for human rights have resulted in barbarous acts which have outraged the conscience of mankind, and the advent of a world in which human beings shall enjoy freedom of speech and belief and freedom from fear and want has been proclaimed as the highest aspiration of the common people,

Whereas it is essential, if man is not to be compelled to have recourse, as a last resort, to rebellion against tyranny and oppression, that human rights should be protected by the rule of law,

Whereas it is essential to promote the development of friendly relations between nations,

Whereas the peoples of the United Nations have in the Charter reaffirmed their faith in fundamental human rights, in the dignity and worth of the human person and in the equal rights of men and women and have determined to promote social progress and better standards of life in larger freedom,

Whereas Member States have pledged themselves to achieve, in co-operation with the United Nations, the promotion of universal respect for and observance of human rights and fundamental freedoms,

Whereas a common understanding of these rights and freedoms is of the greatest importance for the full realization of this pledge,

Now, Therefore THE GENERAL ASSEMBLY proclaims THIS UNIVERSAL DECLARATION OF HUMAN RIGHTS as a common standard of achievement for all peoples and all nations, to the end that every individual and every organ of society, keeping this Declaration constantly in mind, shall strive by teaching and education to promote respect for these rights and freedoms and by progressive measures, national and international, to secure their universal and effective recognition and observance, both among the peoples of Member States themselves and among the peoples of territories under their jurisdiction.

Article 1. All human beings are born free and equal in dignity and rights. They are endowed with reason and conscience and should act towards one another in a spirit of brotherhood.

Article 2. Everyone is entitled to all the rights and freedoms set forth in this Declaration, without distinction of any kind, such as race, colour, sex, language, religion, political or other opinion, national or social origin, property, birth or other status. Furthermore, no distinction shall be made on the basis of the political, jurisdictional or international status of the country or territory to which a person belongs, whether it be independent, trust, non-self-governing or under any other limitation of sovereignty.

Article 3. Everyone has the right to life, liberty and security of person.

Article 4. No one shall be held in slavery or servitude; slavery and the slave trade shall be prohibited in all their forms.

Article 5. No one shall be subjected to torture or to cruel, inhuman or degrading treatment or punishment.

Article 6. Everyone has the right to recognition everywhere as a person before the law.

Article 7. All are equal before the law and are entitled without any discrimination to equal protection of the law. All are entitled to equal protection against any discrimination in violation of this Declaration and against any incitement to such discrimination.

Article 8. Everyone has the right to an effective remedy by the competent national tribunals for acts violating the fundamental rights granted him by the constitution or by law.

Article 9. No one shall be subjected to arbitrary arrest, detention or exile.

Article 10. Everyone is entitled in full equality to a fair and public hearing by an independent and impartial tribunal, in the determination of his rights and obligations and of any criminal charge against him.

Article 11. (1) Everyone charged with a penal offence has the right to be presumed innocent until proved guilty according to law in a public trial at which he has had all the guarantees necessary for his defence. (2) No one shall be held guilty of any penal offence on account of any act or omission which did not constitute a penal offence, under national or international law, at the time when it was committed. Nor shall a heavier penalty be imposed than the one that was applicable at the time the penal offence was committed.

Source: http://www.un.org

3.32 Geneva Conventions, 1949, Article 3

This section of the 1949 Geneva Conventions is common to all three of the 1949 conventions (regarding wounded and sick soldiers on land during war; wounded, sick, and shipwrecked military personnel at sea during war; prisoners of war; and civilians) and is usually referred to as "Common Article 3."

"In all circumstances be treated humanely"

In the case of armed conflict not of an international character occurring in the territory of one of the High Contracting Parties, each Party to the conflict shall be bound to apply, as a minimum, the following provisions:

(1) Persons taking no active part in the hostilities, including members of armed forces who have laid down their arms and those placed hors de combat by sickness, wounds, detention, or any other cause, shall in all circumstances

be treated humanely, without any adverse distinction founded on race, colour, religion or faith, sex, birth or wealth, or any other similar criteria.

To this end, the following acts are and shall remain prohibited at any time and in any place whatsoever with respect to the above-mentioned persons:

(a) violence to life and person, in particular murder of all kinds, mutilation, cruel treatment and torture;

(b) taking of hostages;

(c) outrages upon personal dignity, in particular humiliating and degrading treatment;

(d) the passing of sentences and the carrying out of executions without previous judgment pronounced by a regularly constituted court, affording all the judicial guarantees which are recognized as indispensable by civilized peoples.

(2) The wounded and sick shall be collected and cared for.

Source: http://www.un.org/

4

THE COLD WAR, VIETNAM, AND TORTURE BY THE POLICE

In this time period, government enlisted the academic research community to make interrogation more efficient and effective. The communist threat provided impetus for advances in the political technology of power, and the struggle to contain Soviet influence led the United States to disseminate its interrogation practices in Latin America and Southeast Asia. Meanwhile, at home police used violent and abusive interrogation practices, and courts and agencies were forced to confront "judicial torture" as they reviewed the voluntariness of confessions. While existing law can easily address forced confessions under the constitutional framework of the self-incrimination clause, new issues are presented with regard to another legal doctrine: the Eighth Amendment's prohibition on cruel and unusual punishment. The first document in the chapter is a Supreme Court opinion interpreting the Eighth Amendment.

4.1 Opinion of the U.S. Supreme Court in *Louisiana ex rel. Francis v. Resweber*, 1947

Willie Francis was convicted of murder in Louisiana and sentenced to death. The first attempt to execute him by electrocution failed, and as the state was set to try again, Francis sought relief, arguing that putting him through a second electrocution would amount to cruel and unusual punishment. A majority of the Supreme Court disagreed. They viewed the incident as equivalent to an accident: the repetition of the execution procedure was not deliberate, and it was no one's fault. Thus, the majority focused on the intention of the state rather than the subjective experience of the prisoner.

"We find nothing in what took place here which amounts to cruel and unusual punishment"

MR. JUSTICE REED announced the judgment of the Court in an opinion in which the chief justice, MR. JUSTICE BLACK, and MR. JUSTICE JACKSON join.
    This writ of certiorari brings before this Court a unique situation. The pe-

titioner, Willie Francis, is a colored citizen of Louisiana. He was duly convict- ed of murder and in September, 1945, sentenced to be electrocuted for the crime. Upon a proper death warrant, Francis was prepared for execution and on May 3, 1946, pursuant to the warrant, was placed in the official electric chair of the State of Louisiana in the presence of the authorized witnesses. The executioner threw the switch but, presumably because of some mechani- cal difficulty, death did not result. He was thereupon removed from the chair and returned to prison where he now is. A new death warrant was issued by the Governor of Louisiana, fixing the execution for May 9, 1946. . . .

Applications to the Supreme Court of the state were filed for writs of certio- rari, mandamus, prohibition and habeas corpus, directed to the appropriate officials in the state. Execution of the sentence was stayed. By the applications petitioner claimed the protection of the due process clause of the Fourteenth Amendment on the ground that an execution under the circumstances de- tailed would deny due process to him because of the double jeopardy provi- sion of the Fifth Amendment and the cruel and unusual punishment pro- vision of the Eighth Amendment. These federal constitutional protections, petitioner claimed, would be denied because he had once gone through the difficult preparation for execution and had once received through his body a current of electricity intended to cause death. The Supreme Court of Louisi- ana denied the applications on the ground of a lack of any basis for judicial relief. That is, the state court concluded there was no violation of state or na- tional law alleged in the various applications. It spoke of the fact that no "cur- rent of sufficient intensity to cause death" passed through petitioner's body. It referred specifically to the fact that the applications of petitioner invoked the provisions of the Louisiana Constitution against cruel and inhuman punish- ments and putting one in jeopardy of life or liberty twice for the same offense. We granted certiorari on a petition setting forth the aforementioned conten- tions, to consider the alleged violations of rights under the Federal Constitu- tion in the unusual circumstances of this case. For matters of state law, the opinion and order of the Supreme Court of Louisiana are binding on this Court. So far as we are aware, this case is without precedent in any court.

To determine whether or not the execution of the petitioner may fairly take place after the experience through which he passed, we shall examine the circumstances under the assumption, but without so deciding, that vio- lation of the principles of the Fifth and Eighth Amendments, as to double jeopardy and cruel and unusual punishment, would be violative of the due process clause of the Fourteenth Amendment. As nothing has been brought to our attention to suggest the contrary, we must and do assume that the state officials carried out their duties under the death warrant in a careful and humane manner. Accidents happen for which no man is to blame. We turn to the question as to whether the proposed enforcement of the criminal law of the state is offensive to any constitutional requirements to which reference has been made. . . .

Second. We find nothing in what took place here which amounts to cruel and unusual punishment in the constitutional sense. The case before us does not call for an examination into any punishments except that of death. See *Weems v. United States, 217 U.S. 349.* The traditional humanity of modern Anglo-American law forbids the infliction of unnecessary pain in the execution of the death sentence. Prohibition against the wanton infliction of pain has come into our law from the Bill of Rights of 1688. The identical words appear in our Eighth Amendment. The Fourteenth would prohibit by its due process clause execution by a state in a cruel manner.

Petitioner's suggestion is that because he once underwent the psychological strain of preparation for electrocution, now to require him to undergo this preparation again subjects him to a lingering or cruel and unusual punishment. Even the fact that petitioner has already been subjected to a current of electricity does not make his subsequent execution any more cruel in the constitutional sense than any other execution. The cruelty against which the Constitution protects a convicted man is cruelty inherent in the method of punishment, not the necessary suffering involved in any method employed to extinguish life humanely. The fact that an unforeseeable accident prevented the prompt consummation of the sentence cannot, it seems to us, add an element of cruelty to a subsequent execution. There is no purpose to inflict unnecessary pain nor any unnecessary pain involved in the proposed execution. The situation of the unfortunate victim of this accident is just as though he had suffered the identical amount of mental anguish and physical pain in any other occurrence, such as, for example, a fire in the cell block. We cannot agree that the hardship imposed upon the petitioner rises to that level of hardship denounced as denial of due process because of cruelty.

Third. The Supreme Court of Louisiana also rejected petitioner's contention that death inflicted after his prior sufferings would deny him the equal protection of the laws, guaranteed by the Fourteenth Amendment. This suggestion in so far as it differs from the due process argument is based on the idea that execution, after an attempt at execution has failed, would be a more severe punishment than is imposed upon others guilty of a like offense. That is, since others do not go through the strain of preparation for execution a second time or have not experienced a nonlethal current in a prior attempt at execution, as petitioner did, to compel petitioner to submit to execution after these prior experiences denies to him equal protection. Equal protection does not protect a prisoner against even illegal acts of officers in charge of him, much less against accidents during his detention for execution. See *Lisenba v. California, 314 U.S. 219, 226.* Laws cannot prevent accidents nor can a law equally protect all against them. So long as the law applies to all alike, the requirements of equal protection are met. We have no right to assume that Louisiana singled out Francis for a treatment other than that which has been or would generally be applied. . . .

This court said of a similar clause embodied in the Constitution of New York, *In re Kemmler* (footnote 4): ". . . but the language in question as used in the constitution of the State of New York was intended particularly to operate upon the legislature of the State, to whose control the punishment of crime was almost wholly confided. So that, if the punishment prescribed for an offence against the laws of the State were manifestly cruel and unusual, as burning at the stake, crucifixion, breaking on the wheel, or the like, it would be the duty of the courts to adjudge such penalties to be within the constitutional prohibition." It added, p. 447: "Punishments are cruel when they involve torture or a lingering death; but the punishment of death is not cruel, within the meaning of that word as used in the Constitution. It implies there something inhuman and barbarous, something more than the mere extinguishment of life. Louisiana has the same humane provision in its constitution." Louisiana Constitution, Art. I, § 12. The *Kemmler* case denied that electrocution infringed the federal constitutional rights of a convicted criminal sentenced to execution.

MR. JUSTICE BURTON, with whom MR. JUSTICE DOUGLAS, MR. JUSTICE MURPHY and MR. JUSTICE RUTLEDGE concur, dissenting.

Under circumstances unique in judicial history, the relator asks this Court to stay his execution on the ground that it will violate the due process of law guaranteed to him by the Constitution of the United States. We believe that the unusual facts before us require that the judgment of the Supreme Court of Louisiana be vacated and that this cause be remanded for further proceedings not inconsistent with this opinion. Those proceedings should include the determination of certain material facts not previously determined, including the extent, if any, to which electric current was applied to the relator during his attempted electrocution on May 3, 1946. Where life is to be taken, there must be no avoidable error of law or uncertainty of fact.

If the state officials deliberately and intentionally had placed the relator in the electric chair five times and, each time, had applied electric current to his body in a manner not sufficient, until the final time, to kill him, such a form of torture would rival that of burning at the stake. Although the failure of the first attempt, in the present case, was unintended, the reapplication of the electric current will be intentional. How many deliberate and intentional reapplications of electric current does it take to produce a cruel, unusual and unconstitutional punishment? While five applications would be more cruel and unusual than one, the uniqueness of the present case demonstrates that, today, two separated applications are sufficiently "cruel and unusual" to be prohibited. If five attempts would be "cruel and unusual," it would be difficult to draw the line between two, three, four and five. It is not difficult, however, as we here contend, to draw the line between the one continuous application prescribed by statute and any other application of the current.

Lack of intent that the first application be less than fatal is not material. The intent of the executioner cannot lessen the torture or excuse the result. It was the statutory duty of the state officials to make sure that there was no failure. The procedure in this case contrasts with common knowledge of precautions generally taken elsewhere to insure against failure of electrocutions. The high standard of care generally taken evidences the significance properly attached to the unconditional requirement of a single continued application of the current until death results. In our view of this case, we are giving careful recognition to the law of Louisiana. Neither the Legislature nor the Supreme Court of Louisiana has expressed approval of electrocution other than by one continuous application of a lethal current.

Executive clemency provides a common means of avoiding unconstitutional or otherwise questionable executions. When, however, the unconstitutionality of proposed executive procedure is brought before this Court, as in this case, we should apply the constitutional protection. In this case, final recourse is had to the high trusteeship vested in this Court by the people of the United States over the constitutional process by which their own lives may be taken. . . .

This statement assumed that the relief sought in the Supreme Court of Louisiana was only a review of the judicial proceedings in the lower state courts prior to the passing of sentence upon the relator on September 14, 1945. On the contrary, the issue raised there and here primarily concerns the action of state officials on and after May 3, 1946, in connection with their past and proposed attempts to electrocute the relator. This issue properly presents a federal constitutional question based on the impending deprivation of the life of the relator by executive officials of the State of Louisiana in a manner alleged to be a violation of the due process of law guaranteed by the Fourteenth Amendment. The refusal of the writs necessarily denied the constitutional protection prayed for. In ruling against the relator on the pleadings, in the absence of further evidence, the Supreme Court of Louisiana must be taken to have acted upon the allegations of fact most favorable to the relator.

The petition contains the unequivocal allegation that the official electrocutioner "turned on the switch and a current of electricity was caused to pass through the body of relator, all in the presence of the official witnesses." This allegation must be read in the light of the Louisiana statute which authorized the electrocutioner to apply to the body of the relator only such an electric current as was of "sufficient intensity to cause death." On that record, denial of relief means that the proposed repeated, and at least second, application to the relator of an electric current sufficient to cause death is not, under present circumstances, a cruel and unusual punishment violative of due process of law. It exceeds any punishment prescribed by law. There is no precedent for it. What then is it, if it be not cruel, unusual and unlawful? In spite of the constitutional issue thus raised, the Supreme Court of Louisiana treated it as an executive question not subject to judicial review. We believe that if the facts are as alleged by the relator the proposed action is unconstitutional. We believe also that the Supreme Court of Louisiana should provide for the determination of the facts and then proceed in a manner not inconsistent with this opinion.

Source: *Louisiana ex rel. Resweber v. Francis*, 329 U.S. 459 (1947)

4.2 Interview with A.G., Korean War Veteran, 1999

This interview was conducted by the Rutgers University Oral History Archive.

"It spells out very clearly what you can and cannot do"

AG: I was standing in the sally-port, the sally-port is an entrance way to the enclosure, it's a gate on one side and an open area and another gate before you get to the compounds, walk in, and I see one of the prisoners that has welts on his face. He had obviously been beaten. I said, "All right, I want that man in my office right now and I want the GI on that detail in my office right now. In fact I want all the GIs on that detail," because it was one GI to every fifty prisoners and details were always three hundred, four hundred prisoners at a time. I had my own interpreter. I said, "All right, Kim, I want to know who did it," and I lined up the GIs, and the prisoner walks down the row and there was six or eight GIs, short, tall, fat, thin, whatever, and he said something in Korean to my interpreter and my interpreter started to laugh, in classic military jargon I said, "What the **** is so funny?" And I had given Kim sort of an American sense of humor at this point and he was laughing and he says, "He say they all look alike," which was classic because the GIs said, "All those prisoners, all the gooks, they all look alike," and here was the prisoner coming back and saying that. Well, now maybe he said that because he was afraid of retribution. I said, "Okay, Kim, I'm going to leave here now and I want you to ask him again," and he did and he identified the guy. I submitted papers to have that SOB court-martialed and it was denied by our executive officer—Colonel Brown. Notification would have to be sent to POW Command in Pusan and he didn't want that. Instead, I settled for company punishment and removed him from his station. My exposure to the Geneva Convention, I guess, started at OCS. There was a block of instruction on the Geneva Convention. When I went to branch officer school at Camp Gordon there was more instruction on the Geneva Convention. At Koji, again, exposure to the Geneva Convention, more so there because then I was already involved with prisoners. When I went to my assignment, high in order, the first day or two, each of the GIs were given, it's on the first two pages of the Geneva Convention, "the care and treatment of prisoners," and it spells out very clearly what you can and cannot do, mostly what you cannot do, and it's done in broad stroke conversation, "you shall not humiliate, degrade, physically hurt, damage," whatever, and so on, and I still remember the expression. Each of my guys had to sign a statement that said, "I have read, understand and will comply with the aforementioned paragraphs in the Geneva Convention." There is no excuse for prisoner maltreatment, and when I read about the goings on today, I just wonder what the hell happened. So that's my shtick on that.

SI: Do you think, again, I don't want to break up the narration too much, but do you think that most of the men under your command, and also your fellow officers, felt as strongly as you about the Geneva Convention and the need to treat prisoners humanely?

AG: Well, it's a two-edged sword. There was one case that I knew of in our camp before I got there, this was when they were still living in tents, where one of the GIs was just miserable. You know, the routine, "All right, everybody back into their tents, when I blow the whistle you all run out and line up." He'd blow the whistle, "That wasn't fast enough, do it again," you know, that kind of nonsense, which was completely uncalled for. What the hell was their hurry, you know? And they finally, he was standing in the middle of the little exercise yard in his compound, they ran out, knocked him down and stomped him to death. So I say it's a two edged sword. If you treat them right, they'll treat you right, and it was very easy, I think, to treat them right. Funny, I remember once a detail was doing something and some of these prisoners were early teenagers, they were really kids. Some of them were old men. In my enclosure I had a father and son as prisoners in the same enclosure. This prisoner was carrying something with somebody else and I walked over and I helped them and he said, "Oh, Lieutenant, you like George Washington, you help the prisoner, you help the soldier." So that I think I had the respect of the prisoners. I remember walking through the enclosure one day with this man that I mentioned earlier, Mr. Hong, I have no idea what his rank was in the Korean Army, but when I walked through the enclosure with him, the prisoners would salute me, they would bow to him, and I never really found out what the deal was with Mr. Hong, he was an interesting man.

Source: http://oralhistory.rutgers.edu/

4.3 Opinion of the U.S. Supreme Court in *Rochin v. California*, 1952

In the Rochin *case, the U.S. Supreme Court rules on the legality of forcible stomach pumping used to discover evidence of a crime (here, drug possession). Writing for the Court, Justice Felix Frankfurter finds stomach pumping a violation of the due process clause.*

"Too close to the rack and the screw"

Justice FRANKFURTER delivered the opinion of the Court.

The vague contours of the Due Process Clause do not leave judges at large. We may not draw on our merely personal and private notions and disregard the limits that bind judges in their judicial function. Even though the concept of due process of law is not final and fixed, these limits are derived from considerations that are fused in the whole nature of our judicial process. See Cardozo, *The Nature of the Judicial Process; The Growth of the Law; The Paradoxes of Legal Science.* These are considerations deeply rooted in reason and in the compelling traditions of the legal profession. The Due Process Clause places upon this Court the duty of exercising a judgment, within the narrow confines of judicial power in reviewing State convictions, upon interests of society pushing in opposite directions.

Due process of law thus conceived is not to be derided as resort to a revival of "natural law." To believe that this judicial exercise of judgment could be avoided by freezing "due process of law" at some fixed stage of time or thought is to suggest that the most important aspect of constitutional adjudication is a function for inanimate machines and not for judges, for whom the independence safeguarded by Article III of the Constitution was designed and who are presumably guided by established standards of judicial behavior. Even cybernetics has not yet made that haughty claim. To practice the requisite detachment and to achieve sufficient objectivity no doubt demands of judges the habit of self-discipline and self-criticism, incertitude that one's own views are incontestable and alert tolerance toward views not shared. But these are precisely the presuppositions of our judicial process. They are precisely the qualities society has a right to expect from those entrusted with ultimate judicial power.

Restraints on our jurisdiction are self-imposed only in the sense that there is from our decisions no immediate appeal short of impeachment or constitutional amendment. But that does not make due process of law a matter of judicial caprice. The faculties of the Due Process Clause may be indefinite and vague, but the mode of their ascertainment is not self-willed. In each case "due process of law" requires an evaluation based on a disinterested inquiry pursued in the spirit of science, on a balanced order of facts exactly and fairly stated, on the detached consideration of conflicting claims, see *Hudson County Water Co. v. McCarter,* on a judgment not ad hoc and episodic but duly mindful of reconciling the needs both of continuity and of change in a progressive society.

Applying these general considerations to the circumstances of the present case, we are compelled to conclude that the proceedings by which this conviction was obtained do more than offend some fastidious squeamishness or private sentimentalism about combating crime too energetically. This is conduct that shocks the conscience. Illegally breaking into the privacy of the petitioner, the struggle to open his mouth and remove what was there, the forcible extraction of his stomach's contents—this course of proceeding by agents of government to obtain evidence is bound to offend even hardened sensibilities. They are methods too close to the rack and the screw to permit of constitutional differentiation.

It has long since ceased to be true that due process of law is heedless of the means by which otherwise relevant and credible evidence is obtained. This was not true even before the series of recent cases enforced the constitutional principle that the States may not base convictions upon confessions, however much verified, obtained by coercion. These decisions are not arbitrary exceptions to the comprehensive right of States to fashion their own rules of evidence for criminal trials. They are not sports in our constitutional law but applications of a general principle. They are only instances of the general requirement that States in their prosecutions respect certain decencies of civilized conduct. Due process of law, as a historic and generative principle, precludes defining, and thereby confining, these standards of conduct more precisely than to say that convictions cannot be brought about by methods that offend "a sense of justice." See Mr. Chief Justice Hughes, speaking for a unanimous Court in *Brown v. Mississippi.* It would be a stultification of the responsibility which the course of constitutional history has cast upon this Court to hold that in order to convict a man the police cannot extract by force what is in his mind but can extract what is in his stomach.

To attempt in this case to distinguish what lawyers call "real evidence" from verbal evidence is to ignore the reasons for excluding coerced confessions. Use of involuntary verbal confessions in State criminal trials is constitutionally obnoxious not only because of their unreliability. They are inadmissible under the Due Process Clause even though statements contained in them may be independently established as true. Coerced confessions offend the community's sense of fair play and decency. So here, to sanction the brutal conduct which naturally enough was condemned by the court whose judgment is before us, would be to afford brutality the cloak of law. Nothing would be more calculated to discredit law and thereby to brutalize the temper of a society.

In deciding this case we do not heedlessly bring into question decisions in many States dealing with essentially different, even if related, problems. We therefore put to one side cases which have arisen in the State courts through use of modern methods and devices for discovering wrongdoers and bringing them to book. It does not fairly represent these decisions to suggest that they legalize force so brutal and so offensive to human dignity in securing evidence from a suspect as is revealed by this record. Indeed the California Supreme Court has not sanctioned this mode of securing a conviction. It merely exercised its discretion to decline a review of the conviction. All the California judges who have expressed themselves in this case have condemned the conduct in the strongest language.

We are not unmindful that hypothetical situations can be conjured up, shading imperceptibly from the circumstances of this case and by gradations producing practical differences despite seemingly logical extensions. But the Constitution is "intended to preserve practical and substantial rights, not to maintain theories." *Davis v. Mills.*

On the facts of this case the conviction of the petitioner has been obtained by methods that offend the Due Process Clause. The judgment below must be Reversed.

Source: *Rochin v. California,* 342 U.S. 165 (1952)

4.4 KUBARK Manual, Excerpt no. 1, 1966

The Cold War origins of the KUBARK manual (code name for a CIA instructional manual on interrogation) are apparent in its repeated references to communism and the Soviets. KUBARK was intended to facilitate counterintelligence interrogation, which is referred to in the manual as CI.

"A principal source of aid today is scientific findings"

The interrogation of a resistant source who is a staff or agent member of an Orbit intelligence or security service or of a clandestine Communist organization is one of the most exacting of professional tasks. Usually the odds still favor the interrogator, but they are sharply cut by the training, experience, patience and toughness of the interrogatee. In such circumstances the interrogator needs all the help he can get. And a principal source of aid today is scientific findings. The intelligence service which is able to bring pertinent, modern knowledge to bear upon its problems enjoys huge advantages over a service which conducts its clandestine business in eighteenth century fashion. It is true that American psychologists have devoted somewhat more attention to Communists interrogation techniques, particularly "brainwashing," than to U.S. practices. Yet they have conducted scientific inquiries into many subjects that are closely related to interrogation: the effects of debility and isolation, the polygraph, reactions to pain and fear, hypnosis and heightened suggestibility, narcosis, etc. This work is of sufficient importance and relevance that it is no longer possible to discuss interrogation significantly without reference to the psychological research conducted in the last decade. For this reason a major purpose of this study is to focus relevant scientific findings upon CI interrogation. Every effort has been made to report and interpret these findings in our own language, in place of the terminology employed by the psychologists.

This study is by no means confined to a resume and interpretation of psychological findings. The approach of the psychologists is customarily manipulative; that is, they suggest methods of imposing controls or alterations upon the interrogatees from the outside. Except within the Communist frame of reference, they have paid less attention to the creation of internal controls—i.e., conversion of the source, so that voluntary cooperation results. Moral considerations aside, the imposition of external techniques of manipulating people carries with it the grave risk of later lawsuits, adverse publicity, or other attempts to strike back.

Source: www.gwu.edu/~nsarchiv/NSAEBB/NSAEBB122/, p. 2

4.5 KUBARK Manual, Excerpt no. 2, 1966

In this excerpt from KUBARK, the manual indicates that "medical, chemical or electrical" interrogation methods can be used. It also provides some guidance as to the psychology of interrogation. As McCoy demonstrates, psychological information was obtained in part from CIA-funded academic research. The fruits of some of that research are evident in the following excerpt.

"How can I make him want to tell me what he knows?"

Interrogations conducted under compulsion or duress are especially likely to involve illegality and to entail damaging consequences for KUBARK. Therefore prior Headquarters approval at the KUDOVE level must be obtained for the interrogation of any source against his will and under any of the following circumstances:

1. If bodily harm is to be inflicted.
2. If medical, chemical, or electrical methods or materials are to be used to induce acquiescence.
3. [redacted]

...

The skilled interrogator can save a great deal of time by understanding the emotional needs of the interrogatee. Most people confronted by an official—and dimly powerful representative of a foreign power—will get down to cases much faster if made to feel, from the start, that they are being treated as individuals. So simple a matter as greeting an interrogatee by his name at the opening of the session establishes in his mind the comforting awareness that he is considered as a person, not a squeezable sponge. This is not to say that the egoistic type should be allowed to bask at length in the warmth of individual recognition. But it is important to assuage the fear of denigration which afflicts many people when first interrogated by making it clear that the individuality of the interrogatee is recognized. With this common understanding established, the interrogation can move on to impersonal matters and will not later be thwarted or interrupted—or at least not as often—by irrelevant answers designed not to provide facts but to prove that the interrogatee is a respectable member of the human race.

Although it is often necessary to trick people into telling what we need to know, especially in CI interrogations, the initial question which the interrogator asks of himself should be, "How can I make him want to tell me what he knows?" rather than "How can I trap him into disclosing what he knows?" If the person being questioned is genuinely hostile for ideological reasons, techniques of manipulation are in order. But the assumption of hostility—or at least the use of pressure tactics at the first encounter—may make difficult subjects even out of those who would respond to recognition of individuality and an initial assumption of good will.

Source: www.gwu.edu/~nsarchiv/NSAEBB/NSAEBB122/, pp. 8–12

4.6 KUBARK Manual, Excerpt no. 3, 1966

This section of KUBARK provides specific instructions on coercive investigation.

"The interrogatee's mature defenses crumbles [*sic*] as he becomes more childlike"

THE COERCIVE COUNTERINTELLIGENCE INTERROGATION OF RESISTANT SOURCES
Restrictions.
The purpose of this part of the handbook is to present basic information about coercive techniques available for use in the interrogation situation. It is vital that this discussion not be misconstrued as constituting authorization for the use of coercion at field discretion. As was noted earlier, there is no such blanket authorization.
[redacted]
For both ethical pragmatic reasons no interrogator may take upon himself the unilateral responsibility for using coercive methods. Concealing from the interrogator's Superiors an intent to resort to coercion, or its unapproved employment, does not protect them. It places them, and KUBARK, in unconsidered jeopardy.
The Theory of Coercion.
Coercive procedures are designed not only to exploit the resistant source's internal conflicts and induce him to wrestle with himself but also to bring a superior outside force to bear upon the subject's resistance. Non-coercive methods are not likely to succeed if their selection and use is not predicated upon an accurate psychological assessment of the source. In contrast, the same coercive method may succeed against persons who are very unlike each other. The changes [*sic*] of success rise steeply, nonetheless, if the coercive technique is matched to the source's personality. Individuals react differently

even to such non-discriminatory stimuli as drugs. Moreover, it is a waste of time and energy to apply strong pressures on a hit-or-miss basis if a tap on the psychological jugular will produce compliance. . . .

Conclusion.

A brief summary of the foregoing may help to pull the major concepts of coercive interrogation together.:

1. The principal coercive techniques are arrest, detention, the deprivation of sensory stimuli, threats and fear, debility, pain, heightened suggestibility and hypnosis, and drugs.

2. If a coercive technique is to be used, or if two or more are to be employed jointly, they should be chosen for their effect upon the individual and carefully selected to match his personality.

3. The usual effect of coercion is regression. The interrogatee's mature defenses crumbles [*sic*] as he becomes more childlike. During the process of regression the subject may experience feelings of guilt, and it is usually useful to intensify these.

4. When regression has proceeded far enough so that the subject's desire to yield begins to overbalance his resistance, the interrogator should supply a face-saving rationalization. Like the coercive technique, the rationalization must be carefully chosen to fit the subject's personality.

Source: www.gwu.edu/~nsarchiv/NSAEBB/NSAEBB122/, pp. 82–103.

4.7 Testimony of Paul Meadlo, 1970

On March 16, 1968, U.S. troops killed hundreds of Vietnamese civilians in a massacre at the hamlet of My Lai. It took a year for the incident to become public, and another year for military prosecutions of those involved. Lieutenant William Calley, who was present at the massacre, was charged with specific acts of murder and wounding. Though it was difficult for the prosecution to secure testimony, Paul Meadlo eventually agreed to testify. In his account, he indicates that Calley ordered him to fire on a group of unarmed civilians and that Calley himself began shooting them first. Calley was convicted and sentenced to life in prison but, after appeal, had the sentence reduced from life to twenty years.

"He started shoving them off and shooting them in the ravine"

Direct examination by Aubrey Daniel:
    Q: What did you do in the village?

A: We just gathered up the people and led them to a designated area.

Q: How many people did you gather up?

A: Between thirty and fifty. Men, women, and children.

Q: What kind of children?

A: They were just children.

Q: Where did you get these people?

A: Some of them was in hooches and some was in rice paddies when we gathered them up.

Q: Why did you gather them up?

A: We suspected them of being Viet Cong. And as far as I'm concerned, they're still Viet Cong. . . .

Q: What did you do when you got there?

A: Just guarded them.

Q: Did you see Lieutenant Calley?

A: Yes

Q: What did he do?

A: He came up to me and he said, "You know what to do with them, Meadlo," and I assumed he wanted me to guard them. That's what I did.

Q: What were the people doing?

A: They were just standing there. . . .

A: [Calley] said, "How come they're not dead?" I said, I didn't know we were supposed to kill them. He said, "I want them dead." He backed off twenty or thirty feet and started shooting into the people—the Viet Cong—shooting automatic. He was beside me. He burned four or five magazines. I burned off a few, about three. I helped shoot 'em.

Q: What were the people doing after you shot them?

A: They were lying down.

Q: Why were they lying down?

A: They was mortally wounded.

Q: How were you feeling at that time?

A: I was mortally upset, scared, because of the briefing we had the day before.

Q: Were you crying?

A: I imagine I was. . . .

Q: Were there any Vietnamese there?

A: Yes, there was Viet Cong there. About seventy-five to a hundred, standing outside the ravine. . . .

A: Then Lieutenant Calley said to me, "We've got another job to do, Meadlo."

Q: What happened then?

A: He started shoving them off and shooting them in the ravine.

Q: How many times did he shoot?

A: I can't remember.

Q: Did you shoot?

A: Yes. I shot the Viet Cong. He ordered me to help kill people. I started shoving them off and shooting.

Source: www.law.umkc.edu/faculty/projects/ftrials/mylai/mylai.htm

4.8 Decision of the U.S. Court of Military Appeals, 1973

The Court of Military Appeals affirmed Lieutenant Calley's conviction.

"Lieutenant Calley stands convicted of the premeditated murder of 22 infants, children, women, and old men"

First Lieutenant Calley stands convicted of the premeditated murder of 22 infants, children, women, and old men, and of assault with intent to murder a child of about 2 years of age. All the killings and the assault took place on March 16, 1968, in the area of the village of May Lai in the Republic of South Vietnam. The Army Court of Military Review affirmed the findings of guilty and the sentence, which, as reduced by the convening authority, includes dismissal and confinement at hard labor for 20 years. The accused petitioned this Court for further review, alleging 30 assignments of error. We granted three of these assignments. . . .

Lieutenant Calley was a platoon leader in C Company, a unit that was part of an organization known as Task Force Barker, whose mission was to subdue and drive out the enemy in an area in the Republic of Vietnam known popularly as Pinkville. Before March 16, 1968, this area, which included the village of My Lai 4, was a Viet Cong stronghold. C Company had operated in the area several times. Each time the unit had entered the area it suffered casualties by sniper fire, machine gun fire, mines, and other forms of attack. Lieutenant Calley had accompanied his platoon on some of the incursions.

On March 15, 1968, a memorial service for members of the company killed in the area during the preceding weeks was held. After the service Captain Ernest L. Medina, the commanding officer of C Company, briefed the company on a mission in the Pinkville area set for the next day. C Company was to serve as the main attack formation for Task Force Barker. In that role it would assault and neutralize May Lai 4, 5, and 6 and then mass for an assault on My Lai, 1. Intelligence reports indicated that the unit would be opposed by a veteran enemy battalion, and that all civilians would be absent from the area. The objective was to destroy the enemy. Disagreement exists as to the instructions on the specifics of destruction.

Captain Medina testified that he instructed his troops that they were to destroy My Lai 4 by "burning the hooches, to kill the livestock, to close the wells and to destroy the food crops." Asked if women and children were to be killed, Medina said he replied in the negative, adding that, "You must use common sense. If they have a weapon and are trying to engage you, then you can shoot back, but you must use common sense." However, Lieutenant Calley testified that Captain Medina informed the troops they were to kill every living thing—men, women, children, and animals—and under no circumstances were they to leave any Vietnamese behind them as they passed through the villages en route to their final objective. Other witnesses gave more or less support to both versions of the briefing.

On March 16, 1968, the operation began with interdicting fire. C Company was then brought to the area by helicopters. Lieutenant Calley's platoon was on the first lift. This platoon formed a defense perimeter until the remainder of the force was landed. The unit received no hostile fire from the village.

Calley's platoon passed the approaches to the village with his men firing heavily. Entering the village, the platoon encountered only unarmed, unresisting men, women, and children. The villagers, including infants held in their mothers' arms, were assembled and moved in separate groups to collection points. Calley testified that during this time he was radioed twice by Captain Medina, who demanded to know what was delaying the platoon. On being told that a large number of villagers had been detained, Calley said Medina ordered him to "waste them." Calley further testified that he obeyed the orders because he had been taught the doctrine of obedience throughout his military career. Medina denied that he gave any such order.

One of the collection points for the villagers was in the southern part of the village. There, Private First Class Paul D. Meadlo guarded a group of between 30 to 40 old men, women, and children. Lieutenant Calley approached Meadlo and told him, "You know what to do," and left. He returned shortly and asked Meadlo why the people were not yet dead. Meadlo replied he did not know that Calley had meant that they should be killed. Calley declared that he wanted them dead. He and Meadlo then opened fire on the group, until all but a few children fell. Calley then personally shot these children. He expended 4 or 5 magazines from his M-16 rifle in the incident.

Lieutenant Calley and Meadlo moved from this point to an irrigation ditch on the east side of My Lai 4. There, they encountered another group of civilians being held by several soldiers. Meadlo estimated that this group contained from 75 to 100 persons. Calley stated, "We got another job to do, Meadlo," and he ordered the group into the ditch. When all were in the ditch, Calley and Meadlo opened fire on them. Although ordered by Calley to shoot, Private First Class James J. Dursi refused to join in the killings, and Specialist Four Robert E. Maples refused to give his machine gun to Calley for use in the killings. Lieutenant Calley admitted that he fired into the ditch, with the muzzle of his weapon within 5 feet of people in it. He expended between 10 to 15 magazines of ammunition on this occasion.

With his radio operator, Private Charles Sledge, Calley moved to the north end of the ditch. There, he found an elderly Vietnamese monk, whom he interrogated. Calley struck the man with his rifle butt and then shot him in the head. Other testimony indicates that immediately afterwards a young child was observed running toward the village. Calley seized him by the arm, threw him into the ditch, and fired at him. Calley admitted interrogating and striking the monk, but denied shooting him. He also denied the incident involving the child. . . .

In the stress of combat, a member of the armed forces cannot reasonably be expected to make a refined legal judgment and be held criminally responsible if he guesses wrong on a question as to which there may be considerable disagreement. But there is no disagreement as to the illegality of the order to kill in this case. For 100 years, it has been a settled rule of American law that even in war the summary killing of an enemy, who has submitted to, and is under, effective physical control, is murder. Appellate defense counsel acknowledge that rule of law and its continued viability, but they say that Lieutenant Calley should not be held accountable for the men, women and children he killed because the court-martial could have found that he was a person of "commonest understanding" and such a person might not know what our law provides; that his captain had ordered him to kill these unarmed and submissive people and he only carried out that order as a good disciplined soldier should.

Whether Lieutenant Calley was the most ignorant person in the United States Army in Vietnam, or the most intelligent, he must be presumed to know that he could not kill the people involved here. The United States Supreme Court has pointed out that "[t]he rule that 'ignorance of the law will not excuse' [a positive act that constitutes a crime] . . . is deep in our law." *Lambert v. California.* An order to kill infants and unarmed civilians who were so demonstrably incapable of resistance to the armed might of a military force as were those killed by Lieutenant Calley is, in my opinion, so palpably illegal that whatever conceptional difference there may be between a person of "commonest understanding" and a person of "common understanding,"

that difference could not have had any "impact on a court of lay members receiving the respective wordings in instructions," as appellate defense counsel
contend. In my judgment, there is no possibility of prejudice to Lieutenant
Calley in the trial judge's reliance upon the established standard of excuse of
criminal conduct, rather than the standard of "commonest understanding"
presented by the defense, or by the new variable test postulated in the dissent, which, with the inclusion of such factors for consideration as grade and
experience, would appear to exact a higher standard of understanding from
Lieutenant Calley than that of the person of ordinary understanding.

Source: www.law.umkc.edu/faculty/projects/ftrials/mylai/mylai.htm

---

4.9 Letter from Military Prosecutor Aubrey Daniel to President Richard Nixon, 1970

*Aubrey Daniel was prosecutor in the court-martial trial of William
Calley. When President Richard Nixon intervened and ordered Calley
transferred from prison to house arrest, Daniel wrote the following letter to
the president in protest. Nixon was one of many political leaders who expressed some degree of support for Calley. Ultimately, Calley was paroled
in 1974.*

"For this nation to condone the acts of Lieutenant Calley is to make us
no better than our enemies"

Sir:
It is very difficult for me to know where to begin this letter as I am not accus-
tomed to writing letters of protest. I can only hope that I can find the words
to convey to you my feelings as a United States citizen and as an attorney, who
believes that respect for law is one of the fundamental bases upon which this
nation is founded.

On November 26, 1969, you issued the following statement through your
press secretary, Mr. Ronald Ziegler, in referring to the My Lai incident:

"An incident such as that alleged in this case is in direct violation not only
of United States military policy, but is also abhorrent to the conscience of all
the American people.

"The Secretary of the Army is continuing his investigation. Appropriate
action is and will be taken to assure that illegal and immoral conduct as alleged be dealt with in accordance with the strict rules of military justice.

"This incident should not be allowed to reflect on the some million and a quarter young Americans who have now returned to the United States after having served in Viet-Nam with great courage and distinction."

At the time you issued this statement, a general court-martial had been directed for a resolution of the charges which have been brought against Lieutenant William L. Calley, Jr., for his involvement at My Lai.

On December 8, 1969, you were personally asked to comment on the My Lai incident at a press conference, At that time, you made the following statement:

"What appears was certainly a massacre, and under no circumstances was it justified. One of the goals we are fighting for in Viet-Nam is to keep the people of South Viet-Nam from having imposed upon them a government which has atrocity against civilians as one of its policies. We cannot ever condone or use atrocities against civilians to accomplish that goal."

These expressions of what I believed to be your sentiment were truly reflective of my own feelings when I was given the assignment of prosecuting the charges which had been preferred against Lieutenant Calley. My feelings were generated not by emotionalism or self-indignation but by my knowledge of the evidence in the case, the laws of this nation in which I strongly believe, and my own conscience. I knew that I had been given a great responsibility and I only hoped that I would be able to discharge my duties and represent the United States in a manner which would be a credit to the legal profession and our system of justice.

I undertook the prosecution of the case without any ulterior motives for personal gain, either financial or political. My only desire was to fulfill my duty as a prosecutor and see that justice was done in accordance with the laws of this nation. I dedicated myself to this end from November of 1969 until the trial was concluded.

Throughout the proceedings there was criticism of the prosecution but I lived with the abiding conviction that once the facts and the law had been presented there would be no doubt in the mind of any reasonable person about the necessity for the prosecution of this case and the ultimate verdict. I was mistaken.

The trial of Lieutenant Calley was conducted in the finest tradition of our legal system. It was in every respect a fair trial in which every legal right of Lieutenant Calley was fully protected. It clearly demonstrated that the military justice system which has previously been the subject of much criticism was a fair system.

Throughout the trial, the entire system was under the constant scrutiny of the mass media and the public, and the trial of Lieutenant Calley was also in a very real sense the trial of the military judicial system, which has previously been the subject of much criticism. However, there was never an attack lodged by any member of the media concerning the fairness of the trial. There could be no such allegation justifiably made.

I do not believe that there has ever been a trial in which the accused's rights were more fully protected, the conduct of the defense given greater latitude, the prosecution held to stricter standards. The burden of proof which the Government had to meet in this case was not beyond a reasonable doubt, but beyond possibility. The very fact that Lieutenant Calley was an American officer being tried for the deaths of Vietnamese during a combat operation by fellow officers compels this conclusion.

The jury selection, in which customary procedure was altered by providing both the defense and the prosecution with three peremptory challenges instead of the usual one, was carefully conducted to insure the impartiality of those men who were selected. Six officers, all combat veterans, five having served in Viet-Nam, were selected. These six men who had served their country well, were called upon again to serve their nation as jurors and to sit in judgment of Lieutenant Calley as prescribed by law.

From the time they took their oaths until they rendered their decision, they performed their duties in the very finest tradition of the American legal system. If ever a jury followed the letter of the law in applying it to the evidence presented, they did. They are indeed a credit to our system of justice and to the officer corps of the United States Army.

When the verdict was rendered, I was totally shocked and dismayed at the reaction of many people across the nation. Much of the adverse public reaction I can attribute to people who have acted emotionally and without being aware of the evidence that was presented and perhaps even the laws of this nation regulating the conduct of war.

These people have undoubtedly viewed Lieutenant Calley's conviction simply as the conviction of an American officer for killing the enemy. Others, no doubt out of a sense of frustration, have seized upon the conviction as a means of protesting the war in Viet-Nam. I would prefer to believe that most of the public criticism has come from people who are not aware of the evidence as it was presented, or having followed it they have chosen not to believe it.

Certainly, no one wanted to believe what occurred at My Lai, including the officers who sat in judgment of Lieutenant Calley. To believe, however, that any large percentage of the population could believe the evidence which was presented and approve of the conduct of Lieutenant Calley would be as shocking to my conscience as the conduct itself, since I believe that we are still a civilized nation.

If such be the case, then the war in Viet-Nam has brutalized us more than I care to believe, and it must cease. How shocking it is if so many people across the nation have failed to see the moral issue which was involved in the trial of Lieutenant Calley—that it is unlawful for an American soldier to summarily execute unarmed and unresisting men, women, children, and babies.

But how much more appalling it is to see so many of the political leaders of the nation who have failed to see the moral issue, or, having seen it, to compromise it for political motive in the face of apparent public displeasure with the verdict.

I would have hoped that all leaders of this nation, which is supposed to be the leader within the international community for the protection of the weak and the oppressed regardless of nationality, would have either accepted and supported the enforcement of the laws of this country as reflected by the verdict of the court or not made any statement concerning the verdict until they had had the same opportunity to evaluate the evidence that the members of the jury had.

In view of your previous statements concerning this matter, I have been particularly shocked and dismayed at your decision to intervene in these proceedings in the midst of the public clamor. Your decision can only have been prompted by the response of a vocal segment of our population who while no doubt acting in good faith, cannot be aware of the evidence which resulted in Lieutenant Calley's conviction. Your intervention has, in my opinion, damaged the military judicial system and lessened any respect it may have gained as a result of the proceedings.

You have subjected a judicial system of this country to the criticism that it is subject to political influence, when it is a fundamental precept of our judicial system that the legal processes of this country must be kept free from any outside influences. What will be the impact of your decision upon the future trials, particularly those within the military?

Not only has respect for the legal process been weakened and the critics of the military judicial system been supported for their claims of command influence, the image of Lieutenant Calley, a man convicted of the premeditated murder of at least 22 unarmed and unresisting people, as a national hero has been enhanced, while at the same time support has been given to those people who have so unjustly criticized the six loyal and honorable officers who have done this country a great service by fulfilling their duties as jurors so admirably.

Have you considered those men in making your decisions? The men who since rendering their verdict have found themselves and their families the subject of vicious attacks upon their honor, integrity and loyalty to this nation.

It would seem to me to be more appropriate for you as the President to have said something in their behalf and to remind the nation of the purpose of our legal system and the respect it should command.

I would expect that the President of the United States, a man whom I believed should and would provide the moral leadership for this nation, would stand fully behind the law of this land on a moral issue which is so clear and about which there can be no compromise.

For this nation to condone the acts of Lieutenant Calley is to make us no better than our enemies and make any pleas by this nation for the humane treatment of our own prisoners meaningless.

I truly regret having to have written this letter and wish that no innocent person had died at My Lai on March 16, 1968. But innocent people were killed under circumstances that will always remain abhorrent to my conscience.

While in some respects what took place at My Lai has to be considered a tragic day in the history of our nation, how much more tragic would it have been for this country to have taken no action against those who were responsible.

That action was taken, but the greatest tragedy of all will be if political expediency dictates the compromise of such a fundamental moral principle as the inherent unlawfulness of the murder of innocent persons, making the action and the courage of six honorable men who served their country so well meaningless.

Source: www.law.umkc.edu/faculty/projects/ftrials/mylai/mylai.htm

---

4.10 Interview with C.E., Vietnam War Veteran, 1999

This interview by the Rutgers University Oral History Archive reflects the experience of one veteran in Vietnam.

"How are you going to get a prisoner to talk?"

SI: Did you ever have to work with the South Vietnamese?

CE: You lived with them. I mean, the South Vietnamese Army, . . . the military?

SI: Let us talk about the military first.

CE: . . . My experiences with them, they're . . . chickenshits, the ARVNs [Army of the Republic of Vietnam]. . . .They were nothing but playboys. They'd be the first ones to run. They just played up to the women and stuff like that. They were always; I don't think I've ever seen one that was dirty, got down, you know, . . . right out dirty in fighting. They were always squared away, . . . and they would find the hookers and stuff for the guys, God knows, but, if you were fired at, you had no faith in them. They were absolutely useless to me. Who were good over there? There were a lot of different people I was attached to over there. The Australian Army was; they were very good. I had them attached to us down at Chu Lai, and then, they had the Korean Marines over there. They were called ROK [Republic of Korea] soldiers. They were the Marines that we used to be. They were allowed to do anything and everything, and did do it, and there's things we did that we weren't supposed to do, but you can't say on tape, because, . . . in a way, you could get a lot of people in trouble. Just like today, they torture people and stuff, like, they say, you know, "You can't do that." Well, how are you going to get a prisoner to talk? You going to give him a candy bar and he's going to say, "Oh, you're so sweet. You gave me a candy bar. I'm going to tell you everything you need," you know? . . . That's not part of war. So, the media and the government and all that; . . . I'm getting off of the ROK soldiers and stuff, but the ARVNs, I really held no faith in. I did not want to be attached to them. I thought they were more of a magnet to the Vietcong than anything else, and probably half of them might have been Vietcong dressed in ARVN clothes, but . . . they just didn't have what they needed to have.

Source: http://oralhistory.rutgers.edu/

4.11 Opinion of the U.S. Supreme Court in *Furman v. Georgia*, 1972

In 1972 the Supreme Court outlawed the death penalty, citing the variation in its application and its disproportionate effect on minority defendants. Justices William Brennan and William O. Douglas set forth at length their views on capital punishment. Four years later, in Gregg v. Georgia (1976), *the Court reinstated the death penalty, noting the public support for its application and the newly established guided discretion that post-*Furman *legislative changes would provide. Specifically, the Court in* Gregg *noted that a two-stage proceeding, in which the trial of the offense and the punishment were separated, would reduce the risk of arbitrary and capricious use of the death penalty.*

"Most of those executed were poor, young, and ignorant"

PER CURIAM. Justice DOUGLAS, concurring.

The words "cruel and unusual" certainly include penalties that are barbaric.

But the words, at least when read in light of the English proscription against selective and irregular use of penalties, suggest that it is "cruel and unusual" to apply the death penalty—or any other penalty—selectively to minorities whose numbers are few, who are outcasts of society, and who are unpopular, but whom society is willing to see suffer though it would not countenance general application of the same penalty across the board. Judge Tuttle, indeed, made abundantly clear in *Novak v. Beto,* that solitary confinement may at times be "cruel and unusual" punishment. . . .

A study of capital cases in Texas from 1924 to 1968 reached the following conclusions:

Application of the death penalty is unequal: most of those executed were poor, young, and ignorant. . . .

Seventy-five of the 460 cases involved co-defendants, who, under Texas law, were given separate trials. In several instances where a white and a Negro were co-defendants, the white was sentenced to life imprisonment or a term of years, and the Negro was given the death penalty.

Another ethnic disparity is found in the type of sentence imposed for rape. The Negro convicted of rape is far more likely to get the death penalty than a term sentence, whereas whites and Latins are far more likely to get a term sentence than the death penalty.

Warden Lewis E. Lawes of Sing Sing said: "Not only does capital punishment fail in its justification, but no punishment could be invented with so many inherent defects. It is an unequal punishment in the way it is applied to the rich and to the poor. The defendant of wealth and position never goes to the electric chair or to the gallows. Juries do not intentionally favour the rich, the law is theoretically impartial, but the defendant with ample means is able to have his case presented with every favourable aspect, while the poor defendant often has a lawyer assigned by the court. Sometimes such assignment is considered part of political patronage; usually the lawyer assigned has had no experience whatever in a capital case."

Former Attorney General Ramsey Clark has said, "It is the poor, the sick, the ignorant, the powerless and the hated who are executed." One searches our chronicles in vain for the execution of any member of the affluent strata of this society. The Leopolds and Loebs are given prison terms, not sentenced to death.

Jackson, a black, convicted of the rape of a white woman, was 21 years old. A court-appointed psychiatrist said that Jackson was of average education and average intelligence, that he was not an imbecile, or schizophrenic, or psychotic, that his traits were the product of environmental influences, and that he was competent to stand trial. Jackson had entered the house after the husband left for work. He held scissors against the neck of the wife, demanding money. She could find none and a struggle ensued for the scissors, a battle which she lost; and she was then raped, Jackson keeping the scissors pressed against her neck. While there did not appear to be any long-term traumatic impact on the victim, she was bruised and abrased in the struggle but was not hospitalized. Jackson was a convict who had escaped from a work gang in the area, a result of a three-year sentence for auto theft. He was at large for three days and during that time had committed several other offenses—burglary, auto theft, and assault and battery.

Furman, a black, killed a householder while seeking to enter the home at night. Furman shot the deceased through a closed door. He was 26 years old and had finished the sixth grade in school. Pending trial, he was committed to the Georgia Central State Hospital for a psychiatric examination on his plea of insanity tendered by court-appointed counsel. The superintendent reported that a unanimous staff diagnostic conference had concluded "that this patient should retain his present diagnosis of Mental Deficiency, Mild to Moderate, with Psychotic Episodes associated with Convulsive Disorder." The physicians agreed that "at present the patient is not psychotic, but he is not capable of cooperating with his counsel in the preparation of his defense"; and the staff believed "that he is in need of further psychiatric hospitalization and treatment."

Later, the superintendent reported that the staff diagnosis was Mental Deficiency, Mild to Moderate, with Psychotic Episodes associated with Convulsive Disorder. He concluded, however, that Furman was "not psychotic at present, knows right from wrong and is able to cooperate with his counsel in preparing his defense."

Branch, a black, entered the rural home of a 65-year-old widow, a white, while she slept and raped her, holding his arm against her throat. Thereupon he demanded money and for 30 minutes or more the widow searched for money, finding little. As he left, Jackson said if the widow told anyone what happened, he would return and kill her. The record is barren of any medical or psychiatric evidence showing injury to her as a result of Branch's attack.

He had previously been convicted of felony theft and found to be a borderline mental deficient and well below the average IQ of Texas prison inmates. He had the equivalent of five and a half years of grade school education. He had a "dull intelligence" and was in the lowest fourth percentile of his class.

We cannot say from facts disclosed in these records that these defendants were sentenced to death because they were black. Yet our task is not restricted to an effort to divine what motives impelled these death penalties. Rather, we deal with a system of law and of justice that leaves to the uncontrolled discretion of judges or juries the determination whether defendants committing these crimes should die or be imprisoned. Under these laws no standards govern the selection of the penalty. People live or die, dependent on the whim of one man or of 12.

Irving Brant has given a detailed account of the Bloody Assizes, the reign of terror that occupied the closing years of the rule of Charles II and the opening years of the regime of James II (the Lord Chief Justice was George Jeffreys):

> Nobody knows how many hundreds of men, innocent or of unproved guilt, Jeffreys sent to their deaths in the pseudo trials that followed Monmouth's feeble and stupid attempt to seize the throne. When the ordeal ended, scores had been executed and 1,260 were awaiting the hangman in three counties. To be absent from home during the uprising was evidence of guilt. Mere death was considered much too mild for the villagers and farmers rounded up in these raids. The directions to a high sheriff were to provide an ax, a cleaver, a furnace or cauldron to boil their heads and quarters, and soil to boil therewith, half a bushel to each traitor, and tar to tar them with, and a sufficient number of spears and poles to fix their heads and quarters' along the highways. One could have crossed a good part of northern England by their guidance.
>
> The story of The Bloody Assizes, widely known to Americans, helped to place constitutional limitations on the crime of treason and to produce a bar against cruel and unusual punishments. But in the polemics that led to the various guarantees of freedom, it had no place compared with the tremendous thrust of the trial and execution of Sidney. The hundreds of judicial murders committed by Jeffreys and his fellow judges were totally inconceivable in a free American republic, but any American could imagine himself in Sidney's place—executed for putting on paper, in his closet, words that later on came to express the basic principles of republican government. Unless barred by fundamental law, the legal rulings that permitted this result could easily be employed against any person whose political opinions challenged the party in power." *The Bill of Rights* 154–155 (1965).

Those who wrote the Eighth Amendment knew what price their forebears had paid for a system based, not on equal justice, but on discrimination. In those days the target was not the blacks or the poor, but the dissenters, those who opposed absolutism in government, who struggled for a parliamentary regime, and who opposed governments' recurring efforts to foist a particular religion on the people. But the tool of capital punishment was used with vengeance against the opposition and those unpopular with the regime. One cannot read this history without realizing that the desire for equality was reflected in the ban against "cruel and unusual punishments" contained in the Eighth Amendment.

In a Nation committed to equal protection of the laws there is no permissible "caste" aspect of law enforcement. Yet we know that the discretion of judges and juries in imposing the death penalty enables the penalty to be selectively applied, feeding prejudices against the accused if he is poor and despised, and lacking political clout, or if he is a member of a suspect or unpopular minority, and saving those who by social position may be in a more protected position. In ancient Hindu law a Brahman was exempt from capital punishment, and under that law, "generally, in the law books, punishment increased in severity as social status diminished." We have, I fear, taken in practice the same position, partially as a result of making the death penalty discretionary and partially as a result of the ability of the rich to purchase the services of the most respected and most resourceful legal talent in the Nation.

The high service rendered by the "cruel and unusual" punishment clause of the Eighth Amendment is to require legislatures to write penal laws that are evenhanded, nonselective, and nonarbitrary, and to require judges to see to it that general laws are not applied sparsely, selectively, and spottily to unpopular groups.

A law that stated that anyone making more than $50,000 would be exempt from the death penalty would plainly fall, as would a law that in terms said that blacks, those who never went beyond the fifth grade in school, those who made less than $3,000 a year, or those who were unpopular or unstable should be the only people executed. A law which in the overall view reaches that result in practice has no more sanctity than a law which in terms provides the same.

Thus, these discretionary statutes are unconstitutional in their operation. They are pregnant with discrimination and discrimination is an ingredient not compatible with the idea of equal protection of the laws that is implicit in the ban on "cruel and unusual" punishments.

Any law which is nondiscriminatory on its face may be applied in such a way as to violate the Equal Protection Clause of the Fourteenth Amendment. *Yick Wo v. Hopkins,* 118 U.S. 356. Such conceivably might be the fate of a mandatory death penalty, where equal or lesser sentences were imposed on the elite, a harsher one on the minorities or members of the lower castes. Whether a mandatory death penalty would otherwise be constitutional is a question I do not reach.

I concur in the judgments of the Court. . . .

Justice BRENNAN, concurring.

At bottom, then, the Cruel and Unusual Punishments Clause prohibits the infliction of uncivilized and inhuman punishments. The State, even as it punishes, must treat its members with respect for their intrinsic worth as human beings. A punishment is "cruel and unusual," therefore, if it does not comport with human dignity.

This formulation, of course, does not of itself yield principles for assessing the constitutional validity of particular punishments. Nevertheless, even though "this Court has had little occasion to give precise content to the [Clause]," *ibid.*, there are principles recognized in our cases and inherent in the Clause sufficient to permit a judicial determination whether a challenged punishment comports with human dignity.

The primary principle is that a punishment must not be so severe as to be degrading to the dignity of human beings. Pain, certainly, may be a factor in the judgment. The infliction of an extremely severe punishment will often entail physical suffering. See *Weems v. United States,* 217 U.S., at 366. Yet the Framers also knew "that there could be exercises of cruelty by laws other than those which inflicted bodily pain or mutilation." *Id., at 372.* Even though "there may be involved no physical mistreatment, no primitive torture," *Trop v. Dulles,* severe mental pain may be inherent in the infliction of a particular punishment. That, indeed, was one of the conclusions underlying the holding of the plurality in *Trop v. Dulles* that the punishment of expatriation violates the Clause. And the physical and mental suffering inherent in the punishment of *cadena temporal,* was an obvious basis for the Court's decision in *Weems v. United States* that the punishment was "cruel and unusual." . . .

The question, then, is whether the deliberate infliction of death is today consistent with the command of the Clause that the State may not inflict punishments that do not comport with human dignity. I will analyze the punishment of death in terms of the principles set out above and the cumulative test to which they lead: It is a denial of human dignity for the State arbitrarily to subject a person to an unusually severe punishment that society has indicated it does not regard as acceptable, and that cannot be shown to serve any penal purpose more effectively than a significantly less drastic punishment. Under these principles and this test, death is today a "cruel and unusual" punishment.

Death is a unique punishment in the United States. In a society that so strongly affirms the sanctity of life, not surprisingly the common view is that death is the ultimate sanction. This natural human feeling appears all about us. There has been no national debate about punishment, in general or by imprisonment, comparable to the debate about the punishment of death. No other punishment has been so continuously restricted, nor has any State yet abolished prisons, as some have abolished this punishment. And those States that still inflict death reserve it for the most heinous crimes. Juries, of course, have always treated death cases differently, as have governors exercising their commutation powers. Criminal defendants are of the same view. "As all practicing lawyers know, who have defended persons charged with capital offenses, often the only goal possible is to avoid the death penalty." Some legislatures have required particular procedures, such as two-stage trials and automatic appeals, applicable only in death cases. "It is the universal experience in the administration of criminal justice that those charged with capital offenses are granted special considerations." This Court, too, almost always treats death cases as a class apart. And the unfortunate effect of this punishment upon the functioning of the judicial process is well known; no other punishment has a similar effect.

The only explanation for the uniqueness of death is its extreme severity. Death is today an unusually severe punishment, unusual in its pain, in its finality, and in its enormity. No other existing punishment is comparable to death in terms of physical and mental suffering. Although our information is not conclusive, it appears that there is no method available that guarantees an immediate and painless death. Since the discontinuance of flogging as a constitutionally permissible punishment, *Jackson v. Bishop*, death remains as the only punishment that may involve the conscious infliction of physical pain. In addition, we know that mental pain is an inseparable part of our practice of punishing criminals by death, for the prospect of pending execution exacts a frightful toll during the inevitable long wait between the imposition of sentence and the actual infliction of death. As the California Supreme Court pointed out, "the process of carrying out a verdict of death is often so degrading and brutalizing to the human spirit as to constitute psychological torture." Indeed, as Mr. Justice Frankfurter noted, "the onset of insanity while awaiting execution of a death sentence is not a rare phenomenon." The "fate of ever-increasing fear and distress" to which the expatriate is subjected, *Trop v. Dulles*, can only exist to a greater degree for a person confined in prison awaiting death. . . .

The unusual severity of death is manifested most clearly in its finality and enormity. Death, in these respects, is in a class by itself. Expatriation, for example, is a punishment that "destroys for the individual the political existence that was centuries in the development," that "strips the citizen of his status in the national and international political community," and that puts "his very existence" in jeopardy. Expatriation thus inherently entails "the total destruction of the individual's status in organized society. In short, the expatriate has lost the right to have rights." Yet, demonstrably, expatriation is not "a fate worse than death." Although death, like expatriation, destroys the individual's "political existence" and his "status in organized society," it does more, for, unlike expatriation, death also destroys "his very existence." There is, too, at least the possibility that the expatriate will in the future regain "the right to have rights." Death forecloses even that possibility.

Death is truly an awesome punishment. The calculated killing of a human being by the State involves, by its very nature, a denial of the executed person's humanity. The contrast with the plight of a person punished by imprisonment is evident. An individual in prison does not lose "the right to have rights." A prisoner retains, for example, the constitutional rights to the free exercise of religion, to be free of cruel and unusual punishments, and to treatment as a "person" for purposes of due process of law and the equal protection of the laws. A prisoner remains a member of the human family. Moreover, he retains the right of access to the courts. His punishment is not irrevocable. Apart from the common charge, grounded upon the recognition of human fallibility, that the punishment of death must inevitably be inflicted upon innocent men, we know that death has been the lot of men whose convictions were unconstitutionally secured in view of later, retroactively applied, holdings of this Court. The punishment itself may have been unconstitutionally inflicted, . . . yet the finality of death precludes relief. An executed person has indeed "lost the right to have rights." As one 19th century proponent of punishing criminals by death declared, "When a man is hung, there is an end of our relations with him. His execution is a way of saying, 'You are not fit for this world, take your chance elsewhere.'"

In comparison to all other punishments today, then, the deliberate extinguishment of human life by the State is uniquely degrading to human dignity. I would not hesitate to hold, on that ground alone, that death is today a "cruel and unusual" punishment, were it not that death is a punishment of longstanding usage and acceptance in this country. I therefore turn to the second principle—that the State may not arbitrarily inflict an unusually severe punishment.

The outstanding characteristic of our present practice of punishing criminals by death is the infrequency with which we resort to it. The evidence is conclusive that death is not the ordinary punishment for any crime.

There has been a steady decline in the infliction of this punishment in every decade since the 1930's, the earliest period for which accurate statistics are available. . . .

When a country of over 200 million people inflicts an unusually severe punishment no more than 50 times a year, the inference is strong that the punishment is not being regularly and fairly applied. To dispel it would indeed require a clear showing of nonarbitrary infliction.

Although there are no exact figures available, we know that thousands of murders and rapes are committed annually in States where death is an authorized punishment for those crimes. However the rate of infliction is characterized—as "freakishly" or "spectacularly" rare, or simply as rare—it would take the purest sophistry to deny that death is inflicted in only a minute fraction of these cases. How much rarer, after all, could the infliction of death be?

When the punishment of death is inflicted in a trivial number of the cases in which it is legally available, the conclusion is virtually inescapable that it is being inflicted arbitrarily. Indeed, it smacks of little more than a lottery system. The States claim, however, that this rarity is evidence not of arbitrariness, but of informed selectivity: Death is inflicted, they say, only in "extreme" cases.

Informed selectivity, of course, is a value not to be denigrated. Yet presumably the States could make precisely the same claim if there were 10 executions per year, or five, or even if there were but one. That there may be as many as 50 per year does not strengthen the claim. When the rate of infliction is at this low level, it is highly implausible that only the worst criminals or the criminals who commit the worst crimes are selected for this punishment. No one has yet suggested a rational basis that could differentiate in those terms the few who die from the many who go to prison. Crimes and criminals simply do not admit of a distinction that can be drawn so finely as to explain, on that ground, the execution of such a tiny sample of those eligible. Certainly the laws that provide for this punishment do not attempt to draw that distinction; all cases to which the laws apply are necessarily "extreme." Nor is the distinction credible in fact. If, for example, petitioner Furman or his crime illustrates the "extreme," then nearly all murderers and their murders are also "extreme." Furthermore, our procedures in death cases, rather than resulting in the selection of "extreme" cases for this punishment, actually sanction an arbitrary selection. For this Court has held that juries may, as they do, make the decision whether to impose a death sentence wholly unguided by standards governing that decision. In other words, our procedures are not constructed to guard against the totally capricious selection of criminals for the punishment of death.

Source: *Furman v. Georgia*, 408 U.S. 238 (1972)

4.12 Trial Court Opinion in *Rhem v. Malcolm*, 1974

This U.S. District court case from the 1970s represents a changing judicial attitude toward prison condition suits. The court examines in detail a range of prisoner complaints, on matters from visiting policy to overcrowd-

ing. The court's ruling in favor of the plaintiffs withstood two appeals to the Second Circuit.

"Imprisonment . . . is only for safe custody, not for punishment"

Plaintiffs are unconvicted detainees housed in the Manhattan House of Detention for Men (MHD), popularly but forbiddingly known as the "Tombs." They bring this civil rights action claiming that numerous practices and physical conditions at MHD deprive them of rights under the First, Fifth, Sixth, Eighth and Fourteenth Amendments. Their suit under 42 U.S.C. § 1983 and 28 U.S.C. § 2201 on behalf of all persons confined at MHD originally complained of overcrowding, unsanitary conditions, lack of light and air, excessive noise, mistreatment by guards, arbitrary disciplinary procedures, inadequate medical care, lack of recreation, and restrictions on visiting and mail. . . .

MHD is a twelve floor structure forming part of a complex that includes the Criminal Courts of the City of New York and the offices of the District Attorney of New York County. The complex is located on Centre Street in the heart of Manhattan's Civic Center, heavily populated in the daytime and deserted at night. It consumes all of the city block on which it is built, leaving no open space or outdoor area.

The official capacity of MHD (effective August, 1971) is 902. As of October 6, 1972, its population was 1301. (Stipulation of Facts nos. 8 and 9.) Pursuant to the consent decree, the Department is now housing only one detainee to a cell (of which there are 808). There are approximately 100 convicted misdemeants housed on a dormitory floor, for a total authorized population of something over 900.

Although all the plaintiff class and 80% of persons housed at MHD are unconvicted detainees (the remainder being sentenced misdemeanants who have jobs at MHD), the building is a maximum security institution in every sense. One may surmise that its fortress-like character is the result partly of the penological philosophy in vogue at the time of its construction and partly of concern that its location was believed to provide an easy opportunity for an escapee to melt into the city population during the daytime, or evaporate into the dark of city streets at night. In fact, only one escape has occurred since the institution opened for business some forty years ago. There is no evidence whether this is the result of its maximum security features, or whether it proves that they are not necessary. . . .

Some critical issues presented flow from the maximum security nature of the institution. These include allegations of excessive "lock-in" (in cells), undue restrictions on the length, conditions and number of visits, grossly inadequate opportunity for exercise and recreation and limitations on correspondence and access to reading matter. Others, such as intolerable noise, inadequate ventilation, severe heat in summer and cold in winter and an absence of transparent windows are largely functions of the building's architectural structure (although to some extent they are the result of its maximum security features). Still others are unrelated either to considerations of security or the nature of the building, such as mistreatment by officers—said to be caused by overworking the guards: a fiscal question—and a disciplinary procedure which is claimed to violate due process and which is the child of administrative policy only. . . .

The great majority of prisons in America are municipal or state institutions. Yet in recent years, the assertion of constitutional rights by prisoners has been litigated largely in the federal courts. In earlier times the federal courts withheld action or acted with great caution in such cases, observing the principle of comity and recognizing that the administration of prisons requires an expertise to which courts do not pretend. However, the reluctance to assert authority has rapidly eroded in recent years as one federal court after another has concluded that conditions in America's prisons and jails have sunk below federal constitutionally acceptable levels. As the United States Supreme Court has put it, "Federal courts sit not to supervise prisons but to enforce the constitutional rights of all 'persons,' including prisoners."

The major contentions of the plaintiffs are clean cut. They argue that the City of New York has subjected them to degrading or punitive conditions inconsistent with their status as pre-trial detainees who are presumed innocent, and has thus violated their rights to due process of law, the equal protection of the laws and to be free from cruel and unusual punishment.

In judging the validity of these contentions, we take as our starting point that plaintiffs are unconvicted detainees who, but for their inability to furnish bail, would remain at liberty, enjoying all the rights of free citizens until and unless convicted. We are guided, therefore, not only by the modern judicial view, originating in the seminal declaration of *Coffin v. Reichard,* that all prisoners, convicted or detained, "[retain] all rights of an ordinary citizen except those expressly or by necessary implication taken from [them] by law," but also by the precept that, because of "the presumption of innocence, secured only after centuries of struggle," a *detainee* retains all rights of the ordinary citizen except those necessary to assure his appearance for trial.

The words of Blackstone still express the law: "Upon the whole, if the offense be not bailable, or the party cannot find bail, he is to be committed to the county gaol . . . there to abide till delivered by due course of law. . . . But this imprisonment, as has been said, is only for safe custody, not for punishment: Therefore, in this dubious interval between the commitment and the trial, a prisoner ought to be used with the utmost humanity, and neither be loaded with needless fetters or subjected to other hardships than such as are absolutely requisite for the purpose of confinement only."

It follows from these ancient commands that detainees may not be subjected to punishment (much less cruel and unusual punishment) qua detainees, and that: ". . . it is manifestly obvious that the conditions of incarceration for detainees must, cumulatively, add up to the least restrictive means of achieving the purpose requiring and justifying the deprivation of liberty." . . .

Three years have passed since the "Tombs disturbances." The dismal conditions which still exist in the institution manifestly violate the Constitution and would shock the conscience of any citizen who knew of them. The thousands of inmates who pass through its portals each year, more than 69,000 in 1972 and 49,000 in the first eleven months of 1973, are in some instances subjected to cruel punishment, although the Constitution forbids any punishment of detainees, and are deprived of due process and equal protection of the laws. This state of affairs exists in spite of the humane efforts of the present Departmental administration to afford the "tolerable living conditions" to which prisoners are entitled by law. It exists because the public through its government has not assumed its responsibilities to provide a decent environment within jail walls. Courts are the agency which must enforce the execution of public responsibilities when other branches of government fail to do so: "courts sit not to supervise prisons but to enforce the constitutional rights of all 'persons,' including prisoners."

Source: *Rhem v. Malcolm*, 371 F. Supp. 594 (S.D.N.Y. 1974)

4.13 Federal Appellate Court Opinion in *Filartiga v. Peña-Irala,* 1980

This federal appellate court opinion stands as an important precedent in U.S. law and human rights law because it allows torture victims to sue for acts committed outside the United States based on U.S. law (the Alien Tort Statute) and international law. The plaintiff, Filartiga, successfully sued a Paraguayan official in federal court after that official tortured her brother to death in Paraguay.

"A small but important step in the fulfillment of the ageless dream to free all people from brutal violence"

In the twentieth century the international community has come to recognize the common danger posed by the flagrant disregard of basic human rights and particularly the right to be free of torture. Spurred first by the Great War, and then the Second, civilized nations have banded together to prescribe acceptable norms of international behavior. From the ashes of the Second World War arose the United Nations Organization, amid hopes that an era of peace and cooperation had at last begun. Though many of these aspirations have remained elusive goals, that circumstance cannot diminish the true progress that has been made. In the modern age, humanitarian and practical considerations have combined to lead the nations of the world to recognize that respect for fundamental human rights is in their individual and collective interest. Among the rights universally proclaimed by all nations, as we have noted, is the right to be free of physical torture. Indeed, for purposes of civil liability, the torturer has become like the pirate and slave trader before him hostis humani generis, an enemy of all mankind. Our holding today, giving effect to a jurisdictional provision enacted by our First Congress, is a small but important step in the fulfillment of the ageless dream to free all people from brutal violence.

Source: *Filartiga v. Peña-Irala*, 630 F.2d 876 (2nd Cir. 1980)

4.14 CIA Human Resources Exploitation Training Manual, Excerpt no. 1, A-1 to A-3, 1983

This manual includes some of the language of the KUBARK manual (see documents 4.3, 4.4, and 4.5), but it is also more specific as to certain inter-rogation techniques. According to Blanton and Kornbluh, after Congress began investigating human rights violations by U.S.-trained Honduran intelligence officers, one passage was hand edited to read "while we deplore the use of coercive techniques, we do want to make you aware of them so that you may avoid them."

"While we do not stress the use of coercive techniques, we do want to make you aware of them and the proper way to use them"

PROHIBITION AGAINST USE OF FORCE

The use of force, mental torture, threats, insults, or exposure to unpleasant and inhumane treatment of any kind as an aid to interrogation is prohibited by law, both international and domestic; it is neither approved nor condoned. The interrogator must never take advantage of the source's weaknesses to the extent that the interrogation involves threats, insults, torture or exposure to unpleasant or inhumane treatment of any kind. Experience indicates that the use of force is not necessary to gain cooperation of sources. Use of force is a poor technique, yields unreliable results, may damage subsequent collection efforts, and can induce the source to say what he thinks the interrogator wants to hear. Additionally, the use of force will probably result in adverse publicity and/or legal action against the interrogator (et al.) when the source is released. However, the use of force is not to be confused with psychological ploys, verbal trickery, or other nonviolent and non-coercive ruses employed by the interrogator in the successful interrogation of reticent or uncooperative sources.

INTRODUCTION

OPENING REMARKS

There is nothing mysterious about "questioning." It is no more than obtaining needed information from subjects. These may be prisoners of war, defectors, refugees, illegal immigrants, agents or suspected intelligence agents attempting to operate in your country.

The art of "questioning" has become controversial in many parts of the world. This is because in many countries, the term "questioning" has been identified with the use of torture to obtain information.

Every manual I have read on "questioning" states that information obtained from a subject under torture is not reliable. That the subject will say whatever he thinks you want to hear just to avoid further punishment.

During the Battle of Algiers, the French Army used torture to neutralize a terrorist group within a matter of months. Unfortunately, along with the hundreds of terrorists that were arrested and tortured, were hundreds of innocent civilians. Society will simply not condone this.

The routine use of torture lowers the moral caliber of the organization that uses it and corrupts those that rely on it as the quick and easy way out. We strongly disagree with this approach and instead emphasize the use of psychological techniques designed to persuade the subject to want to furnish us with the information we desire.

Successful "questioning" is based upon a knowledge of the subject matter and upon the use of psychological techniques which are not difficult to understand. We will be discussing two types of techniques, coercive and non-coercive. While we do not stress the use of coercive techniques, we do want to make you aware of them and the proper way to use them.

Psychologists have conducted considerable research in many areas that are closely related to coercive "questioning." During this course we will discuss the following topics as they relate to "questioning":

1. Reactions to pain and fear
2. The effects of debility and isolation
3. Hypnosis and narcosis

Keep in mind "turn around" here [*sic*]

What we are emphasizing throughout this course is that "questioning" is a complicated process involving the interaction of two personalities—that of the questioner and that of the subject. It must be well planned—from the time the subject is arrested through the questioning process to the final disposition of the subject.

Source: www.gwu.edu/~nsarchiv/NSAEBB/NSAEBB122/, A-1 to A-3

4.15 CIA Human Resources Exploitation Training Manual, Excerpt no. 2, K-1 to K-14, 1983

This section of the manual provides detail on the psychology and techniques of coercive interrogation. Hand-edits were made to several sections of the text after 1988; these may be viewed on the website.

"Pain which he feels he is inflicting on himself is more likely to sap his resistance"

THEORY OF COERCION

There are three major principles involved in the successful application of coercive techniques:

Debility (physical weakness)

For centuries "questioners" have employed various methods of inducing physical weaknesses: prolonged constraint; prolonged exertion; extremes of heat, cold or moisture; and deprivation of food or sleep. The assumption is that lowering the subject's physiological resistance will lower his psychological capacity for resistance; however, there has been no scientific investigation of this assumption. Many psychologists consider the threat of inducing debility to be more effective than debility itself. Prolonged constraint or exertion, sustained deprivation of food or sleep, etc. often become patterns to which a subject adjusts by becoming apathetic and withdrawing into himself, in search of escape for the discomfort and tension. In this case debility would be counter-productive.

The questioner should be careful to manipulate the subject's environment to disrupt patterns, not to create them. Meals and sleep should be granted irregularly, in more than abundance and less than adequacy, on no discernible time pattern. This (illegible) disorient the subject and (illegible) destroy (illegible) his capacity to resist.

Dependency

He is helplessly dependent upon the "questioner" for the satisfaction of all basic needs.

Dread (intense fear and anxiety)

Sustained long enough, a strong fear of anything vague or unknown induces regression. On the other hand, materialization of the fear is likely to come as a relief. The subject finds that he can hold out and his resistance is strengthened. A word of caution: if the debility-dependency-dread is unduly prolonged, the subject may sink into a defensive apathy from which it is hard to arouse him. It is advisable to have a psychologist available whenever regression is induced.

OBJECTIONS TO COERCION

There is a profound moral objection to applying duress beyond the point of irreversible psychological damage such as occurs during brainwashing. Brainwashing involves the conditioning of a subject's "stimulus-response bond" through the use of these same techniques, but the objective of brainwashing is directed primarily towards the subject's acceptance and adoption of beliefs, behavior, or doctrine alien to his native cultural environment for propaganda purposes rather than intelligence coercion purposes. Aside from this extreme, we will not judge the validity of other ethical arguments. . . .

COERCIVE TECHNIQUES

Deprivation of sensory stimuli

Solitary confinement acts on most persons as a powerful stress. A person cut off from external stimuli turns his awareness inward and projects his unconscious outward. The symptoms most commonly produced by solitary confinement are superstition, intense love of any other living thing, perceiving inanimate objects as alive, hallucinations, and delusions.

Although conditions identical to those of solitary confinement for the purpose of "questioning" have not been duplicated for scientific experimentation, a number of experiments have been conducted with subjects who volunteered to be placed in "sensory deprivation tanks." They were suspended in water and wore black-out masks, which enclosed the entire head and only allowed breathing. They heard only their own breathing and some faint sounds of water from the piping. . . .

Threats and fear

The threat of coercion usually weakens or destroys resistance more effectively than coercion itself. For example, the threat to inflict pain can trigger fears more damaging than the immediate sensation of pain. In general, direct physical brutality creates only resentment, hostility and further defiance.

The effectiveness of a threat depends on the personality of the subject, whether he believes the "questioner" can and will carry out the threat, and on what he believes to be the reason for the threat. A threat should be delivered coldly, not shouted in anger, or made in response to the subject's own expressions of hostility. Expressions of anger by the "questioner" are often interpreted by the subject as a fear of failure, which strengthens his resolve to resist.

A threat should grant the subject time for compliance and is most effective when joined with a suggested rationale for compliance. It is not enough that a subject be placed under the tension of fear: he must also discern an acceptable escape route.

The threat of death has been found to be worse than useless. The principal reason is that it often induces sheer hopelessness; the subject feels that he is as likely to be condemned after compliance as before. Some subjects recognize that the threat is a bluff and that silencing them forever would defeat the "questioner's" purpose.

If a subject refuses to comply once a threat has been made, it must be carried out. If it is not carried out, then subsequent threats will also prove ineffective.

Pain

Everyone is aware that people react very differently to pain but the reason is not because of a difference in the intensity of the sensation itself. All people have approximately the same threshold at which they begin to feel pain and their estimates of severity are roughly the same. The wide range of individual reactions is based primarily on early conditioning to pain.

The torture situation is an external conflict, a contest between the subject and his tormentor. The pain which is being inflicted upon him from outside himself may actually intensify his will to resist. On the other hand, pain which he feels he is inflicting on himself is more likely to sap his resistance. For example, if he is required to maintain rigid positions such as standing at attention or sitting on a stool for long periods of time, the immediate source of pain is not the "questioner" but the subject himself. His conflict is then an internal struggle. As long as he maintains this position, he is attributing to the "questioner" the ability to do something worse. But there is never a showdown where the "questioner" demonstrates this ability. After a time, the subject is likely to exhaust his internal motivational strength.

Source: www.gwu.edu/~nsarchiv/NSAEBB/NSAEBB122/, K-1 to K-14

4.16 UN International Covenant on Civil and Political Rights, 1966

Though it predates the Convention against Torture (document 4.17), the International Covenant on Civil and Political Rights (ICCPR) similarly prohibits torture as well as cruel, inhuman and degrading treatment, and it sets forth a declaration of individual rights more generally.

"Every human being has the inherent right to life"

Article 6

1. Every human being has the inherent right to life. This right shall be protected by law. No one shall be arbitrarily deprived of his life.

2. In countries which have not abolished the death penalty, sentence of death may be imposed only for the most serious crimes in accordance with the law in force at the time of the commission of the crime and not contrary to the provisions of the present Covenant and to the Convention on the Prevention and Punishment of the Crime of Genocide. This penalty can only be carried out pursuant to a final judgement rendered by a competent court.

3. When deprivation of life constitutes the crime of genocide, it is understood that nothing in this article shall authorize any State Party to the present Covenant to derogate in any way from any obligation assumed under the provisions of the Convention on the Prevention and Punishment of the Crime of Genocide.

4. Anyone sentenced to death shall have the right to seek pardon or commutation of the sentence. Amnesty, pardon or commutation of the sentence of death may be granted in all cases.

5. Sentence of death shall not be imposed for crimes committed by persons below eighteen years of age and shall not be carried out on pregnant women.

6. Nothing in this article shall be invoked to delay or to prevent the abolition of capital punishment by any State Party to the present Covenant.

Article 7

No one shall be subjected to torture or to cruel, inhuman or degrading treatment or punishment. In particular, no one shall be subjected without his free consent to medical or scientific experimentation.

Source: www.un.org

4.17 UN Convention against Torture, 1984

The 1984 Convention against Torture is an important international prohibition on torture. Nonetheless, the convention's language raises some questions. First, it prohibits both torture and cruel/inhuman/degrading treatment (CIDT). While torture is defined by the convention, CIDT is not, which makes enforcement (and even conceptual understanding) difficult. Moreover, the terms of the convention create an exception for "punishment incident to lawful sanctions." Thus, if a signatory to the convention enacts laws permitting a certain form of punishment, it will be difficult to apply the convention in such an instance.

"Any act by which severe pain or suffering, whether physical or mental, is intentionally inflicted on a person"

The States Parties to this Convention,

Considering that, in accordance with the principles proclaimed in the Charter of the United Nations, recognition of the equal and inalienable rights of all members of the human family is the foundation of freedom, justice and peace in the world,

Recognizing that those rights derive from the inherent dignity of the human person,

Considering the obligation of States under the Charter, in particular Article 55, to promote universal respect for, and observance of, human rights and fundamental freedoms,

Having regard to article 5 of the Universal Declaration of Human Rights and article 7 of the International Covenant on Civil and Political Rights, both of which provide that no one shall be subjected to torture or to cruel, inhuman or degrading treatment or punishment,

Having regard also to the Declaration on the Protection of All Persons from Being Subjected to Torture and Other Cruel, Inhuman or Degrading Treatment or Punishment, adopted by the General Assembly on 9 December 1975,

Desiring to make more effective the struggle against torture and other cruel, inhuman or degrading treatment or punishment throughout the world,

Have agreed as follows:

PART I

Article 1

1. For the purposes of this Convention, the term "torture" means any act by which severe pain or suffering, whether physical or mental, is intention-

ally inflicted on a person for such purposes as obtaining from him or a third person information or a confession, punishing him for an act he or a third person has committed or is suspected of having committed, or intimidating or coercing him or a third person, or for any reason based on discrimination of any kind, when such pain or suffering is inflicted by or at the instigation of or with the consent or acquiescence of a public official or other person acting in an official capacity. It does not include pain or suffering arising only from, inherent in or incidental to lawful sanctions.

2. This article is without prejudice to any international instrument or national legislation which does or may contain provisions of wider application.

Article 2

1. Each State Party shall take effective legislative, administrative, judicial or other measures to prevent acts of torture in any territory under its jurisdiction.

2. No exceptional circumstances whatsoever, whether a state of war or a threat of war, internal political instability or any other public emergency, may be invoked as a justification of torture.

3. An order from a superior officer or a public authority may not be invoked as a justification of torture.

Article 3

1. No State Party shall expel, return ("refouler") or extradite a person to another State where there are substantial grounds for believing that he would be in danger of being subjected to torture.

2. For the purpose of determining whether there are such grounds, the competent authorities shall take into account all relevant considerations including, where applicable, the existence in the State concerned of a consistent pattern of gross, flagrant or mass violations of human rights.

Article 4

1. Each State Party shall ensure that all acts of torture are offences under its criminal law. The same shall apply to an attempt to commit torture and to an act by any person which constitutes complicity or participation in torture.

2. Each State Party shall make these offences punishable by appropriate penalties which take into account their grave nature.

Article 5

1. Each State Party shall take such measures as may be necessary to establish its jurisdiction over the offences referred to in article 4 in the following cases:

(a) When the offences are committed in any territory under its jurisdiction or on board a ship or aircraft registered in that State;

(b) When the alleged offender is a national of that State;

(c) When the victim is a national of that State if that State considers it appropriate.

2. Each State Party shall likewise take such measures as may be necessary to establish its jurisdiction over such offences in cases where the alleged offender is present in any territory under its jurisdiction and it does not extradite him pursuant to article 8 to any of the States mentioned in paragraph I of this article.

3. This Convention does not exclude any criminal jurisdiction exercised in accordance with internal law. . . .

Article 16

1. Each State Party shall undertake to prevent in any territory under its jurisdiction other acts of cruel, inhuman or degrading treatment or punishment which do not amount to torture as defined in article 1, when such acts are committed by or at the instigation of or with the consent or acquiescence of a public official or other person acting in an official capacity. In particular, the obligations contained in articles 10, 11, 12 and 13 shall apply with the substitution for references to torture of references to other forms of cruel, inhuman or degrading treatment or punishment.

2. The provisions of this Convention are without prejudice to the provisions of any other international instrument or national law which prohibits cruel, inhuman or degrading treatment or punishment or which relates to extradition or expulsion.

Source: www.un.org

4.18 U.S. Senate Reservations to the UN Convention against Torture, 1990

In ratifying the Convention against Torture, the U.S. Senate stated that it interpreted the convention to contain a "specific intent" requirement: an act must be specifically intended to inflict severe physical or mental pain or suffering to constitute torture. This interpretation would later be taken up by the Bush administration in the "Bybee memo"(document 5.2).

"In order to constitute torture, an act must be specifically intended to inflict severe physical or mental pain or suffering"

[T]he United States understands that, in order to constitute torture, an act must be specifically intended to inflict severe physical or mental pain or suffering and that mental pain or suffering refers to prolonged mental harm caused by or resulting from: (1) the intentional infliction or threatened infliction of severe physical pain or suffering; (2) the administration or application, or threatened administration or application, of mind altering substances or other procedures calculated to disrupt profoundly the senses or the personality; (3) the threat of imminent death; or (4) the threat that another person will imminently be subjected to death, severe physical pain or suffering, or the administration or application of mind altering substances or other procedures calculated to disrupt profoundly the senses or personality. . . .

. . . bound only by the obligation under Article 16 to prevent "cruel, inhuman or degrading treatment or punishment" only insofar as the term "cruel, inhuman or degrading treatment or punishment" means the cruel, inhuman or degrading treatment or punishment prohibited by the Fifth and/or Eighth and/or Fourteenth Amendments to the Constitution of the United States.

Source: 15 *Cong. Rec.* 36, 198 (1990)

4.19 Appellate Court Opinion in *People v. Wilson*, 1987

In this death penalty case from the 1980s, defendant Wilson won reversal of his conviction by showing that his confession was involuntary. It was a product of torture by police commander Jon Burge and others. As time went on, more allegations against Burge would be made, and eventually the fact of systematic torture by some members of the Chicago police would be established conclusively. In his excellent book, Unspeakable Acts, Ordinary People, *John Conroy covers the decades-long case of torture in Chicago's Area 2, from the initial events through the criminal trials of torture victims and the filing of a civil suit against the officers. Conroy shows how certain evidentiary rulings at the civil trial helped to shield Burge and his co-defendants from liability there.*

"He was punched, kicked, smothered with a plastic bag, electrically shocked, and forced against a hot radiator"

The defendant testified that he was punched, kicked, smothered with a plastic bag, electrically shocked, and forced against a hot radiator throughout the day on February 14, until he gave his confession. This began when he arrived at the police station that morning. The defendant testified that when the officers later took him to see the assistant State's Attorney, Hyman, to make a statement, he mentioned the mistreatment, and Hyman told him to leave. Following that, the officers attempted to shock the defendant again. The officers then stretched him against a radiator, with his hands handcuffed to wall rings at opposite ends of the radiator. His face, chest, and legs were touching the radiator. According to the defendant, he incurred his eye injury not at the time of his arrest but rather later that day, when he was kicked by an officer. The defendant testified that he made his confession because of the mistreatment he had suffered. Doris Miller, a friend of the defendant, was also being held at the police station that day, and she testified that she heard the defendant being physically and verbally abused and calling for help. The defendant's brother, Jackie Wilson, testified similarly.

Defense counsel also presented extensive medical testimony and photographic evidence corroborating the defendant's injuries. Patricia Reynolds, a registered nurse, testified that the defendant arrived at the Mercy Hospital emergency room around 10:15 or 10:30 p.m. on February 14 in the company of two Chicago police officers, Ferro and Mulvaney. According to Nurse Reynolds, Officer Ferro said "that if this guy knew what was good for him he would refuse treatment." Reynolds then asked the defendant whether he wished to be treated, and he said that he did not. Later, however, while the officers were looking away, the defendant indicated that he did wish to be treated, and he signed a consent form at 10:50 p.m. Following that, the defendant was given a tetanus shot and was prepared for examination; Nurse Reynolds testified that after the defendant was undressed she observed injuries on his chest and a burn on his right thigh.

The defendant was examined at about 11:15 p.m. by Dr. Geoffrey Korn. Dr. Korn testified that he made note of some 15 separate injuries that were apparent on the defendant's head, chest, and right leg. Two cuts on the defendant's forehead and one on the back of his head required stitches; the defendant's right eye had been blackened, and there was bleeding on the surface of that eye. Dr. Korn also observed bruises on the defendant's chest and several linear abrasions or burns on the defendant's chest, shoulder, and chin area. Finally, Dr. Korn saw on the defendant's right thigh an abrasion from a second-degree burn; it was six inches long and 1 ½ to 2 inches wide.

Dr. Korn testified that as he prepared to suture the defendant's head and face wounds, he saw that Officer Mulvaney had drawn his service revolver. Fearing that the defendant's reaction to the shots of anesthesia might startle the officer, Dr. Korn asked that the weapon be holstered. Mulvaney refused to put the gun away, however, and the doctor therefore left the room. Officer Ferro then went in the examining room and soon came out, explaining to the doctor that the defendant was now going to refuse treatment and would go to a different hospital. Dr. Korn testified that he attempted to persuade the defendant to agree to treatment but that the defendant would not change his mind. At 11:42 p.m. the defendant signed an "against medical advice" form indicating his refusal of treatment, and Officers Ferro and Mulvaney then took the defendant away.

At the suppression hearing Dr. Korn was shown photographs taken of the defendant on February 16, two days after the emergency-room examination. The photographs showed a number of abrasions or burns on the defendant's face, chest, and thigh, and Dr. Korn testified that, apart from having aged a few days, the injuries depicted in the photographs were essentially the same as what he had seen in his examination.

Dr. John M. Raba, medical director of the facility that provides health services for the Cook County jail, also testified in the defendant's behalf at the suppression hearing. Dr. Raba examined the defendant early in the evening on February 15, after receiving from one of his staff physicians a report about the defendant and what was termed his "unusual" injuries. According to Dr. Raba, the defendant explained that he had been beaten, electrically shocked, and held against a radiator. Dr. Raba saw that the defendant had injuries to his right eye, bruises and lacerations on his forehead, and blistering wounds on his face, chest, and right leg.

The trial judge denied the defendant's motion to suppress his confession. The trial judge found that the defendant suffered a cut in the area of his right eye at the time of his arrest but that other facial injuries were shown not to have occurred until after 8:30 p.m., when the confession photograph was taken. The trial judge believed that the injuries to those parts of the defendant's body not visible in the photograph—his shoulder, chest, and leg—were minor or superficial. In making that assessment, the trial judge apparently was relying on Dr. Korn's statement, on cross-examination, that the defendant's wounds could be termed superficial because they did not require major surgery. The trial judge concluded that the defendant's confession was voluntary.

The State must establish, by a preponderance of the evidence, the voluntary nature of a defendant's confession.

Source: *People v. Wilson*, 116 Ill. 2d. 29 (1987)

4.20 Appellate Court Opinion in *U.S. ex rel. Maxwell v. Gilmore*, 1999

The federal appellate court considers the claim of another criminal defendant in Chicago who argues that the systematic torture in the Chicago

Police Department's Area 2 bears on his case. The court states that the police torture in Area 2 is "common knowledge."

"Regularly engaged in the physical abuse and torture of prisoners to extract confessions"

Maxwell's next contention is that the prosecutors violated *Brady v. Maryland* by withholding exculpatory information about police officers' widespread (and indeed systematic) physical abuse of prisoners in the Area 2 Violent Crimes division. It is now common knowledge that in the early to mid-1980s Chicago Police Commander Jon Burge and many officers working under him regularly engaged in the physical abuse and torture of prisoners to extract confessions. Both internal police accounts and numerous lawsuits and appeals brought by suspects alleging such abuse substantiate that those beatings and other means of torture occurred as an established practice, not just on an isolated basis. Maxwell has asserted since before his trial that the officers who interrogated him at Area 2 in November 1986 beat a confession out of him. In fact, the public defender initially assigned to Maxwell's case states that he had photographs taken of Maxwell's bruises a week after the interrogation occurred, although that evidence is now missing.

Source: *U.S. ex rel. Maxwell v. Gilmore*, 37 F. Supp.2d 1078 (N.D. Ill. 1999)

4.21 Chicago Police Department Office of Professional Standards Report, 1991

This internal report adopts findings related to the Wilson case (document 4.19). The chief administrator, who recommends termination of Commander Burge, concludes that Burge did, in fact, torture Wilson and that he also permitted others to torture Wilson. Burge was ultimately fired and faced a civil suit by one of the detainees alleging torture. He won that suit but was convicted in June 2010 of perjury and obstruction of justice as a result of statements he made denying involvement in torture.

"Repeatedly administering electrical stimulation"

On 14 Feb 1982, during the morning and/or early afternoon hours, at Area Two Headquarters . . . Police Commander Jon Burge, while on duty and the commanding officer, brought discredit upon the Department and failed to promote the Department's efforts to implement its policy or accomplish its goals by his overall actions and conduct in that he actively participated in the mistreatment of Andrew Wilson, a prisoner in custody of Area Two personnel, and that he was aware of the continued mistreatment of Mr. Wilson by other Department members in his command but failed to report this mistreatment in direct violation of his assigned supervisory responsibility which requires that he do so. . . .

Commander Jon Burge did maltreat Andrew Wilson by repeatedly administering electrical stimulation to Mr. Wilson's body in order to create pain and he held Mr. Wilson, while handcuffed, against a hot radiator causing burns to Mr. Wilson's face, chest and thigh. Further, Police Commander Jon Burge engaged Andrew Wilson in several unjustified physical altercations during which Mr. Wilson was handcuffed and incapable of providing any resistance. Police Commander Jon Burge was inattentive to duty in that, while in a supervisory capacity, as the assigned commanding officer of the Area Two Violent Crimes Unit, he failed to provide prompt medical attention to Andrew Wilson, who was suffering from multiple injuries and who upon release from Area Two custody, was refused in the Central Detention lockup as a result of these injuries.

RECOMMENDATION: Based on the above and foregoing facts, it is the recommendation of the Chief Administrator of the Office of Professional Standards that Police Commander Jon Burge . . . be separated from the Department of Police, City of Chicago.

Source: www.humanrights.uchicago.edu/chicagotorture/ops.shtml

---

4.22 Department of Defense Memo for Secretary of Defense Cheney, 1992

This memo, prepared for Secretary of Defense Richard Cheney during the George H. W. Bush administration, warns that the manuals contained "offensive and objectionable materials." According to Thomas Blanton and Peter Kornbluh, "The Army investigators traced the origins of the instructions on use of beatings, false imprisonment, executions and truth serums back to 'Project X'—a program run by the Army Foreign Intelligence unit in the 1960s." It documents what the manuals taught to U.S. personnel and to clients in other countries. Blanton and Kornbluh note that Cheney concurred that these manuals should be retrieved and destroyed.

"The manual . . . refers to motivation by fear, payment of bounties for enemy dead, beatings, false imprisonment, executions and the use of truth serum"

Our inquiry revealed that seven Spanish-language manuals had been compiled from outdated instructional material without the required doctrinal reviews or approval. They had evolved from lesson plans used in an intelligence course at the USASOA. They were based, in part, on old material dating back to the 1960's from the Army's Foreign Intelligence Assistance Program, entitled "Project X." This material had been retained in the files of the Army Intelligence School at Fort Huachuca, Arizona. . . .

An Army review, dated 21 Feb 1992, conducted at our request, concluded that five of the seven manuals contained language and statements in violation of legal, regulatory and policy prohibitions. These manuals are: Handling of Sources, Revolutionary War and Communist Ideology, Terrorism and the Urban Guerilla, Interrogation and Combat Intelligence. To illustrate, the manual Handling of Sources, in depicting the recruitment and control of HUMINT sources, refers to motivation by fear, payment of bounties for enemy dead, beatings, false imprisonment, executions and the use of truth serum. The manual also discloses classified HUMINT methodology that could compromise Army clandestine intelligence modus operandi. A sixth manual, Counterintelligence, includes statements that also could be interpreted to be in violation of legal, regulatory, or policy prohibitions, and contains sensitive Army counterintelligence tactics, techniques, and procedures. Only the manual entitled Analysis I does not appear to violate any restrictions; however, the information therein is considered obsolete. . . .

The service schools and components play an important role in the development for training and courses. For example, the CI training for foreign military students should be developed by the Army Intelligence School and approved through Army channels. In addition, the combatant commander had the inherent responsibility to ensure that such training conducted in his area of responsibility is consistent with U.S. and DoD policy. To illustrate, we were told by USCINSCO that one of his major priorities is the emphasis on adherence to human policies by Latin American armed forces. Obviously, the offensive and objectionable material in the manuals contradicts this policy, undermines U.S. credibility, and could result in significant embarrassment.

In theory, the offending and improper language in the materials should have been discovered during the Army's existing review and approval process. It is incredible that the use of the lesson plans since 1982, and the manuals since 1987, evaded the established system of doctrinal controls. Nevertheless, we could find no evidence that this was a deliberate and orchestrated attempt to violate DoD or Army policies.

Source: www.gwu.edu/~nsarchiv/NSAEBB/NSAEBB122/

4.23 U.S. Code Criminal Provision (18 U.S.C. Section 2340), 1994

The U.S. Code provision criminalizing torture tracks the language of the Convention against Torture(document 4.18). For the Bush administration's narrow interpretation of 18 U.S.C. Section 2340, see document 5.2.

"Other than pain or suffering incidental to lawful sanctions"

As used in this chapter—

(1) "torture" means an act committed by a person acting under the color of law specifically intended to inflict severe physical or mental pain or suffering (other than pain or suffering incidental to lawful sanctions) upon another person within his custody or physical control;

(2) "severe mental pain or suffering" means the prolonged mental harm caused by or resulting from—

(A) the intentional infliction or threatened infliction of severe physical pain or suffering;

(B) the administration or application, or threatened administration or application, of mind-altering substances or other procedures calculated to disrupt profoundly the senses or the personality;

(C) the threat of imminent death; or

(D) the threat that another person will imminently be subjected to death, severe physical pain or suffering, or the administration or application of mind-altering substances or other procedures calculated to disrupt profoundly the senses or personality;

Source: 18 U.S.C. Section 2340

4.24 Statement by President Bill Clinton, 1999

President Bill Clinton's public apology for U.S. actions in Guatemala was an official acknowledgment of what many people already knew: that the United States had worked with and supported the Guatemalan government for decades as that government and its associated paramilitary forces engaged in executions, torture, rape, and other human rights violations on a massive scale.

"The United States must not repeat that mistake"

For the United States it is important that I state clearly that support for military forces and intelligence units which engaged in violence and widespread repression was wrong, and the United States must not repeat that mistake.

Source: www.nytimes.com/1999/03/11/world/clinton-offers-his-apologies-to -guatemala.html?pagewanted=1

4.25 Opinion of the U.S. Supreme Court in *Hope v. Pelzer*, 2002

In 2002 the Supreme Court ruled that handcuffing an inmate to a hitching post as punishment violated the Eighth Amendment. The petitioner here had been handcuffed to the post for seven hours in the sun, exposed to thirst, and taunted. Under civil rights law, a state actor is entitled to immunity if the rights violation in question was not "clearly established" by existing law. Thus, even if a constitutional violation occurred, the state actor could still be immune from liability because the law provided insufficient guidance as to the contours of the victim's rights. Writing for the majority, Justice John Paul Stevens explained that case law, a Department of Justice report, and an Alabama Corrections regulation provided fair warning to the defendants that their actions were unlawful. Significantly, the corrections regulation does not prohibit all use of the hitching post but merely limits its use: it may not be employed as punishment, but it may be used as a tool for coercing inmates to work.

Justice Clarence Thomas dissented, arguing that the hitching post was not clearly unlawful in 1995, when the case arose.

"This punitive treatment amounts to gratuitous infliction of 'wanton and unnecessary' pain"

"The unnecessary and wanton infliction of pain . . . constitutes cruel and un-usual punishment forbidden by the Eighth Amendment." We have said that "among 'unnecessary and wanton' inflictions of pain are those that are 'totally without penological justification.'" In making this determination in the context of prison conditions, we must ascertain whether the officials involved acted with "deliberate indifference" to the inmates' health or safety. We may infer the existence of this subjective state of mind from the fact that the risk of harm is obvious.

As the facts are alleged by Hope, the Eighth Amendment violation is obvious. Any safety concerns had long since abated by the time petitioner was handcuffed to the hitching post because Hope had already been subdued, handcuffed, placed in leg irons, and transported back to the prison. He was separated from his work squad and not given the opportunity to return to work. Despite the clear lack of an emergency situation, the respondents knowingly subjected him to a substantial risk of physical harm, to unnecessary pain caused by the handcuffs and the restricted position of confinement for a 7-hour period, to unnecessary exposure to the heat of the sun, to prolonged thirst and taunting, and to a deprivation of bathroom breaks that created a risk of particular discomfort and humiliation. The use of the hitching post under these circumstances violated the "basic concept underlying the Eighth Amendment[, which] is nothing less than the dignity of man." This punitive treatment amounts to gratuitous infliction of "wanton and unnecessary" pain that our precedent clearly prohibits. . . .

The use of the hitching post as alleged by Hope "unnecessarily and wantonly inflicted pain," and thus was a clear violation of the Eighth Amendment. See Part II, supra. Arguably, the violation was so obvious that our own Eighth Amendment cases gave the respondents fair warning that their conduct violated the Constitution. Regardless, in light of binding Eleventh Circuit precedent, an Alabama Department of Corrections (ADOC) regulation, and a DOJ report informing the ADOC of the constitutional infirmity in its use of the hitching post, we readily conclude that the respondents' conduct violated "clearly established statutory or constitutional rights of which a reasonable person would have known." . . .

Relevant to the question whether [an earlier case] provided fair warning to respondents that their conduct violated the Constitution is a regulation promulgated by ADOC in 1993. The regulation authorizes the use of the hitching post when an inmate refuses to work or is otherwise disruptive to a work squad. It provides that an activity log should be completed for each such inmate, detailing his responses to offers of water and bathroom breaks every 15 minutes. Such a log was completed and maintained for petitioner's shackling in May, but the record contains no such log for the 7-hour shackling in June and the record indicates that the periodic offers contemplated by the regulation were not made. The regulation also states that an inmate "will be allowed to join his assigned squad" whenever he tells an officer "that he is ready to go to work." The findings in as well as the record in this case, indicate that this important provision of the regulation was frequently ignored by corrections officers. If regularly observed, a requirement that would effectively give the inmate the keys to the handcuffs that attached him to the hitching post would have made this case more analogous to the practice upheld in *Ort,* rather than the kind of punishment *Ort* described as impermissible. A course of conduct that tends to prove that the requirement was merely a sham, or that respondents could ignore it with impunity, provides equally strong support for the conclusion that they were fully aware of the wrongful character of their conduct. . . .

The respondents violated clearly established law. Our conclusion that "a reasonable person would have known," of the violation is buttressed by the fact that the DOJ specifically advised the ADOC of the unconstitutionality of its practices before the incidents in this case took place. The DOJ had conducted a study in 1994 of Alabama's use of the hitching post. Among other findings, the DOJ report noted that ADOC's officers consistently failed to comply with the policy of immediately releasing any inmate from the hitching post who agrees to return to work. The DOJ concluded that the systematic use of the restraining bar in Alabama constituted improper corporal punishment. Accordingly, the DOJ advised the ADOC to cease use of the hitching post in order to meet constitutional standards. The ADOC replied that it thought the post could permissibly be used "to preserve prison security and discipline." Ibid. In response, the DOJ informed the ADOC that, "although an emergency situation may warrant drastic action by corrections staff, our experts found that the 'rail' is being used systematically as an improper punishment for relatively trivial offenses. Therefore, we have concluded that the use of the 'rail' is without penological justification." Ibid. Although there is nothing in the record indicating that the DOJ's views were communicated to respondents, this exchange lends support to the view that reasonable officials in the ADOC should have realized that the use of the hitching post under the circumstances alleged by Hope violated the Eighth Amendment prohibition against cruel and unusual punishment.

The obvious cruelty inherent in this practice should have provided respondents with some notice that their alleged conduct violated Hope's constitutional protection against cruel and unusual punishment. Hope was treated in a way antithetical to human dignity—he was hitched to a post for an extended period of time in a position that was painful, and under circumstances that were both degrading and dangerous. This wanton treatment was not done of necessity, but as punishment for prior conduct. Even if there might once have been a question regarding the constitutionality of this practice, the Eleventh Circuit precedent of *Gates* and *Ort*, as well as the DOJ report condemning the practice, put a reasonable officer on notice that the use of the hitching post under the circumstances alleged by Hope was unlawful. The "fair and clear warning," that these cases provided was sufficient to preclude the defense of qualified immunity at the summary judgment stage.

Source: *Hope v. Pelzer*, 536 U.S. 730 (2002)

5

After the terror attacks of September 11, 2001, the need to defend against future attacks made the definition of torture and its use a focus of public debate. Consequently, documents were generated concerning the legal standards for interrogation of suspected terrorists, which involved review of existing standards for lawful interrogations and prisoner treatment, including some of the provisions of U.S. and international law cited in chapter 4. Those legal limits had to be discussed in government memos and reports, even when those documents were classified. The Bush administration sought ways to circumvent the Geneva Convention, the Convention against Torture, and the U.S criminal statute prohibiting torture to permit consideration of such techniques as "walling," "close confinement," and waterboarding. In addition, the administration's lawyers opposed application of the Geneva Convention to those they classified as "unlawful enemy combatants."

5.1 Legal Memorandum by Alberto Gonzales, 2002

White House Counsel Alberto Gonzales outlines the legal arguments for declining to adhere to the standards of the Geneva Convention for treatment of prisoners.

"This new paradigm renders obsolete Geneva's strict limitations on questioning of enemy prisoners and renders quaint some of its provisions"

On January 18, I advised you that the Department of Justice had issued a formal legal opinion concluding that the Geneva Convention III on the Treatment of Prisoners of War (GPW) does not apply to the conflict with al Qaeda. I also advised you that DOJ's opinion concludes that there are reasonable grounds for you to conclude that GPW does not apply with respect to the conflict with the Taliban. I understand that you decided that GPW does not apply, and accordingly, that al Qaeda and Taliban detainees are not prisoners of war under the GPW....

The consequences of a decision to adhere to what I understood to be your earlier determination that the GPW does not apply to the Taliban include the following:

Preserves flexibility:

As you have said, the war against terrorism is a new kind of war. It is not the traditional clash between nations adhering to the laws of war that formed the backdrop for the GPW. The nature of the new war places a high premium on other factors, such as the ability to quickly obtain information from captured terrorists and their sponsors in order to avoid further atrocities against American civilians, and the need to try terrorists for war crimes such as wantonly killing civilians. In my judgment, this new paradigm renders obsolete Geneva's strict limitations on questioning of enemy prisoners and renders quaint some of its provisions requiring that captured enemy be afforded such things as commissary privileges, scrip (i.e., advances on monthly pay), athletic uniforms and scientific instruments. . . .

Substantially reduces the threat of domestic criminal prosecution under the War Crimes Act (18 2441)

Adhering to your determination that GPW does not apply would guard effectively against misconstruction or misapplication of Section 2441 for several reasons:

First, some of the language of GPW is undefined (it prohibits, for example, "outrages upon personal dignity" and "inhuman treatment"), and it is difficult to predict with confidence what actions might be deemed to constitute violations of the relevant portions of GPW.

Second, it is difficult to predict the needs or circumstances that could arise in the war on terrorism.

Third, it is difficult to predict the motives of prosecutors and independent counsels who may in the future decide to pursue unwarranted charges based on Section 2441. Your determination would create a reasonable basis in law that Section 2441 does not apply, which would provide a solid defense to any future prosecution. . . .

In the treatment of the detainees, the US will continue to be constrained by (i) its commitment to treat the detainees humanely and, to the extent appropriate and consistent with military necessity, in a manner consistent with the principle of GPW, (ii) its applicable treaty obligations, (iii) minimum standards of treatment universally recognized by the nations of the world, and (iv) applicable military regulations regarding the treatment of detainees. . . .

Source: www.washingtonpost.com/wp-srv/politics/documents/cheney/gonzales_addington_memo_jan252001.pdf

5.2 Legal Memorandum by Jay Bybee, 2002

In 2002 Assistant Attorney General Jay Bybee sent a memo to the White House entitled Re: Standards of Conduct for Interrogation under 18 U.S.C.§§2340-2340A. The "Bybee memo" interprets the U.S. criminal prohibition against torture, suggesting what scenarios would (or would not) meet the statutory definition of torture. Because Bybee was a member of the Office of Legal Counsel within the Department of Justice, he was in a position to provide binding legal advice to the president, and it was in that capacity that he reported his opinion on the interpretation of the U.S. antitorture law. The cited statute, 18 U.S.C. Section 2340, defines the act of torture as an "act committed by a person acting under the color of law specifically intended to inflict severe physical or mental pain or suffering (other than pain or suffering incidental to lawful sanctions) upon another person within his custody or physical control." The question of "standards of conduct for interrogation" arose in the context of the Bush administration's "war on terror" following the September 11, 2001, terror attacks on the United States as the federal government sought to obtain information from detainees.

"Such damage must rise to the level of death, organ failure, or the permanent impairment of a significant body function"

To violate Section 2340A, the statute requires that severe pain and suffering must be inflicted with specific intent. In order for a defendant to have acted with specific intent, he must expressly intend to achieve the forbidden act. See *United States v. Carter. Black's Law Dictionary* (defining specific intent as "[t]he intent to accomplish the precise criminal act that one is later charged with"). For example, in *Ratzlaf v. United States,* the statute at issue was construed to require that the defendant act with the "specific intent to commit the crime." As a result, the defendant had to act with the express "purpose to disobey the law" in order for the *mens rea* element to be satisfied. Ibid. Here, because Section 2340 requires that a defendant act with the specific intent to inflict severe pain, the infliction of such pain must be the defendant's precise objective. If the statute had required only general intent, it would be sufficient to establish guilt by showing that the defendant "possessed knowledge with respect to the *actus reus* of the crime." *Carter,* 530 U.S. at 268. If the defendant acted knowing that severe pain or suffering was reasonably likely to result from his actions, but no more, he would have acted only with general intent. *Black's Law Dictionary* (explaining that general intent "usu[ally] takes the form of recklessness (involving actual awareness of a risk and the culpable taking of that risk) or negligence (involving blameworthy inadvertence)"). . . .

As a theoretical matter, therefore, knowledge alone that a particular result is certain to occur does not constitute specific intent. As the Supreme Court explained in the context of murder, "the . . . common law of homicide distinguishes . . . between a person who knows that another person will be killed as a result of his conduct and a person who acts with the specific purpose of taking another's life[.]" *United States v. Bailey*. "Put differently, the law distinguishes actions taken 'because of' a given end from actions taken in spite of their unintended but foreseen consequences." *Vacco v. Quill*. Thus, even if the defendant knows that severe pain will result from his actions, if causing such harm is not his objective, he lacks the requisite specific intent even though the defendant did not act in good faith. Instead, a defendant is guilty of torture only if he acts with the express purpose of inflicting severe pain or suffering on a person within his custody or physical control. . . .

Further, a showing that an individual acted with a good faith belief that his conduct would not produce the result that the law prohibits negates specific intent. See, e.g., *South Atl. Lmtd. Ptrshp. of Tenn. v. Riese*. . . .

The key statutory phrase in the definition of torture is the statement that acts amount to torture if they cause "severe physical or mental pain or suffering." . . .

Section 2340 makes plain that the infliction of pain or suffering per se, whether it is physical or mental, is insufficient to amount to torture. Instead, the text provides that pain or suffering must be "severe." The statute does not, however, define the term "severe." "In the absence of such a definition, we construe a statutory term in accordance with its ordinary or natural meaning." The dictionary defines "severe" as "[u]nsparing in exaction, punishment, or censure" or "[I]nflicting discomfort or pain hard to endure; sharp; afflictive; distressing; violent; extreme; as severe pain, anguish, torture." *Webster's New International Dictionary*; *American Heritage Dictionary of the English Language* ("extremely violent or grievous: severe pain"); *The Oxford English Dictionary* ("Of pain, suffering, loss, or the like: Grievous, extreme" and "of circumstances . . . hard to sustain or endure"). Thus, the adjective "severe" conveys that the pain or suffering must be of such a high level of intensity that the pain is difficult for the subject to endure.

Congress's use of the phrase "severe pain" elsewhere in the United States Code can shed more light on its meaning. . . . Significantly, the phrase "severe pain" appears in statutes defining an emergency medical condition for the purpose of providing health benefits. These statutes define an emergency condition as one "manifesting itself by acute symptoms of sufficient security (including severe pain) such that a prudent lay person, who possesses an average knowledge of health and medicine, could reasonably expect the absence of immediate medical attention to result in—placing the health of the individual . . . (i) in serious jeopardy, (ii) serious impairment to bodily functions, or (iii) serious dysfunction of any bodily organ or part." . . . Although these statutes address a substantially different subject from Section 2340, they are nonetheless helpful for understanding what constitutes severe physical pain. They treat severe pain as an indicator of ailments that are likely to result in permanent and serious physical damage in the absence of immediate medical treatment. Such damage must rise to the level of death, organ failure, or the permanent impairment of a significant body function. These statutes suggest that "severe pain," as used in Section 2340, must rise to a similarly high level—the level that would ordinarily be associated with a sufficiently serious physical condition or injury such as death, organ failure, or serious impairment of body functions—in order to constitute torture.

Source: http://www.washingtonpost.com /wp-srv/nation/documents/ dojinterrogationmemo20020801.pdf

---

5.3 Memo from William Haynes II to Secretary of Defense Donald Rumsfeld, 2002

In November 2002 Department of Defense general counsel William Haynes II wrote to Secretary of Defense Rumsfeld requesting approval of certain interrogation techniques. Appended to his memo were requests of others in the military chain of command detailing the techniques they wanted to employ. Of the Category III (most severe) techniques, only "mild" physical contact was recommended for use. Rumsfeld signed off and approved the memo. In handwritten notation, he added, "However, I stand for 8–10 hours a day. Why is standing limited to 4 hours?"

"A standard of interrogation that reflects a tradition of restraint"

The Commander of USSOUTHCOM has forwarded a request by the Commander of Joint Task Force 170 (now JTF GTMO) for approval of counterresistance techniques to aid in the interrogation of detainees at Guantanamo Bay.

The request contains three categories of counter resistance techniques, with the first category the least aggressive and the third category the most aggressive.

I have discussed this with the Deputy, Doug Feith and General Myers. I believe that all join in my recommendation that, as a matter of policy, you authorized the Commander of USSOUTHCOM to employ, in his discretion, only Category I and II and the fourth technique listed in Category III ("Use of mild, non-injurious physical contact such as grabbing, poking in the chest with the finger, and light pushing").

While all Category III techniques may be legally available, we believe that, as a matter of policy, a blanket approval of Category III techniques is not warranted at this time. Our Armed Forces are trained to a standard of interrogation that reflects a tradition of restraint.

RECOMMENDATION: That SECDEF approve the USSOUTHCOM Commander's use of those counter-resistance techniques listed in Category I and II and the fourth technique listed in Category III during the interrogation of detainees at Guantanamo.

[Editor's note: The techniques referred to in the memo are listed in attachments to the memo. Category I techniques are yelling, deception, "multiple interrogator techniques," and posing as an official from a foreign nation where torture might be practiced. Category II techniques are stress positions, false documents, 30 days isolation, alternative locations for interrogation, light and sensory stimuli, hooding, 28-hour interrogation, removal of comfort items, cold meals, forced grooming, use of phobias. Category III techniques include death threats and waterboarding, but the approved technique here is "mild, non-injurious physical contact."]

Source: http://www.gwu.edu/~nsarchiv/NSAEBB/NSAEBB127/02.12.02.pdf

---

5.4 Memo from Donald Rumsfeld to Commander, USSOUTHCOM, 2003

In this memo dated April 16, 2003, Secretary of Defense Rumsfeld lists the specific interrogation techniques he has approved for use against "unlawful combatants" detained at Guantanamo Bay, Cuba. Rumsfeld states several times that the Geneva Convention does not apply to these detainees, although he notes that other nations may disagree.

"The provisions of the Geneva Convention are not applicable to the interrogation of unlawful combatants"

MEMORANDUM FOR THE COMMANDER US SOUTHERN COMMAND
SUBJECT: Counter-Resistance Techniques in the War on Terrorism

I have considered the report of the Working Group that I directed be established on January 15, 2003. I approve the use of specified counter-resistance techniques, subject to the following:

a. The techniques I authorize are those lettered A–X set out at Tab A.

b. These techniques must be used with all the safeguards described at Tab B.

c. Use of these techniques is limited to interrogations of unlawful combatants held at Guantanamo Bay, Cuba.

d. Prior to the use of these techniques, the Chairman of the Working Group on Detainee Interrogations in the Global War on Terrorism must brief you and your staff.

I reiterate that US Armed Forces shall continue to treat detainees humanely and, to the extent appropriate and consistent with military necessity, in a manner consistent with the principles of the Geneva Conventions. In addition, if you intend to use techniques B, I, O, or X, you must specifically determine that military necessity requires its use and notify me in advance.

If, in your view, you require additional interrogation techniques for a particular detainee, you should provide me, via the Chairman of the Joint Chiefs of Staff, a written request describing the proposed technique, recommended safeguards, and the rationale for applying it with an identified detainee. Nothing in this memorandum in any way restricts your existing authority to maintain good order and discipline among detainees.

TAB A
INTERROGATION TECHNIQUES

The use of techniques A–X is subject to the general safeguards as provided below as well as specific implementation guidelines to be provided by the appropriate authority. Specific implementation guidance with respect to techniques A–Q is provided in Army Field Manual 34-52. Further implementation guidance with respect to techniques R–X will need to be developed by the appropriate authority.

Of the techniques set forth below, the policy aspects of certain techniques should be considered to the extent those policy aspects reflect the views of other major U.S. partner nations. Where applicable, the description of the technique is annotated to include a summary of the policy issues that should be considered before application of the technique.

A. Asking straightforward questions.

B. Incentive/Removal of Incentive: Providing a reward or removing a privilege above and beyond those that are required by the Geneva Convention, from detainees. [Caution: Other nations that believe that detainees are entitled to POW protections may consider that provision and retention of religious items (e.g., the Koran) are protected under international law (see, Geneva III, Article 34). Although the provisions of the Geneva Convention are not applicable to the interrogation of unlawful combatants, consideration should be given to these views prior to application of the technique.]

C. Emotional Love: Playing on the love a detainee has for an individual or group.

D. Emotional Hate: Playing on the hatred a detainee has for an individual or group.

E. Fear Up Harsh: Significantly increasing the fear level in a detainee.

F. Fear Up Mild: Moderately increasing the fear level in a detainee.

G. Reduced Fear: Reducing the fear level in a detainee.

H. Pride and Ego Up: Boosting the ego of a detainee.

I. Pride and Ego Down: Attacking or insulting the ego of a detainee, not beyond the limits that would apply to a POW. [Caution: Article 17 of Geneva III provides, "Prisoners of war who refuse to answer may not be threatened, insulted, or exposed to any unpleasant or disadvantageous, treatment of any kind." Other nations that believe that detainees are entitled to POW protections may consider this technique inconsistent with the provisions of Geneva. Although the provisions of Geneva are not applicable to the interrogation of unlawful combatants, consideration should be given to these views prior to application of the technique.]

J. Futility: Invoking the feeling of futility of a detainee.

K. We Know All: Convincing the detainee that the interrogator knows the answer to questions he asks the detainee.

L. Establish your identity: Convincing the detainee that the interrogator has mistaken the detainee for someone else.

M. Repetition Approach: Continuously repeating the same question to the detainee within interrogation periods of normal duration.

N. File and Dossier: Convincing detainee that the interrogator has a damning and inaccurate file, which must be fixed.

O. Mutt and Jeff team consisting of a friendly and harsh interrogator. The harsh interrogator might employ the Pride and Ego Down technique. [Caution: Other nations that believe that POW protections apply to detainees may view this technique as inconsistent with Geneva III, Article 13 which provides that POWs must be protected against acts of intimidation. Although the provisions of Geneva are not applicable to the interrogation of unlawful combatants, consideration should be given to these views prior to application of the technique.]

P. Rapid Fire: Questioning in rapid succession without allowing detainee to answer.

Q. Silence: Staring at the detainee to encourage discomfort.

R. Change of Scenery Up: Removing the detainee from the standard interrogation setting (generally to a location more pleasant, but no worse).

S. Change of Scenery Down: Removing the detainee from the standard interrogation setting and placing him in a setting that may be less comfortable; would not constitute a substantial change in environmental quality.

T. Dietary Manipulation: Changing the diet of a detainee; no intended deprivation of food or water; no adverse medical or cultural effect and without intent to deprive subject of food or water, e.g., hot rations to MREs.

U. Environmental Manipulation: Altering the environment to create moderate discomfort (e.g., adjusting temperature or introducing an unpleasant smell). Conditions would not be such that they would injure the detainee. Detainee would be accompanied by interrogator at all times. [Caution: Based on court cases in other countries, some nations may view application of this technique in certain circumstances to be inhumane. Consideration of these views should be given prior to use of this technique.]

V. Sleep Adjustment: Adjusting the sleeping times of the detainee (e.g., reversing sleep cycles from night to day). This technique is NOT sleep deprivation.

W. False Flag: Convincing the detainee that individuals from a country other than the United States are interrogating him.

X. Isolation: Isolating the detainee from other detainees while still complying with basic standards of treatment. [Caution: The use of isolation as an interrogation technique requires detailed implementation instructions, including specific guidelines regarding the length of isolation, medical and psychological review, and approval for extensions of the length of isolation by the appropriate level in the chain of command. This technique is not known to have been generally used for interrogation purposes for longer than 30 days. Those nations that believe detainees are subject to POW protection may view use of this technique as inconsistent with the requirements of Geneva III Article 13 which provides that POWs must be protected against acts of intimidation; Article 14 which provides, that POWs are entitled to respect for their person; Article 34 which prohibits coercion and Article 126 which ensures access and basic standards of treatment. Although the provisions of Geneva are not applicable to the interrogation of unlawful combatants, consideration should be given to these views prior to application of the technique.]

Source: www.gwu.edu/~nsarchiv/NSAEBB/NSAEBB127/03.04.16.pdf

5.5 Memo from Lieutenant General Ricardo Sanchez to Combined Joint Task Force 7, Baghdad (no. 1), 2003

In a memo dated September 14, 2003, General Ricardo Sanchez approved the interrogation techniques listed in the Rumsfeld memo (document 5.4 regarding Guantanamo detainees) for use in Iraq, where, as Sanchez notes, "the Geneva Conventions are applicable." He adds several techniques that Rumsfeld did not approve at Guantanamo and refers to a set of safeguards, which include guidance for effective interrogation but say little about protecting detainees during interrogation. Note also that "DD" is referenced in the memo but not provided.

"CJTF-7 is operating in a theater of war in which the Geneva Conventions are applicable"

SUBJECT: CJTF-7 Interrogation and Counter-Resistance Policy

1. This memorandum establishes the interrogation and counter-resistance policy for CJTF-7.

2. I approve the use of specified interrogation and counter-resistance techniques A-DD, as described in enclosure 1, subject to the following:

a. These techniques must be used with the safeguards described in enclosure 2.

b. Use of these techniques is limited to interrogations of detainees, security internees and enemy prisoners of war under the control of CJTF-7.

c. Use of techniques B, I, O, X, Y, AA and CC on enemy prisoners of war must be approved by me personally prior to use. Submit written requests for use of these techniques, with supporting rationale, to me through the CJTF-7 C2. A legal review from the CJFT-7 SJA must accompany each request.

3. CJTF-7 is operating in a theater of war in which the Geneva Conventions are applicable. Coalition forces will continue to treat all persons under their control humanely.

4. Requests for use of those techniques not listed in enclosure 1 will be

submitted to me through the CJTF-7 C2, and include a description of the proposed techniques and recommended safeguards. A . A legal review from the CJFT-7 SJA must accompany each request.

5. Nothing in this policy limits existing authority for maintenance of good order and discipline among detainees.

[Editor's Note: The list of techniques here is substantially similar to the one provided in the Rumsfeld memo, in document 5.4. However, the following techniques are added.]

Y. Presence of Military Working Dog: Exploits Arab fear of dogs while maintaining security during interrogation. Dogs will be muzzled and under control of MWD handler at all times to prevent contact with detainee.

Z. Sleep Management: Detainee provided minimum 4 hours of sleep per 24 hour period, not to exceed 72 continuous hours.

AA. Yelling, Loud music, and Light Control: Used to create fear, disorient detainee and prolong capture shock. Volume controlled to prevent injury.

BB. Deception: Use of falsified representations including documents and reports.

CC. Stress positions: Use of physical postures (sitting, standing, kneeling prone, etc.) for no more than 1 hour per use. Use of techniques(s) will not exceed 4 hours and adequate rest between use of each position will be provided.

GENERAL SAFEGUARDS

Application of these interrogation techniques is subject to the following general safeguards: (i) limited to use at interrogation facilities only; (ii) there is a reasonable basis to believe that the detainee possesses critical intelligence; (iii) the detainee is medically and operationally evaluated as suitable (considering all techniques to be used in combination); (iv) interrogators are specifically trained for the technique(s); (v) a specific interrogation plan (including reasonable safeguards, limits on duration, intervals between applications, termination criteria and the presence or availability of qualified medical personnel) has been developed; (vi) there is appropriate supervision; and, (vii) there is appropriate specified senior approval as identified by 205th MI BDB Commander for use with any specific detainee (after considering the foregoing and receiving legal advice).

The purpose of all interviews and interrogations is to get the most information from detainee with the least intrusive method, always applied in a humane and lawful manner with sufficient oversight by trained investigators or interrogators. Operating instructions must be developed based on command policies to insure uniform, careful and safe application of interrogations of detainees.

Interrogations must always be planned, deliberate actions that take into account factors such as a detainee's current and past performance in both decoration and interrogation; a detainee's emotional and physical strengths and weakness; assessment of possible approaches that may work on a certain detainee in an effort to gain the trust of the detainee; strength and weakness of interrogators; and augmentation by other personnel for a certain detainee based on other factors.

Interrogation approaches are designed to manipulate the detainee's emotions and weaknesses to gain his willing cooperation. Interrogation operations are never conducted in a vacuum; they are conducted in close cooperation with the unit detaining the individuals. The policies established by the detaining units that pertain to marching, silencing and segregating also play a role in the interrogation of the detainee. Detainee interrogation involves developing a plan tailored to an individual and approved by senior interrogations. Strict adherence to policies/standard operating procedures governing the administration or interrogation techniques and oversight is essential.

It is important that the interrogators be provided reasonable latitude to vary techniques depending on the detainee's culture, strengths and weaknesses, environment, extent of training in resistance techniques as well as the urgency of obtaining information that the detainee is believed to have.

While techniques are considered individually within this analysis, it must be understood that in practice, techniques are usually used in combination. The cumulative effect of all techniques to be employed must be considered before any decisions are made regarding approval for particular situations. The title of a particular technique is not always fully descriptive of a particular technique. 205 MI BDE Commander is responsible for oversight of all techniques involving physical contact.

Source: Jameel Jaffer and Amrit Singh, *Administration of Torture: A Documentary Record from Washington to Abu Ghraib and Beyond* (New York: Columbia University Press, 2007), p. A-232.

5.6 Memo from Lieutenant General Ricardo Sanchez to Combined Joint Task Force 7, Baghdad (no. 2), 2003

This memo, also written by General Sanchez, was issued a month later, on October 12, 2003. Here, General Sanchez limits the authorized interroga-

*tion techniques listed in the previous memo in two ways: by referring only
to "security internees" as persons to whom the techniques may be applied
(he omits "detainees and prisoners of war"), and by removing techniques
R-DD from the list of approved techniques.*

"Security internees under definite suspicion"

SUBJECT: CJTF-7 Interrogation and Counter-Resistance Policy

1. This memorandum establishes the interrogation and counter-resistance
policy for security internees under the control of CJTF-7. Security internees
are civilians who are detained pursuant to Articles 5 and 78 of the Geneva
Convention Relative to the protection of Civilian Persons in Time of War of
August 12, 1949 (hereinafter, Geneva Convention).

2. I approve the use of specified interrogation and counter-resistance techniques A–Q, as described in enclosure 1, relating to security internees, subject to the following:

> a. Use of these techniques is limited to interrogations of security in-
> ternees and under the control of CJTF-7.
> b. These techniques must be used with the safeguards described in
> enclosure 2.
> c. Segregation of security internees will be required in many instances
> to ensure the success of interrogations and to prevent the sharing of
> interrogation methods among internees. Segregation may also be nec-
> essary to protect sources from other detainees or otherwise provide for
> their security. Additionally, the Geneva Convention provides that secu-
> rity internees under definite suspicion of activity hostile to the security
> of Coalition forces shall, where absolute military necessity requires,
> be regarded as having forfeited rights of communication. Accordingly,
> these security internees may be segregated. I must approve segregation
> in all cases where such segregation will exceed 30 days in duration,
> whether consecutive or non-consecutive. Submit written requests with
> supporting rationale to me through CJTF-& C2. A legal review from
> the CJFT-7 SJA must accompany each request.
> d. In employing each of the authorized approaches, the interrogator
> must maintain control of the interrogation: The interrogator should ap-
> pear to be the one who controls all aspects of the interrogation, to in-
> clude the lighting, heating and configuration of the interrogation room,
> as well as the food, clothing and shelter given to the security internee.

3. Requests for use of approaches not listed in enclosure 1 will be submitted to me through the CJTF-7 C2, and include a description of the proposed

approach and recommended safeguards. A legal review from the CJFT-7 SJA must accompany each request.

4. Nothing in this policy limits existing authority for maintenance of good order and discipline among persons under Coalition control.

5. This policy supersedes the CJTF-7 Interrogation and Counter-Resistance Policy signed on 14 September 2003.

Source: Jameel Jaffer and Amrit Singh, *Administration of Torture: A Documentary Record from Washington to Abu Ghraib and Beyond* (New York: Columbia University Press, 2007), p. A-238

5.7 OLC Memorandum to the CIA (no. 1), 2002

The CIA has solicited a legal opinion as to whether certain coercive interrogation techniques may be used on detainee Abu Zubaydah without violating U.S. criminal law. The interrogators want to put an insect in a box with Zubaydah and then tell him the insect stings. Jay Bybee of the Office of Legal Counsel (see document 5.2) advises that this action would not violate criminal law because it does not make the detainee believe death or serious bodily harm is imminent. The interrogators also want to waterboard Zubaydah. Bybee says that waterboarding does, in fact, create the impression of imminent death. However, according to Bybee, the waterboarding procedure does not violate criminal law because it does not produce lasting harm.

"You also would like to introduce an insect into one of the boxes"

You have asked for this Office's views on whether certain proposed conduct would violate the prohibition against torture found at Section 2340A of Title 18 of the United States Code. You have asked for this advice in the course of conducting interrogations of Abu Zubaydah. As we understand it, Zubaydah is one of the highest ranking members of the al Qaeda terrorist organization, with which the United States is currently engaged in an international armed conflict following the attacks on the World Trade Center and the Pentagon on September 11, 2001. This letter memorializes our previous oral advice, given on July 24, 2002, and July 26, 2002, that the proposed conduct would not violate this prohibition. . . .

In addition to using confinement boxes alone, you also would like to introduce an insect into one of the boxes with Zubaydah. As we understand it, you plan to inform Zubaydah that you are going to place a stinging insect in the box, but you will actually place a harmless insect in the box, such as a caterpillar. If you do so, to ensure that you are outside the predicate act requirement, you must inform him that the insect will not have a sting that will produce death or severe pain. If, however, you were to place the insect in the box without informing him that you are doing so, then in order not to commit a predicate act, you should not affirmatively lead him to believe that any insect is present which has a sting that could produce severe pain or suffering or even cause his death. [redacted] so long as you take either of the approaches we have described, the insect's placement in the box would not constitute a threat of severe physical pain or suffering to a reasonable person in his condition. An individual, even an individual with a fear of insects, would not reasonably feel threatened with severe physical pain or suffering if a caterpillar was placed in the box. . . .

We find that the use of the waterboard constitutes a threat of imminent death. As you have explained the waterboard procedure to us, it creates in the subject the uncontrollable physiological sensation that the subject is drowning. . . . From the vantage point of any reasonable person undergoing this procedure in such circumstances, he would feel as if he is drowning at the very moment of the procedure due to the uncontrollable physiological sensation he is experiencing. Thus, this procedure cannot be viewed as too uncertain to satisfy the imminence requirement. Accordingly, it constitutes a threat of imminent death and fulfills the predicate act requirement under the statute.

Although the waterboard constitutes a threat of imminent death, prolonged mental harm must nonetheless result to violate the statutory prohibition on infliction of severe mental pain or suffering . . . . We have previously concluded that prolonged mental harm is mental harm of some lasting duration, e.g., mental harm lasting months or years. . . . [Y]ou have advised us that relief is almost immediate when the cloth is removed from the nose and mouth. In the absence of prolonged mental harm, no severe mental pain or suffering would have been inflicted, and the use of these procedures would not constitute torture within the meaning of the statute.

Source: http://documents.nytimes.com/justice-department-memos-on-interrogation -techniques#p=85

5.8 Report by Office of the Inspector General, Department of Justice, 2003

The Inspector General at the Department of Justice reviewed allegations by detainees at the Metropolitan Detention Center (MDC) in Brooklyn, New York, and the Passaic County Jail in Paterson, New Jersey. The detainees were housed at these facilities following 9/11. The OIG found more evidence substantiating abuse at the MDC.

"An officer bent his finger back until it touched his wrist"

VI. ALLEGATIONS OF PHYSICAL AND VERBAL ABUSE

Based on our interviews of 19 September 11 detainees and our investigation of allegations of abuse raised by several detainees, we believe the evidence indicates a pattern of physical and verbal abuse against some September 11 detainees held at the MDC by some correctional officers, particularly during the first months after the terrorist attacks. Although the allegations have been declined for criminal prosecution, the OIG is continuing to investigate these matters administratively.

In this section of the report, we describe our interviews of 19 September 11 detainees during our inspection visit in May 2002, the investigation conducted by the OIG's Investigations Division regarding specific complaints of abuse, and other allegations of abuse that were referred to the FBI or BOP for investigation.

A. OIG Site Visit

In connection with this review of the treatment of September 11 detainees, our inspection team interviewed 19 detainees who were being held at the MDC when we visited the facility in May 2002. All 19 detainees complained of some form of abuse. Twelve complained about physical abuse and 10 complained about verbal abuse. The complaints of physical abuse ranged from painfully tight handcuffs to allegations they were slammed against the wall by MDC staff. The detainees told us that the physical abuse usually occurred upon their arrival at the MDC, while being moved to and from their cells, or when the hand-held surveillance camera was turned off.

Ten of the 19 detainees we interviewed during our inspection visit alleged they had been subjected to verbal abuse by MDC staff, consisting of slurs and threats. According to detainees, the verbal abuse included taunts such as "Bin Laden Junior" or threats such as "you're going to die here," "you're never going to get out of here," and "you will be here for 20-25 years like the Cuban people." They said most of the verbal abuse occurred during intake and during movement to and from the detainees' cells.

Our inspection team interviewed 12 correctional officers about the detainees' allegations of physical abuse. All 12 officers denied witnessing or committing any acts of abuse. Further, they denied knowledge of any rumors about allegations of abuse. The correctional officers we interviewed also denied they verbally abused the detainees and denied making these specific comments to the detainees.

B. OIG Investigation of Abuse

On October 30, 2001, the OIG reviewed a newspaper article in which a September 11 detainee alleged he was physically abused when he arrived at the MDC on October 4, 2001. Based on the allegations in the article, the OIG's Investigations Division initiated an investigation into the matter. When we interviewed the detainee, he complained that MDC officers repeatedly slammed him against walls while twisting his arm behind his back. He also alleged officers dragged him by his handcuffed arms and frequently stepped on the chain between his ankle cuffs. The detainee stated his ankles and wrists were injured as a result of the officers' abuse. He also identified three other September 11 detainees who allegedly had been abused by MDC staff members.

We interviewed these three other September 11 detainees. They stated that when they arrived at the MDC, they were forcefully pulled out of the vehicle and slammed against walls. One detainee further alleged that his handcuffs were painfully tight around his wrists and that MDC officers repeatedly stepped on the chain between his ankle cuffs. Another detainee alleged officers dragged him by his handcuffs and twisted his wrist every time they moved him. All three detainees alleged that officers verbally abused them with racial slurs and threats like "you will feel pain" and "someone thinks you have something to do with the World Trade Center so don't expect to be treated well."

During our investigation of these complaints, we received similar allegations from other September 11 detainees. On February 11, 2002, four September 11 detainees held at the MDC (including one of the detainees we interviewed previously) told MDC officers that certain MDC officers were physically and verbally abusing them. Those complaints were provided to us. In interviews with our investigators, these detainees alleged that when they arrived at the MDC in September and October 2001, MDC officers forcefully pulled them from the car, slammed them into walls, dragged them by their arms, stepped on the chain between their ankle cuffs, verbally abused them, and twisted their arms, hands, wrists, and fingers. One of the detainees alleged that when he was being taken to the MDC's medical department following a 4-day hunger strike, an officer bent his finger back until it touched his wrist. Another detainee alleged that when he arrived at the MDC, officers repeatedly twisted his arm, which was in a cast, and finger, which was healing from a recent operation. He also alleged that when he was transferred to another cell in December 2001, officers slammed him into a wall and twisted his wrist. One detainee claimed his chin was cut open and he had to receive stitches because officers slammed him against a wall.

During our investigation, the OIG asked the detainees individually to identify the officers who had committed the abuse through photographic lineups. The detainees identified many of the same officers as the perpetrators, and the OIG focused its investigation on eight officers. The OIG interviewed seven of these officers. Six of them denied physically or verbally abusing any of the detainees or witnessing any other officer abuse the detainees. Five remembered at least one of the detainees and some of them remembered a few of the detainees. Two officers described two detainees as disruptive and uncooperative. One of the officers explained that the high-security procedures in place during the weeks following the September 11 attacks required four officers to physically control inmates during all escorts; face them toward the wall while waiting for doors, elevators, or the application and removal of leg restraints; and place them against the wall if they became aggressive during these escorts.

The seventh officer interviewed by the OIG told us that he witnessed officers "slam" inmates against walls and stated this was a common practice before the MDC began videotaping the detainees. He said he did not believe these actions were warranted. He said he told MDC officers to "ease up" and not to be so aggressive when escorting detainees. He also said he witnessed a supervising officer slam detainees against walls, but when he spoke with the officer about this practice the officer told him it was all part of being in jail and not to worry about it. The seventh officer signed a sworn affidavit to this effect. In a subsequent interview with the OIG, this officer recharacterized the action as "placing" the detainees against the wall, and said he did not want to use the word "slam." He denied that the officers acted in an abusive or inappropriate manner.

The OIG reviewed the detainees' medical records. The medical records do not indicate that most of the detainees received medical treatment for the injuries they asserted they received from officers. Two of the detainees' medical records indicate they were treated for injuries that they later claimed were caused by officers, but the medical records did not indicate that they alleged their injuries were caused by officers at the time they were treated.

One detainee's records do not mention the cause of the injury and the other detainee's records state the detainee said he was injured when he fell. In his interview with the OIG, the detainee alleged his chin was badly cut when detention officers slammed him against the wall. He said that nobody ever asked him how his injury occurred. The other five detainees did not seek treatment for their alleged injuries.

Based on the scarcity of medical records documenting injuries and the lack of evidence of serious injuries to most of the detainees, the U.S. Attorney's Office for the Eastern District of New York and the Civil Rights Division declined criminal prosecution in this case. All of the detainees, with the exception of one, now have been removed from the United States. Nevertheless, the OIG is continuing its investigation of these allegations as an administrative matter. Because this case is ongoing, we are not describing in detail all the evidence in the case about the detainees' allegations. However, we believe there is evidence supporting the detainees' claims of abuse, including the fact that similar—although not identical—allegations of abuse have been raised by other detainees, which we describe in the next section.

Source: www.justice.gov/oig/special/0306/chapter8.htm#V

5.9 Opinion of the U.S. Supreme Court in *Chavez v. Martinez*, 2003

The Chavez case, regarding domestic law enforcement but cited in at least one interrogation memo on terrorism, arose when the police interrogated a dying suspect (he survived in the end but was blinded and paralyzed), ignoring his pleas for treatment. The Court ruled that the victim's civil rights were not violated because the officers' conduct did not meet the "shocking to the conscience" standard. Justice John Paul Stevens dissented, and part of his dissent is excerpted here.

"I am dying, please"

Justice THOMAS announced the judgment of the Court and delivered an opinion.

This case involves a § 1983 suit arising out of petitioner Ben Chavez's allegedly coercive interrogation of respondent Oliverio Martinez. The United States Court of Appeals for the Ninth Circuit held that Chavez was not entitled to a defense of qualified immunity because he violated Martinez's clearly established constitutional rights. We conclude that Chavez did not deprive Martinez of a constitutional right.

On November 28, 1997, police officers Maria Pena and Andrew Salinas were near a vacant lot in a residential area of Oxnard, California, investigating suspected narcotics activity. While Pena and Salinas were questioning an individual, they heard a bicycle approaching on a darkened path that crossed the lot. They ordered the rider, respondent Martinez, to dismount, spread his legs, and place his hands behind his head. Martinez complied. Salinas then conducted a patdown frisk and discovered a knife in Martinez's waistband. An altercation ensued.

There is some dispute about what occurred during the altercation. The officers claim that Martinez drew Salinas' gun from its holster and pointed it at them; Martinez denies this. Both sides agree, however, that Salinas yelled, "He's got my gun!" App. to Pet. for Cert. 3a. Pena then drew her gun and shot Martinez several times, causing severe injuries that left Martinez permanently blinded and paralyzed from the waist down. The officers then placed Martinez under arrest.

Petitioner Chavez, a patrol supervisor, arrived on the scene minutes later with paramedics. Chavez accompanied Martinez to the hospital and then questioned Martinez there while he was receiving treatment from medical personnel. The interview lasted a total of about 10 minutes, over a 45-minute period, with Chavez leaving the emergency room for periods of time to permit medical personnel to attend to Martinez.

At first, most of Martinez's answers consisted of "I don't know," "I am dying," and "I am choking." App. 14, 17, 18. Later in the interview, Martinez admitted that he took the gun from the officer's holster and pointed it at the police. Id., at 16. He also admitted that he used heroin regularly. Id., at 18. At one point, Martinez said "I am not telling you anything until they treat me," yet Chavez continued the interview. Id., at 14. At no point during the interview was Martinez given Miranda warnings under *Miranda v. Arizona*. Martinez was never charged with a crime, and his answers were never used against him in any criminal prosecution. Nevertheless, Martinez filed suit under Rev Stat § 1979, 42 USC § 1983, maintaining that Chavez's actions violated his Fifth Amendment right not to be "compelled in any criminal case to be a witness against himself," as well as his Fourteenth Amendment substantive due process right to be free from coercive questioning. The District Court granted summary judgment to Martinez as to Chavez's qualified immunity defense on both the Fifth and Fourteenth Amendment claims. Chavez took an interlocutory appeal to the Ninth Circuit, which affirmed the District Court's denial of qualified immunity. . . .

The Ninth Circuit then concluded that the Fifth and Fourteenth Amendment rights asserted by Martinez were clearly established by federal law, explaining that a reasonable officer "would have known that persistent interrogation of the suspect despite repeated requests to stop violated the suspect's Fifth and Fourteenth Amendment right to be free from coercive interrogation." Id., at 858.

We are satisfied that Chavez's questioning did not violate Martinez's due process rights. Even assuming, arguendo, that the persistent questioning of Martinez somehow deprived him of a liberty interest, we cannot agree with Martinez's characterization of Chavez's behavior as "egregious" or "conscience shocking." As we noted in Lewis, the official conduct "most likely to rise to the conscience-shocking level," is the "conduct intended to injure in some way unjustifiable by any government interest." Here, there is no evidence that Chavez acted with a purpose to harm Martinez by intentionally interfering with his medical treatment. Medical personnel were able to treat Martinez throughout the interview, App. to Pet. for Cert. 4a, 18a, and Chavez ceased his questioning to allow tests and other procedures to be performed. Id., at 4a. Nor is there evidence that Chavez's conduct exacerbated Martinez's injuries or prolonged his stay in the hospital. Moreover, the need to investigate whether there had been police misconduct constituted a justifiable government interest given the risk that key evidence would have been lost if Martinez had died without the authorities ever hearing his side of the story.
. . .

Justice STEVENS, concurring in part and dissenting in part.

As a matter of fact, the interrogation of respondent was the functional equivalent of an attempt to obtain an involuntary confession from a prisoner by torturous methods. As a matter of law, that type of brutal police conduct constitutes an immediate deprivation of the prisoner's constitutionally protected interest in liberty. Because these propositions are so clear, the District Court and the Court of Appeals correctly held that petitioner is not entitled to qualified immunity.

What follows is an English translation of portions of the tape-recorded questioning in Spanish that occurred in the emergency room of the hospital when, as is evident from the text, both parties believed that respondent was about to die:

Chavez: What happened? Oliverio, tell me what happened.
O[liverio] M[artinez]: I don't know
Chavez: I don't know what happened (sic)?
O. M.: Ay! I am dying. Ay! What are you doing to me? No, . . . !
    (unintelligible scream).
Chavez: What happened, sir?

O. M.: My foot hurts . . .

Chavez: Oliverio. Sir, what happened?

O. M.: I am choking.

Chavez: Tell me what happened.

O. M.: I don't know.

Chavez: "I don't know."

O. M.: My leg hurts.

Chavez: I don't know what happened (sic)?

O. M.: It hurts. . .

Chavez: Hey, hey look.

O. M.: I am choking.

Chavez: Can you hear? look listen, I am Benjamin Chavez with the police here in Oxnard, look.

O. M.: I am dying, please.

Chavez: OK, yes, tell me what happened. If you are going to die, tell me what happened. Look I need to tell (sic) what happened.

O. M.: I don't know.

Chavez: You don't know, I don't know what happened (sic)? Did you talk to the police?

O. M.: Yes.

Chavez: What happened with the police?

O. M.: We fought.

Chavez: Huh? What happened with the police?

O. M.: The police shot me.

Chavez: Why?

O. M.: Because I was fighting with him.

Chavez: Oh, why were you fighting with the police?

O. M.: I am dying. . .

Chavez: OK, yes you are dying, but tell me why you are fighting, were you fighting with the police? . . .

O. M.: Doctor, please I want air, I am dying.

Chavez: OK, OK. I want to know if you pointed the gun [to yourself] (sic) at the police.

O. M.: Yes.

Chavez: Yes, and you pointed it [to yourself]? (sic) at the police pointed the gun? (sic) Huh?

O. M.: I am dying, please. . . .

Chavez: OK, listen, listen I want to know what happened, ok??

O. M.: I want them to treat me.

Chavez: OK, they are do it (sic), look when you took out the gun from the tape (sic) of the police. . .

O. M.: I am dying. . . .

Chavez: Ok, look, what I want to know if you took out (sic) the gun of the police?

O. M.: I am not telling you anything until they treat me.

Chavez: Look, tell me what happened, I want to know, look well don't you want the police know (sic) what happened with you?

O. M.: Uuuggghhh! my belly hurts. . . .

Chavez: Nothing, why did you run (sic) from the police?

O. M.: I don't want to say anything anymore.

Chavez: No?

O. M.: I want them to treat me, it hurts a lot, please.

Chavez: You don't want to tell (sic) what happened with you over there?

O. M.: I don't want to die, I don't want to die.

Chavez: Well if you are going to die tell me what happened, and right now you think you are going to die?

O. M.: No.

Chavez: No, do you think you are going to die?

O. M.: Aren't you going to treat me or what?

Chavez: Look, think you are going to die, (sic) that's all I want to know, if you think you are going to die? Right now, do you think you are going to die?

O. M.: My belly hurts, please treat me.

Chavez: Sir?

O. M.: If you treat me I tell you everything, if not, no.

Chavez: Sir, I want to know if you think you are going to die right now?

O. M.: I think so.

Chavez: You think (sic) so? Ok. Look, the doctors are going to help you with all they can do, Ok? That they can do.

O. M.: Get moving, I am dying, can't you see me? come on.

Chavez: Ah, huh, right now they are giving you medication. App. 8-22.

The sound recording of this interrogation, which has been lodged with the Court, vividly demonstrates that respondent was suffering severe pain and mental anguish throughout petitioner's persistent questioning.

The Due Process Clause of the 14th Amendment protects individuals against state action that either "'shocks the conscience,' or interferes with rights 'implicit in the concept of ordered liberty.'" In *Palko*, the majority of the Court refused to hold that every violation of the Fifth Amendment satisfied the second standard. In a host of other cases, however, the Court has held that unusually coercive police interrogation procedures do violate that standard. By its terms, the Fifth Amendment itself has no application to the States. It is, however, one source of the protections against state actions that deprive individuals of rights "implicit in the concept of ordered liberty" that the Fourteenth Amendment guarantees. Indeed, as I pointed out in my dissent in *Oregon v. Elstad,* it is the most specific provision in the Bill of Rights "that protects all citizens from the kind of custodial interrogation that was once employed by the Star Chamber, by 'the Germans of the 1930's and early 1940's,' and by some of our own police departments only a few decades ago." Whenever it occurs, as it did here, official interrogation of that character is a classic example of a violation of a constitutional right "implicit in the concept of ordered liberty."

Source: *Chavez v. Martinez,* 538 U.S. 760 (2003)

5.10 Fay-Jones Report, 2004

This 2004 report followed a military investigation of incidents at the Abu Ghraib prison. The report condemns the incidents, including those that constitute torture.

"The climate created at Abu Ghraib provided the opportunity for such abuse to occur"

5. Summary of Abuses at Abu Ghraib

a. (U) Several types of detainee abuse were identified in this investigation: physical and sexual abuse; improper use of military working dogs; humiliating and degrading treatments; and improper use of isolation.

(1) (U) Physical Abuse. Several Soldiers reported that they witnessed physical abuse of detainees. Some examples include slapping, kicking, twisting the hands of a detainee who was hand-cuffed to cause pain, throwing balls at restrained internees, placing gloved hand over the nose and mouth of an internee to restrict breathing, "poking" at an internee's injured leg, and forcing an internee to stand while handcuffed in such a way as to dislocate his shoulder. These actions are clearly in violation of applicable laws and regulations.

(2) (U) Use of Dogs. The use of military working dogs in a confinement facility can be effective and permissible under AR 190-12 as a means of controlling the internee population. When dogs are used to threaten and terrify detainees, there is a clear violation of applicable laws and regulations. One

such impermissible practice was an alleged contest between the two Army dog handlers to see who could make the internees urinate or defecate in the presence of the dogs.

An incident of clearly abusive use of the dogs occurred when a dog was allowed in the cell of two male juveniles and allowed to go "nuts." Both juveniles were screaming and crying with the youngest and smallest trying to hide behind the other juvenile. (Reference Annex B, Appendix 1,SOLDIER-17)

(3) (U) Humiliating and Degrading Treatments. Actions that are intended to degrade or humiliate a detainee are prohibited by GC IV, Army policy and the UCMJ. The following are examples of such behavior that occurred at Abu Ghraib, which violate applicable laws and regulations.

(4) (U) Nakedness. Numerous statements, as well as the ICRC report, discuss the seemingly common practice of keeping detainees in a state of undress. A number of statements indicate that clothing was taken away as a punishment for either not cooperating with interrogators or with MPs. In addition, male internees were naked in the presence of female Soldiers. Many of the Soldiers who witnessed the nakedness were told that this was an accepted practice. Under the circumstances, however, the nakedness was clearly degrading and humiliating.

(5) (U) Photographs. A multitude of photographs show detainees in various states of undress, often in degrading positions.

(6) (U) Simulated Sexual Positions. A number of Soldiers describe incidents where detainees were placed in simulated sexual positions with other internees. Many of these incidents were also photographed.

(7) (U) Improper Use of Isolation. There are some legitimate purposes for the segregation (or isolation) of detainees, specifically to prevent them from sharing interrogation tactics with other detainees or other sensitive information. Article 5 of Geneva Convention IV supports this position by stating that certain individuals can lose their rights of communication, but only when absolute military security requires. The use of isolation at Abu Ghraib was often done as punishment, either for a disciplinary infraction or for failure to cooperate with an interrogation.

These are improper uses of isolation and depending on the circumstances amounted to violation of applicable laws and regulations. Isolation could properly be a sanction for a disciplinary infraction if applied through the proper process set out in AR 190-8 and the Geneva Conventions.

(8) (U) Failure to Safeguard Detainees. The Geneva Conventions and Army Regulations require that detainees be "protected against all acts of violence and threats thereof and against insults and public curiosity." Geneva Convention IV, Article 27 and AR 190-8, paragraph 5-1(a)(2). The duty to protect

imposes an obligation on an individual who witnesses an abusive act to intervene and stop the abuse. Failure to do so may be a violation of applicable laws and regulations.

(9) (U) Failure to Report Detainee Abuse. The duty to report detainee abuse is closely tied to the duty to protect. The failure to report an abusive incident could result in additional abuse. Soldiers who witness these offenses have an obligation to report the violations under the provision of Article 92, UCMJ. Soldiers who are informed of such abuses also have a duty to report violations. Depending on their position and their assigned duties, the failure to report detainee abuse could support a charge of dereliction of duty, a violation of the UCMJ. Civilian contractors employed as interrogators and translators would also have a duty to report such offenses as they are also bound by the Geneva Conventions and are charged with protecting the internees.

(10) (U) Other traditional prison guard issues were far less clear. MPs are responsible for the clothing of detainees; however, MI interrogators started directing nakedness at Abu Ghraib as early as 16 September 2003 to humiliate and break down detainees. MPs would also sometimes discipline detainees by taking away clothing and putting detainees in cells naked. A severe shortage of clothing during the September, October, November 2003, time frame was frequently mentioned as the reason why people were naked. Removal of clothing and nakedness were being used to humiliate detainees at the same time there was a general level of confusion as to what was allowable in terms of MP disciplinary measures and MI interrogation rules, and what clothing was available. This contributed to an environment that would appear to condone depravity and degradation rather than the humane treatment of detainees. . . .

e. (U) The physical and sexual abuses of detainees at Abu Ghraib are by far the most serious. The abuses spanned from direct physical assault, such as delivering head blows rendering detainees unconscious, to sexual posing and forced participation in group masturbation. At the extremes were the death of a detainee in OGA custody, an alleged rape committed by a US translator and observed by a female Soldier, and the alleged sexual assault of an unknown female. They were perpetrated or witnessed by individuals or small groups. Such abuse can not be directly tied to a systemic US approach to torture or approved treatment of detainees. The MPs being investigated claim their actions came at the direction of MI. Although self-serving, these claims do have some basis in fact. The climate created at Abu Ghraib provided the opportunity for such abuse to occur and to continue undiscovered by higher authority for a long period of time. What started as undressing and humiliation, stress and physical training (PT), carried over into sexual and physical assaults by a small group of morally corrupt and unsupervised Soldiers and civilians. Twenty-four (24) serious incidents of physical and sexual abuse occurred from 20 September through 13 December 2003. The incidents identified in this investigation include some of the same abuses identified in the MG Taguba investigation; however, this investigation adds several previously unreported events. A direct comparison cannot be made of the abuses cited in the MG Taguba report and this one.

Source: www. news.bbc.co.uk/nol/shared/bsp/hi/pdfs/26_08_04_fayreport.pdf

---

5.11 Statement of Senator Charles Schumer (D-NY) before Senate Judiciary Subcommittee, 2004

In the course of questioning Attorney General John Ashcroft at a subcommittee hearing, Senator Schumer indicates that he would support the use of torture in certain circumstances, and he states a variation of the "ticking bomb" hypothetical as an instance where he (and, he says, most Americans) would approve its use.

"There are probably very few people in this room or in America who would say that torture should never, ever be used"

SCHUMER: Mr. Chairman, thank you.

And, Mr. Attorney General, I know this hasn't been an easy day for you. And we respect your being here. But in all due respect, I have to say sometimes you're your own worst enemy.

And I'd like to interject a note of balance here. There are times when we all get in high dudgeon. We ought to be reasonable about this. I think there are probably very few people in this room or in America who would say that torture should never, ever be used, particularly if thousands of lives are at stake.

Take the hypothetical: If we knew that there was a nuclear bomb hidden in an American city and we believed that some kind of torture, fairly severe maybe, would give us a chance of finding that bomb before it went off, my guess is most Americans and most senators, maybe all, would say, "Do what you have to do."

So it's easy to sit back in the armchair and say that torture can never be used. But when you're in the foxhole, it's a very different deal.

And I respect—I think we all respect the fact that the president's in the foxhole every day. So he can hardly be blamed for asking you or his White House counsel or the Department of Defense to figure out when it comes to torture, what the law allows and when the law allows it and what there is permission to do.

The problem is not in asking the question. The problem isn't with the issues being explored. The problem is there has to be very careful guidance, and it should be made public. And most people are reasonable and would understand that. If it doesn't, it has no legitimacy.

Source: www.washingtonpost.com/wp-dyn/articles/A25211-2004Jun8.html

5.12 Legal Memorandum by Daniel Levin, 2004

The "Levin memo" was issued late in 2004 to replace the "Bybee memo" (document 5.2). Levin notes that the Bybee memo's reference to "organ failure" as the standard for severe pain constituting torture is no longer the administration's legal position.

"We decided to withdraw the August 2002 Memorandum"

Torture is abhorrent both to American law and values and to international norms. This universal repudiation of torture is reflected in our criminal law, for example, 18 U.S.C. §§ 2340-2340A; international agreements, exemplified by the United Nations Convention against Torture (the "CAT"); customary international law; centuries of Anglo-American law; and the longstanding policy of the United States, repeatedly and recently reaffirmed by the President.

This Office interpreted the federal criminal prohibition against torture—codified at 18 U.S.C. §§ 2340–2340A—in *Standards of Conduct for Interrogation under 18 U.S.C. §§ 2340–2340A* (Aug. 1, 2002) ("August 2002 Memorandum"). The August 2002 Memorandum also addressed a number of issues beyond interpretation of those statutory provisions, including the President's Commander-in-Chief power, and various defenses that might be asserted to avoid potential liability under sections 2340–2340A. *See id.* at 31–46.

Questions have since been raised, both by this Office and by others, about the appropriateness and relevance of the non-statutory discussion in the August 2002 Memorandum, and also about various aspects of the statutory analysis, in particular the statement that "severe" pain under the statute was limited to pain "equivalent in intensity to the pain accompanying serious physical injury, such as organ failure, impairment of bodily function, or even death." *Id.* at 1. We decided to withdraw the August 2002 Memorandum, a decision you announced in June 2004. At that time, you directed this Office to prepare a replacement memorandum. Because of the importance of—and public interest in—these issues, you asked that this memorandum be prepared in a form that could be released to the public so that interested parties could understand our analysis of the statute.

This memorandum supersedes the August 2002 Memorandum in its entirety. Because the discussion in that memorandum concerning the President's Commander-in-Chief power and the potential defenses to liability was—and remains—unnecessary, it has been eliminated from the analysis that follows. Consideration of the bounds of any such authority would be inconsistent with the President's unequivocal directive that United States personnel not engage in torture.

We have also modified in some important respects our analysis of the legal standards applicable under 18 U.S.C. §§ 2340-2340A. For example, we disagree with statements in the August 2002 Memorandum limiting "severe" pain under the statute to "excruciating and agonizing" pain, *id.* at 19, or to pain "equivalent in intensity to the pain accompanying serious physical injury, such as organ failure, impairment of bodily function, or even death," *id.* at 1. There are additional areas where we disagree with or modify the analysis in the August 2002 Memorandum, as identified in the discussion below.

Source: www.justice.gov/olc/18usc23402340a2.htm

5.13 OLC Memorandum to the CIA (no. 2), 2005

The CIA has requested an opinion on the legality of the interrogation tactics it is using. The author of the memo, Stephen Bradbury, was appointed to the DOJ's Office of Legal Counsel in 2005. Part of Bradbury's response is a recitation of what he understands to be the steps followed in a "prototypical interrogation."

"Stripped of his clothes, shackled, and hooded, with the walling collar over his head"

A Prototypical Interrogation

In a "prototypical interrogation, the detainee begins his first interrogation session stripped of his clothes, shackled, and hooded, with the walling collar over his head and around his neck." *Background Paper* at 9–10. The interrogators remove the hood and explain that the detainee can improve his situation by cooperating, and may say that the interrogators "will do what it takes to get important information." *Id.* As soon as the detainee does anything inconsistent with the interrogator's instructions, the interrogators use an insult slap or abdominal slap. They employ walling if it becomes clear that the detainee is not cooperating in the interrogation. This sequence "may continue for several more iterations as the interrogators continue to measure the [detainee's] resistance posture and apply a negative consequence to [his] resistance efforts." *Id.* The interrogators and security officers then out the detainee into position for standing sleep deprivation, begin dietary manipulation through a liquid diet, and keep the detainee nude (except for a diaper). *See Id.* at 10-11. The first interrogation session, which could have lasted from thirty minutes to several hours, would then be at an end. *See Id.* at 11.

If the interrogation team determines there is a need to continue, and if the medical and psychological personnel advise that there are no contraindications, a second session may begin, *See Id.* at 12. The interval between sessions could be as short as an hour or as long as twenty four hours. *See Id.* at 11. At the start of the second session, the detainee is released from the position for standing sleep deprivation, is hooded, and is positioned against the walling wall, with the walling collar over his head and around his neck. *See Id.* Even before removing the hood, the interrogator, the interrogators use the attention grasp to startle the detainee. The interrogators take off the hood and begin questioning. If the detainee does not give appropriate answers to the first questions, the interrogators use an insult slap or abdominal slap. *See Id.* They employ walling if they determine that the detainee "is intent on maintaining his resistance posture." *Id.* at 13. This sequence "may continue for multiple iterations as the interrogators continue to measure the [detainee's] resistance posture." *Id.* Then interrogators then increase the pressure on the detainee by using a hose to douse the detainee with water for several minutes. They stop and start the dousing as they continue the interrogation. *See Id.* They then end the session by placing the detainee into the same circumstances as at the end of the first session: the detainee is in the standing position for sleep deprivation, is nude (except for a diaper), and is subjected to dietary manipulation. Once again, the session could have lasted from thirty minutes to several hours. *See Id.*

Again, if the interrogation team determines there is a need to continue, and if the medical and psychological personnel find no contraindications, a third session may follow. The session begins with the detainee positioned as at the beginning of the second. *See Id.* at 14. If the detainee continues to resist, the interrogators continue to use walling and water dousing. The corrective techniques—the insult slap, the abdominal slap, the facial hold, the attention grasp—"may be used several times during this sessions based on the responses and actions of the [detainee]." *Id.* The interrogators integrate stress positions and wall standing into the session. Furthermore, "[i]ntense questioning and walling would be repeated multiple times." *Id.* Interrogators "use one technique to support another." *Id.* For example, they threaten the use of walling unless the detainee holds a stress position, thus inducing the detainee to remain in the position longer than he otherwise would. At the end of the session, the interrogators and security personnel place the detainee into the same circumstances as at the end of the first two sessions, with the detainee subject to sleep deprivation, nudity, and dietary manipulation. *Id.*

In later sessions, the interrogators use those techniques that are proving most effective and drop the others. Sleep deprivation "may continue to the 70 to 120 hour range, or possibly beyond for the hardest resisters, but in no case exceed the 180-hour time limit." *Id.* at 15. If the medical or psychological personnel find contraindications, sleep deprivation will end earlier. *See Id.* at 15–16. While continuing the use of deprivation, nudity and dietary manipulation, the interrogators may add cramped confinement. As the detainee begins to cooperate "begin gradually to decrease the use of interrogation techniques." *Id.* at 16. They may permit the detainee to sit, supply clothes, and supply more appetizing food. See *Id.*

The entire process in this "prototypical interrogation may last thirty days. If additional time is required, and a new approval is obtained from headquarters, interrogation may go longer than thirty days. Nevertheless, "[o]n average, the actual use of interrogation techniques covers a period of three to seven days, but can vary upwards of fifteen days, based on the resilience of the [detainee]. *Id.* As in *Techniques,* our advice here is limited to an interrogation process lasting no more than thirty days. *See Techniques* at 5.
Use of the Waterboard in Combination with other Techniques.

We understand that for a small number of detainees in very limited circumstances, the CIS may wish to use the waterboard technique. You have previously explained that the waterboard technique would be used only if: (1) the CIA has credible intelligence that a terrorist attack is imminent; (2) there are "substantial and credible indicators that the subject has actionable intelligence that can prevent, disrupt or delay this attack; and (3) other interrogation methods have failed or are unlikely to yield actionable intelligence in time to prevent the attack.

Source: http://documents.nytimes.com/justice-department-memos-on-interrogation-techniques#p=85

5.14 OLC Memorandum to CIA (no. 3), 2005

This is another memo requested by the CIA in which a legal opinion as to the legality of coercive interrogation techniques is provided.

"Extended sleep deprivation and use of the waterboard present more substantial questions"

In sum, based on the information you have provided and the limitations, procedures and safeguards that would be in place, we conclude that—although extended sleep deprivation and use of the waterboard present more substantial questions in certain respects under the statute and the use of the waterboard raises the most substantial issue—none of these specific techniques, considered individually, would violate the prohibitions in Sections 2340 and 2340A. The universal rejection of torture and the president's unequivocal directive that the United States not engage in torture warrant great care in analyzing whether particular interrogation techniques are consistent with the requirements of 2340-2340A, and we have attempted to employ such care throughout our analysis. We emphasize that these are issues about which reasonable persons may disagree.

Source: http://documents.nytimes.com/justice-department-memos-on-interrogation
-techniques#p=85

5.15 OLC Memorandum to CIA (no. 4), 2005

In this memo, Bradbury determines that the interrogation techniques being used by the CIA, including "walling" and the waterboarding, do not violate the Convention against Torture. The memo details how each technique is performed.

"The interrogator pulls the detainee towards him and then slams the detainee against the false wall"

You have asked us to consider whether certain "enhanced interrogation techniques" employed by the Central Intelligence Agency ("CIA") in the interrogation of high value al Qaeda detainees are consistent with United States obligations under Article 16 of the United Nations Convention against Torture and other Cruel, Inhuman or Degrading Treatment or Punishment. . . . We conclude that use of the techniques, subject to the CIA's careful screening criteria and limitations and its medical safeguards, is consistent with United States obligations under Article 16. . . .

Consistent with its heightened standard for use of the waterboard, the CIA has used this technique in the interrogation of only three detainees to date (KSM, Zubaydah and "Abd al-Rashim al-Nashiri") and has not used it since the March 2003 interrogation of KSM. . . .

Coercive techniques "place the detainee in more physical and psychological stress" than the other techniques and are generally "considered to be more effective tools in persuading a resistant [detainee] to participate with CIA interrogators. *Background Paper at 7.* These techniques are typically not used simultaneously. The Background Paper lists walling, water dousing, stress positions, wall standing, and cramped confinement in this category. We will also treat the waterboard as a coercive tactic.

Walling is performed by placing the detainee against what seems to be a normal wall but is in fact a flexible false wall. *See Techniques at 8.* The interrogator pulls the detainee towards him and then slams the detainee against the false wall. The false wall is designed, and a C-collar or similar device is used, to help avoid whiplash or similar injury. *See Id.* The technique is designed to create a loud sound and to shock the detainee without causing significant pain. The CIA regards walling as "one of the most effective interrogation techniques because it wears down the [detainee] physically, heightens uncertainty in the detainee about what the interrogator may do to him, and creates a sense of dread when the [detainee] knows he is about to be walled again." *Background Paper at 7.* A detainee "may be walled one time (one impact with the wall) to make a point or twenty or thirty times consecutively when the interrogator requires a more significant response to a question," and "will be walled multiple times during a session designed to be intense." *Id.* At no time, however, is the technique employed in such a way that could cause severe physical pain. *See Techniques* at 32 n.38.

In the water dousing technique, potable cold water is poured on the detainee either from a container or a hose without a nozzle. Ambient air temperatures are kept above 64 degrees Fahrenheit. The maximum permissible duration of water exposure depends on the water temperature, which may be no lower than 41 degrees Fahrenheit, and is usually no lower than 50 degrees Fahrenheit. *See Id.* at 10. Maximum exposure durations have been "set at 2/3 the time at which, based on extensive medical literature and experience, hypothermia could be expected to develop in healthy individuals who are submerged in water of the same temperature" in order to provide adequate safety margins against hypothermia. *Id.* This technique can easily be used in combination with other techniques and "is intended to weaken the detainee's resistance and persuade him to cooperate with interrogators." *Id.* at 9.

Stress positions and wall standing are used to induce muscle fatigue and the attendant discomfort. *See Techniques* at 9 (describing techniques); *See also PREAL Manual* at 20 (explaining that stress positions are sued "to create a distracting pressure" and "to humiliate or insult"). The use of these techniques is "usually self-limiting in that temporary muscle fatigue usually leads to the [detainee's] being unable to maintain this stress position after a period of time." *Background Paper* at 8. We understand that these techniques are used only to induce temporary muscle fatigue; neither of these techniques is designed or expected to cause severe physical pain. *See Techniques* at 33-34.

Cramped confinement involves placing the detainee in an uncomfortable small container. Such confinement may last up to eight hours in a relatively large container, or up to two hours in a smaller container. *See Background Paper* at 8; *Techniques* at 9. The technique "accelerate(s) the physical and psychological stress of captivity." *PRWAL Manual* at 22. In OMS's view, however, cramped confinement "ha(s) not proved particularly effective" because it provides "a safe haven offering respite for interrogation." *OMS Guidelines* at 16.

The waterboard is generally considered to be "the most traumatic of the enhanced interrogation techniques, *Id.* at 17, a conclusion with which we have readily agreed, *See Techniques* at 41. In this technique, the detainee is placed face up on a gurney with his head inclined downward. A cloth is placed over his face on which cold water is then poured for periods of, at most, forty seconds. This creates a barrier through which it is either difficult or impossible to breathe. The techniques "thereby induce(s) a sensation of drowning." *Id.* at 13. The water board may be authorized for, at most, one thirty-day period, during which the technique can actually be applied on no more than five days. *See Id.* at 14.

Source: http://documents.nytimes.com/justice-department-memos-on-interrogation -techniques#p=85

5.16 Congressional Testimony of FBI Agent Ali Soufan, 2009

FBI agent Ali Soufan stated his opposition to coercive interrogation, expressing his opposition in both practical and moral terms. Soufan testified that he had interrogated a number of terror suspects in the course of his work.

"I protested to my superiors in the FBI and refused to be a part of what was happening"

Mr. Chairman, Committee members, thank you for inviting me to appear before you today. I know that each one of you cares deeply about our nation's security. It was always a comfort to me during the most dangerous of situations that I faced, from going undercover as an al Qaeda operative, to unraveling terrorist cells, to tracking down the killers of the 17 U.S. sailors murdered in the USS *Cole* bombing, that those of us on the frontline had your support and the backing of the American people. So I thank you.

From my experience—and I speak as someone who has personally interrogated many terrorists and elicited important actionable intelligence—I strongly believe that it is a mistake to use what has become known as the "enhanced interrogation techniques," a position shared by many professional operatives, including the CIA officers who were present at the initial phases of the Abu Zubaydah interrogation.

These techniques, from an operational perspective, are ineffective, slow and unreliable, and as a result harmful to our efforts to defeat al Qaeda. (This is aside from the important additional considerations that they are un-American and harmful to our reputation and cause.)

My interest in speaking about this issue is not to advocate the prosecution of anyone. People were given misinformation, half-truths, and false claims of successes; and reluctant intelligence officers were given instructions and assurances from higher authorities. Examining a past we cannot change is only worthwhile when it helps guide us towards claiming a better future that is yet within our reach.

And my focus is on the future. I wish to do my part to ensure that we never again use these harmful, slow, ineffective, and unreliable techniques instead of the tried, tested, and successful ones—the ones that are also in sync with our values and moral character. Only by doing this will we defeat the terrorists as effectively and quickly as possible.

Most of my professional career has been spent investigating, studying, and interrogating terrorists. I have had the privilege of working alongside, and learning from, some of the most dedicated and talented men and women our nation has—individuals from the FBI, and other law enforcement, military, and intelligence agencies.

In my capacity as a FBI Agent, I investigated and supervised highly sensitive and complex international terrorism cases, including the East Africa bombings, the USS *Cole* bombing, and the events surrounding the attacks of

9/11. I also coordinated both domestic and international counter-terrorism operations on the Joint Terrorist Task Force, FBI New York Office.

I personally interrogated many terrorists we have in our custody and elsewhere, and gained confessions, identified terror operatives, their funding, details of potential plots, and information on how al Qaeda operates, along with other actionable intelligence. Because of these successes, I was the government's main witness in both of the trials we have had so far in Guantanamo Bay—the trial of Salim Ahmed Hamdan, a driver and bodyguard for Osama Bin Laden, and Ali Hamza Al Bahlul, Bin Laden's propagandist. In addition I am currently helping the prosecution prepare for upcoming trials of other detainees held in Guantanamo Bay.

There are many examples of successful interrogations of terrorists that have taken place before and after 9/11. Many of them are classified, but one that is already public and mirrors the other cases, is the interrogation of al Qaeda terrorist Nasser Ahmad Nasser al-Bahri, known as Abu Jandal. In the immediate aftermath of 9/11, together with my partner Special Agent Robert McFadden, a first-class intelligence operative from the Naval Criminal Investigative Service (NCIS), (which, from my experience, is one of the classiest agencies I encountered in the intelligence community), I interrogated Abu Jandal.

Through our interrogation, which was done completely by the book (including advising him of his rights), we obtained a treasure trove of highly significant actionable intelligence. For example, Abu Jandal gave us extensive information on Osama Bin Laden's terror network, structure, leadership, membership, security details, facilities, family, communication methods, travels, training, ammunitions, and weaponry, including a breakdown of what machine guns, rifles, rocket launchers, and anti-tank missiles they used. He also provided explicit details of the 9/11 plot operatives, and identified many terrorists who we later successfully apprehended.

The information was important for the preparation of the war in Afghanistan in 2001. It also provided an important background to the 9/11 Commission report; it provided a foundation for the trials so far held in Guantanamo Bay; and it also has been invaluable in helping to capture and identify top al Qaeda operatives and thus disrupt plots.

The approach used in these successful interrogations can be called the Informed Interrogation Approach. Until the introduction of the "enhanced" technique, it was the sole approach used by our military, intelligence, and law enforcement community.

It is an approach rooted in experiences and lessons learned during World

War II and from our Counter-insurgency experience in Vietnam—experiences and lessons that generated the Army Field Manual. This was then refined over the decades to include how to interrogate terrorism suspects specifically, as experience was gained from interrogations following the first World Trade Center bombing, the East Africa Embassy bombings, and the USS *Cole* bombing. To sum up, it is an approach derived from the cumulative experiences, wisdom, and successes of the most effective operational people our country has produced.

Before I joined the Bureau, for example, traditional investigative strategies along with intelligence derived from human sources successfully thwarted the 1993 New York City Landmark Bomb Plot (TERRSTOP), a plot by the Blind Sheikh Omar Abdel-Rahman, to attack the UN Headquarters, the FBI's New York office, and tunnels and bridges across New York City—as a follow-up to the 1993 World Trade Center bombings. That remains to this day the largest thwarted attack on our homeland. I had the privilege of working with, and learning from, those who conducted this successful operation.

The Informed Interrogation Approach is based on leveraging our knowledge of the detainee's culture and mindset, together with using information we already know about him. The interrogator knows that there are three primary points of influence on the detainee:

First, there is the fear that the detainee feels as a result of his capture and isolation from his support base. People crave human contact, and this is especially true in some cultures more than others. The interrogator turns this knowledge into an advantage by becoming the one person the detainee can talk to and who listens to what he has to say, and uses this to encourage the detainee to open up.

In addition, acting in a non-threatening way isn't how the detainee is trained to expect a U.S. interrogator to act. This adds to the detainee's confusion and makes him more likely to cooperate.

Second, and connected, there is the need the detainee feels to sustain a position of respect and value to the interrogator. As the interrogator is the one person speaking to and listening to the detainee, a relationship is built—and the detainee doesn't want to jeopardize it. The interrogator capitalizes on this and compels the detainee to give up more information.

And third, there is the impression the detainee has of the evidence against him. The interrogator has to do his or her homework and become an expert in every detail known to the intelligence community about the detainee. The interrogator then uses that knowledge to impress upon the detainee that everything about him is known and that any lie will be easily caught.

For example, in my first interrogation of the terrorist Abu Zubaydah, who had strong links to al Qaeda's leaders and who knew the details of the 9/11 plot before it happened, I asked him his name. He replied with his alias. I then asked him, "how about if I call you Hani?" That was the name his mother nicknamed him as a child. He looked at me in shock, said "ok," and we started talking.

The Army Field Manual is not about being nice or soft. It is a knowledge-based approach. It is about outwitting the detainee by using a combination of interpersonal, cognitive, and emotional strategies to get the information needed. If done correctly it's an approach that works quickly and effectively because it outwits the detainee using a method that he is not trained, or able, to resist.

This Informed Interrogation Approach is in sharp contrast with the harsh interrogation approach introduced by outside contractors and forced upon CIA officials to use. The harsh technique method doesn't use the knowledge we have of the detainee's history, mindset, vulnerabilities, or culture, and instead tries to subjugate the detainee into submission through humiliation and cruelty. The approach applies a force continuum, each time using harsher and harsher techniques until the detainee submits.

The idea behind the technique is to force the detainee to see the interrogator as the master who controls his pain. It is an exercise in trying to gain compliance rather than eliciting cooperation. A theoretical application of this technique is a situation where the detainee is stripped naked and told: "Tell us what you know."

If the detainee doesn't immediately respond by giving information, for example he asks: "what do you want to know?" the interviewer will reply: "you know," and walk out of the interrogation room. Then the next step on the force continuum is introduced, for example sleep deprivation, and the process will continue until the detainee's will is broken and he automatically gives up all information he is presumed to know.

There are many problems with this technique.

A major problem is that it is ineffective. Al Qaeda terrorists are trained to resist torture. As shocking as these techniques are to us, the al Qaeda training prepares them for much worse—the torture they would expect to receive if caught by dictatorships for example. This is why, as we see from the recently released Department of Justice memos on interrogation, the contractors had to keep getting authorization to use harsher and harsher methods, until they reached waterboarding and then there was nothing they could do but use that technique again and again. Abu Zubaydah had to be waterboarded 83 times and Khalid Shaikh Mohammed 183 times. In a democracy there is a glass ceiling of harsh techniques the interrogator cannot breach, and a detainee can eventually call the interrogator's bluff.

In addition the harsh techniques only serve to reinforce what the detainee has been prepared to expect if captured. This gives him a greater sense of control and predictability about his experience, and strengthens his will to resist.

A second major problem with this technique is that evidence gained from it is unreliable. There is no way to know whether the detainee is being truthful, or just speaking to either mitigate his discomfort or to deliberately provide false information. As the interrogator isn't an expert on the detainee or the subject matter, nor has he spent time going over the details of the case, the interrogator cannot easily know if the detainee is telling the truth. This unfortunately has happened and we have had problems ranging from agents chasing false leads to the disastrous case of Ibn Sheikh al-Libby who gave false information on Iraq, al Qaeda, and WMD.

A third major problem with this technique is that it is slow. It takes place over a long period of time, for example preventing the detainee from sleeping for 180 hours as the memos detail, or waterboarding 183 times in the case of KSM. When we have an alleged "ticking timebomb" scenario and need to get information quickly, we can't afford to wait that long.

A fourth problem with this technique is that it ignores the end game. In our country we have due process, which requires evidence to be collected in a certain way. The CIA, because of the sensitivity of its operations, by necessity, operates secretly. These two factors mean that by putting the CIA in charge of interrogations, either secrecy is sacrificed for justice and the CIA's operations are hampered, or justice is not served. Neither is a desirable outcome.

Another disastrous consequence of the use of the harsh techniques was that it reintroduced the "Chinese Wall" between the CIA and FBI—similar to the wall that prevented us from working together to stop 9/11. In addition, the FBI and the CIA officers on the ground during the Abu Zubaydah interrogation were working together closely and effectively, until the contractors' interferences. Because we in the FBI would not be a part of the harsh techniques, the agents who knew the most about the terrorists could have no part in the investigation. An FBI colleague of mine, for example, who had tracked KSM and knew more about him than anyone in the government, was not allowed to speak to him.

Furthermore, the CIA specializes in collecting, analyzing, and interpreting intelligence. The FBI, on the other hand, has a trained investigative branch. Until that point, we were complimenting each other's expertise, until the imposition of the "enhanced methods." As a result people ended doing what they were not trained to do.

It is also important to realize that those behind this technique are outside contractors with no expertise in intelligence operations, investigations, terrorism, or al Qaeda. Nor did the contractors have any experience in the art of interview and interrogation. One of the contractors told me this at the time, and this lack of experience has also now been recently reported on by sources familiar with their backgrounds.

The case of the terrorist Abu Zubaydah is a good example of where the success of the Informed Interrogation Approach can be contrasted with the failure of the harsh technique approach. I have to restrict my remarks to what has been unclassified. (I will note that there is documented evidence supporting everything I will tell you today.)

Immediately after Abu Zubaydah was captured, a fellow FBI agent and I were flown to meet him at an undisclosed location. We were both very familiar with Abu Zubaydah and have successfully interrogated al-Qaeda terrorists. We started interrogating him, supported by CIA officials who were stationed at the location, and within the first hour of the interrogation, using the Informed Interrogation Approach, we gained important actionable intelligence. The information was so important that, as I later learned from open sources, it went to CIA Director George Tenet who was so impressed that he initially ordered us to be congratulated. That was apparently quickly withdrawn as soon as Mr. Tenet was told that it was FBI agents, who were responsible. He then immediately ordered a CIA CTC interrogation team to leave DC and head to the location to take over from us.

During his capture Abu Zubaydah had been injured. After seeing the extent of his injuries, the CIA medical team supporting us decided they were not equipped to treat him and we had to take him to a hospital or he would die. At the hospital, we continued our questioning as much as possible, while taking into account his medical condition and the need to know all information he might have on existing threats.

We were once again very successful and elicited information regarding the role of KSM as the mastermind of the 9/11 attacks, and lots of other information that remains classified. (It is important to remember that before this we had no idea of KSM's role in 9/11 or his importance in the al Qaeda leadership structure.) All this happened before the CTC team arrived.

A few days after we started questioning Abu Zubaydah, the CTC interrogation team finally arrived from DC with a contractor who was instructing them on how they should conduct the interrogations, and we were removed. Immediately, on the instructions of the contractor, harsh techniques were introduced, starting with nudity. (The harsher techniques mentioned in the memos were not introduced or even discussed at this point.)

The new techniques did not produce results as Abu Zubaydah shut down and stopped talking. At that time nudity and low-level sleep deprivation (between 24 and 48 hours) was being used. After a few days of getting no information, and after repeated inquiries from DC asking why all of sudden no information was being transmitted (when before there had been a steady stream), we again were given control of the interrogation.

We then returned to using the Informed Interrogation Approach. Within a few hours, Abu Zubaydah again started talking and gave us important actionable intelligence.

This included the details of Jose Padilla, the so-called "dirty bomber." To remind you of how important this information was viewed at the time, the then-Attorney General, John Ashcroft, held a press conference from Moscow to discuss the news. Other important actionable intelligence was also gained that remains classified.

After a few days, the contractor attempted to once again try his untested theory and he started to re-implementing the harsh techniques. He moved this time further along the force continuum, introducing loud noise and then temperature manipulation.

Throughout this time, my fellow FBI agent and I, along with a top CIA interrogator who was working with us, protested, but we were overruled. I should also note that another colleague, an operational psychologist for the CIA, had left the location because he objected to what was being done.

Again, however, the technique wasn't working and Abu Zubaydah wasn't revealing any information, so we were once again brought back in to interrogate him. We found it harder to reengage him this time, because of how the techniques had affected him, but eventually, we succeeded, and he reengaged again.

Once again the contractor insisted on stepping up the notches of his experiment, and this time he requested the authorization to place Abu Zubaydah in a confinement box, as the next stage in the force continuum. While everything I saw to this point were nowhere near the severity later listed in the memos, the evolution of the contractor's theory, along with what I had seen till then, struck me as "borderline torture."

As the Department of Justice IG report released last year states, I protested to my superiors in the FBI and refused to be a part of what was happening. The Director of the FBI, Robert Mueller, a man I deeply respect, agreed passing the message that "we don't do that," and I was pulled out.

As you can see from this timeline, many of the claims made in the memos about the success of the enhanced techniques are inaccurate. For example, it is untrue to claim Abu Zubaydah wasn't cooperating before August 1, 2002.

The truth is that we got actionable intelligence from him in the first hour of interrogating him.

In addition, simply by putting together dates cited in the memos with claims made, falsehoods are obvious. For example, it has been claimed that waterboarding got Abu Zubaydah to give up information leading to the capture of Jose Padilla. But that doesn't add up: Waterboarding wasn't approved until 1 August 2002 (verbally it was authorized around mid July 2002), and Padilla was arrested in May 2002.

The same goes for KSM's involvement in 9/11: That was discovered in April 2002, while waterboarding was not introduced until almost three months later. It speaks volumes that the quoted instances of harsh interrogation methods being a success are false.

Nor can it be said that the harsh techniques were effective, which is why we had to be called back in repeatedly. As we know from the memos, the techniques that were apparently introduced after I left did not appear to work either, which is why the memos granted authorization for harsher techniques. That continued for several months right till waterboarding was introduced, which had to be used 83 times—an indication that Abu Zubaydah had called the interrogator's bluff knowing the glass ceiling that existed.

Authoritative CIA, FBI, and military sources have also questioned the claims made by the advocates of the techniques. For example, in one of the recently released Justice Department memos, the author, Stephen Bradbury, acknowledged a (still classified) internal CIA Inspector General report that had found it "difficult to determine conclusively whether interrogations have provided information critical to interdicting specific imminent attacks."

In summary, the Informed Interrogation Approach outlined in the Army Field Manual is the most effective, reliable, and speedy approach we have for interrogating terrorists. It is legal and has worked time and again.

It was a mistake to abandon it in favor of harsh interrogation methods that are harmful, shameful, slower, unreliable, ineffective, and play directly into the enemy's handbook. It was a mistake to abandon an approach that was working and naively replace it with an untested method. It was a mistake to abandon an approach that is based on the cumulative wisdom and successful tradition of our military, intelligence, and law enforcement community, in favor of techniques advocated by contractors with no relevant experience.

The mistake was so costly precisely because the situation was, and remains, too risky to allow someone to experiment with amateurish, Hollywood style interrogation methods that in reality taints sources, risks outcomes, ignores the end game, and diminishes our moral high ground in a battle that is impossible to win without first capturing the hearts and minds around the world. It was one of the worst and most harmful decisions made in our efforts against al Qaeda.

For the last seven years, it was not easy objecting to these methods when they had powerful backers. I stood up then for the same reason I'm willing to take on critics now, because I took an oath swearing to protect this great nation. I could not stand by quietly while our country's safety was endangered and our moral standing damaged.

I know you are motivated by the same considerations, and I hope you help ensure that these grave mistakes are never made again.

Thank You.

Source: http://judiciary.senate.gov/hearings/testimony.cfm?id=3842&wit_id=7906

5.17 Detainee Treatment Act, 2005

The Detainee Treatment Act prohibits torture and cruel, inhuman, or degrading treatment (CIDT) irrespective of location. It also establishes the Army Field Manual (documents 5.18 and 5.19) as the standard for interrogations. However, the law also contains a provision that protects U.S. personnel from suit in interrogation-related cases by providing a statutory defense in such cases. One aspect of the defense is that reliance on advice of counsel tends to protect U.S. officials.

"It shall be a defense that such officer, employee, member of the Armed Forces, or other agent did not know that the practices were unlawful"

SEC. 1002. UNIFORM STANDARDS FOR THE INTERROGATION OF PERSONS UNDER THE DETENTION OF THE DEPARTMENT OF DEFENSE.

(a) In General—No person in the custody or under the effective control of the Department of Defense or under detention in a Department of Defense facility shall be subject to any treatment or technique of interrogation not authorized by and listed in the United States Army Field Manual on Intelligence Interrogation.

(b) Applicability—Subsection (a) shall not apply with respect to any person in the custody or under the effective control of the Department of Defense pursuant to a criminal law or immigration law of the United States.

(c) Construction—Nothing in this section shall be construed to affect the rights under the United States Constitution of any person in the custody or under the physical jurisdiction of the United States.

THE WAR ON TERROR · 227

SEC. 1003. PROHIBITION ON CRUEL, INHUMAN, OR DEGRADING TREAT-
MENT OR PUNISHMENT OF PERSONS UNDER CUSTODY OR CONTROL OF
THE UNITED STATES GOVERNMENT.

(a) In General—No individual in the custody or under the physical control of the United States Government, regardless of nationality or physical location, shall be subject to cruel, inhuman, or degrading treatment or
punishment.

(b) Construction—Nothing in this section shall be construed to impose
any geographical limitation on the applicability of the prohibition against
cruel, inhuman, or degrading treatment or punishment under this section.

(c) Limitation on Supersedure—The provisions of this section shall not be
superseded, except by a provision of law enacted after the date of the enactment of this Act which specifically repeals, modifies, or supersedes the provisions of this section.

(d) Cruel, Inhuman, or Degrading Treatment or Punishment Defined—In
this section, the term "cruel, inhuman, or degrading treatment or punishment" means the cruel, unusual, and inhumane treatment or punishment
prohibited by the Fifth, Eighth, and Fourteenth Amendments to the Constitution of the United States, as defined in the United States Reservations,
Declarations and Understandings to the United Nations Convention Against
Torture and Other Forms of Cruel, Inhuman or Degrading Treatment or Punishment done at New York, December 10, 1984.

SEC. 1004. PROTECTION OF UNITED STATES GOVERNMENT PERSONNEL
ENGAGED IN AUTHORIZED INTERROGATIONS.

(a) Protection of United States Government Personnel—In any civil action
or criminal prosecution against an officer, employee, member of the Armed
Forces, or other agent of the United States Government who is a United States
person, arising out of the officer, employee, member of the Armed Forces,
or other agent's engaging in specific operational practices, that involve detention and interrogation of aliens who the President or his designees have
determined are believed to be engaged in or associated with international
terrorist activity that poses a serious, continuing threat to the United States,
its interests, or its allies, and that were officially authorized and determined
to be lawful at the time that they were conducted, it shall be a defense that
such officer, employee, member of the Armed Forces, or other agent did not
know that the practices were unlawful and a person of ordinary sense and
understanding would not know the practices were unlawful. Good faith reliance on advice of counsel should be an important factor, among others, to
consider in assessing whether a person of ordinary sense and understanding

would have known the practices to be unlawful. Nothing in this section shall be construed to limit or extinguish any defense or protection otherwise available to any person or entity from suit, civil or criminal liability, or damages, or to provide immunity from prosecution for any criminal offense by the proper authorities.

(b) Counsel—The United States Government may provide or employ counsel, and pay counsel fees, court costs, bail, and other expenses incident to the representation of an officer, employee, member of the Armed Forces, or other agent described in subsection (a), with respect to any civil action or criminal prosecution arising out of practices described in that subsection, under the same conditions, and to the same extent, to which such services and payments are authorized under section 1037 of title 10, United States Code. . . .

SEC. 1006. TRAINING OF IRAQI FORCES REGARDING TREATMENT OF DETAINEES.

(a) Required Policies—

(1) In General—The Secretary of Defense shall ensure that policies are prescribed regarding procedures for military and civilian personnel of the Department of Defense and contractor personnel of the Department of Defense in Iraq that are intended to ensure that members of the Armed Forces, and all persons acting on behalf of the Armed Forces or within facilities of the Armed Forces, ensure that all personnel of Iraqi military forces who are trained by Department of Defense personnel and contractor personnel of the Department of Defense receive training regarding the international obligations and laws applicable to the humane detention of detainees, including protections afforded under the Geneva Conventions and the Convention Against Torture.

Source: Pub. L. No. 109-148, §§ 1001–1006 (2005), http://thomas.loc.gov/cgi-bin/cpquery/T?&report=hr359&dbname=109&

5.18 U.S. Army Field Manual 34-52, 1992

The Army Field Manual is mentioned in the Detainee Treatment Act (document 5.17) and the Executive Order prohibiting torture (document 5.24). The 1992 version of the manual states that prisoners are protected by the Geneva Convention until their status can be determined. More-

over, it prohibits coercive questioning, including several techniques such as stress positions, sleep deprivation, and mock execution (in the form of waterboarding) that the United States had used.

"US policy expressly prohibits acts of violence or intimidation, including physical or mental torture, threats, insults, or exposure to inhumane treatment as a means of or aid to interrogation"

These persons are protected by the Geneva Conventions for the Protection of War Victims of August 12, 1949, as they relate to captured wounded and sick enemy personnel (GWS), retained enemy medical personnel and chaplains (GWS), enemy prisoners of war (GPW), and civilian internees (GC). Captured insurgents and other detained personnel whose status is not clear, such as suspected terrorists, are entitled to PW protection until their precise status has been determined by competent authority. . . .

The GWS, GPW, GC, and US policy expressly prohibit acts of violence or intimidation, including physical or mental torture, threats, insults, or exposure to inhumane treatment as a means of or aid to interrogation.

Such illegal acts are not authorized and will not be condoned by the US Army. Acts in violation of these prohibitions are criminal acts punishable under the UCMJ. If there is doubt as to the legality of a proposed form of interrogation not specifically authorized in this manual, the advice of the command judge advocate should be sought before using the method in question.

Experience indicates that the use of prohibited techniques is not necessary to gain cooperation of interrogation sources. Use of torture and other illegal methods is a poor technique that yields unreliable results, may damage subsequent collection efforts, and can induce the source to say what he thinks the interrogator wants to hear.

Revelation of use of torture by US personnel will bring discredit on the US and its armed forces while undermining domestic and international support for the war effort. It may also place US and allied personnel in enemy hands at a greater risk of abuse by their captors. Conversely, knowing the enemy has abused US and allied PWs does not justify using methods of interrogation specifically prohibited by the GWS, GPW, or GC, and US policy.

Limitations on the use of methods identified herein as expressly prohibited should not be confused with psychological ploys, verbal trickery, or other nonviolent or coercive ruses used by the interrogator in the successful interrogation of hesitant or uncooperative sources.

The psychological techniques and principles in this manual should neither be confused with, nor construed to be synonymous with, unauthorized techniques such as brainwashing, physical or mental torture, or any other form of mental coercion to include drugs that may induce lasting and permanent mental alteration and damage.

Physical or mental torture revolve around eliminating the source's free will, and are expressly prohibited by GWS, Article 13; GPW, Articles 13 and 17; and GC, Articles 31 and 32. Torture is defined as the infliction of intense pain to body or mind to extract a confession or information, or for sadistic pleasure.

Examples of physical torture include:

Electric shock
Infliction of pain through chemicals or bondage (other than legitimate use of restraints to prevent escape)
Forcing an individual to stand, sit or kneel in abnormal positions for prolonged periods of time
Food deprivation
Any form of beating

Examples of mental torture include:

Mock execution
Abnormal sleep deprivation
Chemically induced psychosis

Coercion is defined as actions designed to unlawfully induce another to compel an act against one's will. Examples of coercion include:-

Threatening or implying physical or mental torture to the subject, his family, or others to whom he owes loyalty
Intentionally denying medical assistance or care in exchange for the information sought or other cooperation.
Threatening or implying that other rights guaranteed by the GWS, GPW or GC will not be provided unless cooperation is forthcoming.

Source: www.fas.org/irp/doddir/army/fm34-52.pdf

5.19 U.S. Army Field Manual 2-22.3, 2006

This revised version of the AFM places further limits on the interrogation methods that can be used by U.S. military personnel. The Obama administration adopted this version of the manual as the uniform standard in 2009 (see document 5.24).

"[T]he only interrogation approaches and techniques that are authorized for use against any detainee, regardless of status or characterization, are those authorized and listed in this Field Manual."

This manual expands upon the information contained in FM 2-0. It supersedes FM 34-52 and rescinds ST 2-22.7. It is consistent with doctrine in FM 3-0, FM 5-0, FM 6-0, and JP 2-0. In accordance with the Detainee Treatment Act of 2005, the only interrogation approaches and techniques that are authorized for use against any detainee, regardless of status or characterization, are those authorized and listed in this Field Manual. Some of the approaches and techniques authorized and listed in this Field Manual also require additional specified approval before implementation. . . .

Interrogation, the HUMINT subdiscipline responsible for MI exploitation of enemy personnel and their documents to answer the supported specific information requirements (SIRs), requires the HUMINT collector to be fully familiar with both the classification of the source and applicable law. The principles and techniques of HUMINT collection are to be used within the constraints established by US law including the following:

The Uniform Code of Military Justice (UCMJ).

Geneva Convention for the Amelioration of the Condition of the Wounded and Sick in Armed Forces in the Field (including Common Article III), August 12,1949; hereinafter referred to as GWS.

Geneva Convention Relative to the Treatment of Prisoners of War (including Common Article III), August 12, 1949; hereinafter referred to as GPW.

Geneva Convention Relative to the Protection of Civilian Persons in Time of War (including Common Article III), August 12, 1949; hereinafter referred to as GC.

Detainee Treatment Act of 2005, Public Law No. 109-163, Title XIV. . . .

Protected Persons: Include civilians entitled to protection under the GC, including those we retain in the course of a conflict, no matter what the reason.

Enemy Combatant: In general, a person engaged in hostilities against the United States or its coalition partners during an armed conflict. The term "enemy combatant" includes both "lawful enemy combatants" and "unlawful enemy combatants." All captured or detained personnel, regardless of status, shall be treated humanely, and in accordance with the Detainee Treatment Act of 2005 and DOD Directive 2310.1E, "Department of Defense Detainee Program," and no person in the custody or under the control of DOD, regardless of nationality or physical location, shall be subject to torture or cruel, inhuman, or degrading treatment or punishment, in accordance with and as defined in US law.

Lawful Enemy Combatant: Lawful enemy combatants, who are entitled to protections under the Geneva Conventions, include members of the regular armed forces of a State Party to the conflict; militia, volunteer corps, and organized resistance movements belonging to a State Party to the conflict, which are under responsible command, wear a fixed distinctive sign recognizable at a distance, carry their arms openly, and abide by the laws of war; and members of regular armed forces who profess allegiance to a government or an authority not recognized by the detaining power.

Unlawful Enemy Combatant: Unlawful enemy combatants are persons not entitled to combatant immunity, who engage in acts against the United States or its coalition partners in violation of the laws and customs of war during an armed conflict. For the purposes of the war on terrorism, the term "unlawful enemy combatant" is defined to include, but is not limited to, an individual who is or was part of or supporting Taliban or al Qaeda forces, or associated forces that are engaged in hostilities against the United States or its coalition partners. . . .

RESTRICTED INTERROGATION TECHNIQUE—SEPARATION

INTRODUCTION M-1. As part of the Army's efforts to gain actionable intelligence in the war on terrorism, HUMINT collectors may be authorized, in accordance with this appendix, to employ the separation interrogation technique, by exception, to meet unique and critical operational requirements. The purpose of separation is to deny the detainee the opportunity to communicate with other detainees in order to keep him from learning counter-resistance techniques or gathering new information to support a cover story; decreasing the detainee's resistance to interrogation. Separation, further described in paragraphs M-2 and M-28, is the only restricted interrogation technique that may be authorized for use. Separation will only be used during the interrogation of specific unlawful enemy combatants for whom proper approvals have been granted in accordance with this appendix. However, separation may *not* be employed on detainees covered by Geneva Convention Relative to the Treatment of Prisoners of War (GPW), primarily enemy prisoners of war (EPWs). The separation technique will be used only at COCOM-approved locations. Separation may be employed in combination with authorized interrogation approaches—

On specific unlawful enemy combatants.
To help overcome resistance and gain actionable intelligence.
To safeguard US and coalition forces.
To protect US interests.

GENERAL M-2. This appendix provides doctrinal guidance for the use of separation as an interrogation technique. Separation involves removing the detainee from other detainees and their environment, while still complying with the basic standards of humane treatment and prohibitions against torture or cruel, inhuman, or degrading treatment or punishment, as defined in the Detainee Treatment Act of 2005 and addressed in GPW Article 3 (Common Article III). Separation is to be distinguished from segregation, which refers to removing a detainee from other detainees and their environment for legitimate purposes unrelated to interrogation, such as when necessary for the movement, health, safety and/or security of the detainee, or the detention facility or its personnel. This appendix—

Will be reviewed annually and may be amended or updated from time to time to account for changes in doctrine, policy, or law, and to address lessons learned.

Is not a stand-alone doctrinal product and must be used in conjunction with the main portion of this manual.

M-3. Careful consideration should be given prior to employing separation as an interrogation technique in order to mitigate the risks associated with its use. The use of separation should not be confused with the detainee-handling techniques approved in Appendix D. Specifically, the use of segregation during prisoner handling (Search, Silence, Segregate, Speed, Safeguard, and Tag [5 S's and a T]) should not be confused with the use of separation as a restricted interrogation technique.

M-4. Members of all DOD Components are required to comply with the law of war during all armed conflicts, however such conflicts are characterized, and in all other military operations. Proper application of separation as a restricted interrogation technique in selective cases involving specific unlawful enemy combatants and in accordance with the safeguards outlined in this manual is consistent with the minimum humane standards of treatment required by US law, the law of war; and does not constitute cruel, inhuman, or degrading treatment or punishment as defined in the Detainee Treatment Act of 2005 and addressed in GPW Common Article III.

M-5. Use of separation for interrogation is authorized by exception. Separation will be applied on a case-by-case basis when there is a good basis to believe that the detainee is likely to possess important intelligence and the interrogation approach techniques provided in Chapter 8 are insufficient. Separation should be used as part of a well-orchestrated strategy involving the innovative application of unrestricted approach techniques. Separation requires special approval, judicious execution, special control measures, and rigorous oversight.

M-6. Additionally, the use of separation as a restricted interrogation technique shall be conducted humanely in accordance with applicable law and policy. Applicable law and policy for purposes of this appendix include US law; the law of war; relevant international law; relevant directives including DOD Directive 3115.09, "DOD Intelligence Interrogations, Detainee Debriefings, and Tactical Questioning"; DOD Directive 2310.1E, "The Department of Defense Detainee Program"; DOD instructions; and military execute orders including FRAGOs.

M-7. More stringent than normal safeguards must be applied when using the separation technique. Use of separation is subject to USD(I) oversight. Compared to approach techniques, there are two additional steps in the approval process (see Figure M-l) for the use of the separation technique:

First, the COCOM Commander approves (after SJA review) use of the separation technique in theater.

Second, following the COCOM Commander's approval, the first General Officer/Flag Officer (GO/FO) in an interrogator's chain of command approves each specific use of separation and the interrogation plan that implements separation (this is non-delegable). Interrogation supervisors shall have their servicing SJA review the interrogation plan before submitting it to the GO/FO for approval. . . .

GENERAL CONTROLS AND SAFEGUARDS HUMANE TREATMENT

M-15. All captured or detained personnel shall be treated humanely at all times and in accordance with DOD Directive 3115.09, "DOD Intelligence Interrogations, Detainee Debriefings, and Tactical Questioning"; DOD Directive 2310.1E, "Department of Defense Detainee Program," and no person in the custody or under the control of the DOD, regardless of nationality or physical location, shall be subject to cruel, inhuman, or degrading treatment or punishment as defined in US law, including the Military Treatment Act of 2005. All intelligence interrogations, debriefings, or tactical questioning to gain intelligence from captured or detained personnel shall be conducted in accordance with applicable law and policy.

M-16. Any inhumane treatment—including abusive practices, torture, or cruel, inhuman, or degrading treatment or punishment as defined in US law, including the Detainee Treatment Act of 2005—is prohibited and all instances of such treatment will be reported immediately in accordance with paragraph 5-69 thru 5-72. Beyond being impermissible, these unlawful and unauthorized forms of treatment are unproductive because they may yield unreliable results, damage subsequent collection efforts, and result in extremely negative consequences at national and international levels. Review by the servicing SJA is required prior to using separation. Each interrogation plan must include specific safeguards to be followed: limits on duration, interval between applications, and termination criteria. Medical personnel will be available to respond in the event a medical emergency occurs.

FM 2-22.3 REQUIREMENTS

M-17. Separation must be employed in accordance with the standards in this manual. These standards include the following:

Prohibitions against abusive and unlawful actions (see para 5-75) and against the employment of military working dogs in the conduct of interrogation (see paras 5-59 and 8-2).

Requirement for non-DOD agencies to observe the same standards for the conduct of interrogation operations and treatment of detainees when in DOD facilities (see para 5-55).

Prohibition on guards conducting intelligence interrogations or taking any actions to set the conditions for interrogations. Humane treatment, evacuation, custody and control (reception, processing, administration, internment, and safety) of detainees; force protection; and the operation of the internment facility are discussed in paragraphs 5-57 through 5-66. (FM 3-19 .40 and JP 3-63 also thoroughly discuss detainee operations.)

Assignment of ISNs to all detainees in DOD control, whether or not interrogation has commenced, as soon as possible; normally within 14 days of capture. (See AR 190-8 and Secretary of Defense Memorandum dated 20 September 2005, "(S//NF) Policy on Assigning Detainee Internment Serial Numbers (ISN)(U)."

Access to detainees by the ICRC.

REPORTING OF ABUSES AND SUSPECTED ABUSES

M-18. As an interrogation technique, separation is particularly sensitive due to the possibility that it could be perceived as an impermissible act. Interrogators applying the separation technique and the chain of command supervising must be acutely sensitive to the application of the technique to ensure that the line between permissible or lawful actions and impermissible or unlawful actions is distinct and maintained. Therefore, HUMINT collectors should have heightened awareness and understanding of the risks, control measures, and safeguards associated with the use of separation. Any interrogation technique that appears to be cruel, inhuman, or degrading as defined in US law; or impermissibly coercive, or is not listed in this manual, is prohibited and should be reported immediately to the chain of command or other appropriate channels for resolution. Orders given to treat detainees inhumanely are unlawful. Every interrogator must know how to respond to orders that the individual interrogator perceives to be unlawful (see paras 5-80 through 5-82).

M-19. If the order is a lawful order, it should be obeyed. Failure to obey a lawful order is an offense under the UCMJ. . . .

APPLICATION OF SEPARATION TECHNIQUE

M-26. The purpose of separation is to deny the detainee the opportunity to communicate with other detainees in order to keep him from learning counter-resistance techniques or gathering new information to support a cover story, decreasing the detainee's resistance to interrogation. Separation does not constitute sensory deprivation, which is prohibited. For the purposes of this manual, sensory deprivation is defined as an arranged situation causing significant psychological distress due to a prolonged absence, or significant reduction, of the usual external stimuli and perceptual opportunities. Sensory deprivation may result in extreme anxiety, hallucinations, bizarre thoughts, depression, and anti-social behavior. Detainees will not be subjected to sensory deprivation.

M-27. Physical separation is the best and preferred method of separation. As a last resort, when physical separation of detainees is not feasible, goggles or blindfolds and earmuffs may be utilized as a field expedient method to generate a perception of separation.

M-28. Objectives:

Physical Separation: Prevent the detainee from communicating with other detainees (which might increase the detainee's resistance to interrogation) and foster a feeling of futility.

Field Expedient Separation: Prolong the shock of capture. Prevent the detainee from communicating with other detainees (which might increase the detainee's resistance to interrogation) and foster a feeling of futility.

M-29. Safeguards:

Duration: Self-explanatory.

Physical Separation: Limited to 30 days of initial duration.

Field Expedient Separation: Limited to 12 hours of initial duration at the initial interrogation site. This limit on duration does not include the time that goggles or blindfolds and earmuffs are used on detainees for security purposes during transit and evacuation.

Oversight Considerations for Field Expedient Separation: The intended use of field expedient means of separation must be specified on the interrogation plan that is submitted to the GO/FO for approval. Detainees must be protected from self-injury when field expedient means of separation are used. The effect of the application of field expedient separation means on the detainee must be monitored to detect any possible health concerns.

M-30. The following safeguards apply to both Physical Separation and Field Expedient Separation.

Break: Additional periods of separation will not be applied without the approving GO/FO's determination of the length of a break between iterations.

Extension:

Physical Separation Method: Extensions of this technique past 30 days must be reviewed by the servicing SJA and approved by the original approving GO/FO or his replacement in that position.

Field Expedient Method: Extensions past 12 hours of initial duration at the initial interrogation site must be reviewed by the servicing SJA and approved by the original approving/replacement GO/FO.

Medical: Detainees will be checked periodically in accordance with command health care directives, guidance, and SOPs applicable to all detainees.

Custody and Control: The interrogation chain of command must coordinate the interrogation plan with the Detention Operations Commander. The Detention Operations Commander (in conjunction with the MI commander) may convene a multidiscipline custody and control oversight team including, but not limited to, MP, MI, BSC (if available), and legal representatives. The team can advise and provide measures to ensure effective custody and control in compliance with the requirements of applicable law and policy.

Oversight Considerations: Use of hoods (sacks) over the head, or of duct tape or adhesive tape over the eyes, as a separation method is prohibited. If separation has been approved, and the interrogator subsequently determines that there may be a problem, the interrogator should seek further guidance through the chain of command before applying the technique.

Care should be taken to protect the detainee from exposure (in accordance with all appropriate standards addressing excessive or inadequate environmental conditions) to . . .

Excessive noise.

Excessive dampness.

Excessive or inadequate heat, light, or ventilation.

Inadequate bedding and blankets.

Interrogation activity leadership will periodically monitor the application of this technique.

Use of separation must not preclude the detainee getting four hours of continuous sleep every 24 hours.

Oversight should account for moving a detainee from one environment to another (thus a different location) or arrangements to modify the environment within the same location in accordance with the approved interrogation plan.

M-31. Suggested Approach Combinations:

Futility.
Incentive.
Fear Up.

Source: http://www.army.mil/institution/armypublicaffairs/pdf/fm2-22-3.pdf

5.20 Military Commissions Act, 2006

In June 2006, the Supreme Court decided Hamdan v. Rumsfeld, *invalidating the military tribunals used by the Bush administration. This legislation countered the Court's objections to those commissions raised in* Hamdan. *In the MCA, some statements obtained through torture would again be admissible in commission proceedings, and the Geneva Convention would not apply to unlawful combatants.*

"No alien enemy unlawful combatant . . . may invoke the Geneva Conventions as a source of rights"

(f) GENEVA CONVENTIONS NOT ESTABLISHING SOURCE OF RIGHTS.— No alien enemy unlawful combatant subject to trial by military commission under this chapter may invoke the Geneva Conventions as a source of rights at his trial by military commission. . . .

(a) In General—No person shall be required to testify against himself at a proceeding of a military commission under this chapter.

(b) Exclusion of Statements Obtained by Torture—A statement obtained by use of torture shall not be admissible in a military commission under this chapter, except against a person accused of torture as evidence that the statement was made.

(c) Statements Obtained before Enactment of Detainee Treatment Act of 2005—A statement obtained before December 30, 2005 (the date of the enactment of the Defense Treatment Act of 2005) in which the degree of coercion is disputed may be admitted only if the military judge finds that—

(1) the totality of the circumstances renders the statement reliable and possessing sufficient probative value; and

(2) the interests of justice would best be served by admission of the statement into evidence.

(d) Statements Obtained after Enactment of Detainee Treatment Act of 2005—A statement obtained on or after December 30, 2005 (the date of the enactment of the Defense Treatment Act of 2005) in which the degree of coercion is disputed may be admitted only if the military judge finds that—

(1) the totality of the circumstances renders the statement reliable and possessing sufficient probative value;

(2) the interests of justice would best be served by admission of the statement into evidence; and

(3) the interrogation methods used to obtain the statement do not amount to cruel, inhuman, or degrading treatment prohibited by section 1003 of the Detainee Treatment Act of 2005.

§ 949s. Cruel or Unusual Punishments Prohibited. Punishment by flogging, or by branding, marking, or tattooing on the body, or any other cruel or unusual punishment, may not be adjudged by a military commission under this chapter or inflicted under this chapter upon any person subject to this chapter. The use of irons, single or double, except for the purpose of safe custody, is prohibited under this chapter.

§ 949t. Maximum Limits. The punishment which a military commission under this chapter may direct for an offense may not exceed such limits as the President or Secretary of Defense may prescribe for that offense.

Source: Publ. L. No. 109-336, 120 Stat. 2600 (2005)

5.21 Appellate Court Opinion in *El-Masri v. U.S.*, 2007

This case involved a German citizen who was captured and taken to Afghanistan, where he was held for nearly six months, beaten, and tortured. El-Masri sued the U.S. government, claiming that he was seized as part of the "extraordinary rendition" program, in which the United States captured and transported interrogation subjects to foreign countries, where they could be held in secret and tortured.[1] The U.S. government success-

1. For a thorough description and analysis of extraordinary rendition, see the Committee of International Rights of the Association of the Bar of the City of New York, *Torture by Proxy:*

*fully moved for dismissal of the suit, claiming that the rendition program
was a "state secret," which would threaten national security if details were
released in court. On appeal, the U.S. Court of Appeals for the Fourth
Circuit affirmed dismissal.*

"The state secrets doctrine protects sensitive military intelligence"

On December 6, 2005, El-Masri, a German citizen of Lebanese descent, filed
his Complaint in this case, alleging, in substance, as follows: on December
31, 2003, while travelling in Macedonia, he was detained by Macedonian law
enforcement officials; after twenty-three days in Macedonian custody, he was
handed over to CIA operatives, who flew him to a CIA-operated detention
facility near Kabul, Afghanistan; he was held in this CIA facility until May 28,
2004, when he was transported to Albania and released in a remote area; and
Albanian officials then picked him up and took him to an airport in Tirana,
Albania, from which he travelled to his home in Germany. The Complaint
asserted that El-Masri had not only been held against his will, but had also
been mistreated in a number of other ways during his detention, including
being beaten, drugged, bound, and blindfolded during transport; confined in
a small, unsanitary cell; interrogated several times; and consistently prevented from communicating with anyone outside the detention facility, including
his family or the German government. El-Masri alleged that his detention
and interrogation were carried out pursuant to an unlawful policy and practice devised and implemented by defendant Tenet known as "extraordinary
rendition": the clandestine abduction and detention outside the United States
of persons suspected of involvement in terrorist activities, and their subsequent interrogation using methods impermissible under U.S. and international laws.

According to the Complaint, the corporate defendants provided the CIA
with an aircraft and crew to transport El-Masri to Afghanistan, pursuant to
an agreement with Director Tenet, and they either knew or reasonably should
have known that "Mr. El-Masri would be subjected to prolonged arbitrary
detention, torture and cruel, inhuman, or degrading treatment in violation of
federal and international laws during his transport to Afghanistan and while
he was detained and interrogated there."

International and Domestic Law Applicable to "Extraordinary Renditions," Report by the New
York City Bar Association and NYU Law School (2004), www.nyuhr.org (accessed December
12, 2007; and J. Mayer, "Annals of Justice: Outsourcing Torture," *New Yorker,* February 14, 2005,
www.newyorker.com/printables/fact/050214fa_fact6.

El-Masri also alleges that CIA officials "believed early on that they had the wrong person," and that Director Tenet was notified in April 2004 that "the CIA had detained the wrong person" in El-Masri. Id. P 43.

To summarize, our analysis of the Executive's interposition of the state secrets privilege is governed primarily by two standards. First, evidence is privileged pursuant to the state secrets doctrine if, under all the circumstances of the case, there is a reasonable danger that its disclosure will expose military (or diplomatic or intelligence) matters which, in the interest of national security, should not be divulged. Second, a proceeding in which the state secrets privilege is successfully interposed must be dismissed if the circumstances make clear that privileged information will be so central to the litigation that any attempt to proceed will threaten that information's disclosure. With these controlling principles in mind, and being cognizant of the delicate balance to be struck in applying the state secrets doctrine, we proceed to our analysis of El-Masri's contentions.

B.

1. The question before us is whether the facts of this proceeding satisfy the governing standard for dismissal of an action on state secrets grounds, as the district court ruled. El-Masri essentially accepts the legal framework described above. He acknowledges that the state secrets doctrine protects sensitive military intelligence information from disclosure in court proceedings, and that dismissal at the pleading stage is appropriate if state secrets are so central to a proceeding that it cannot be litigated without threatening their disclosure. El-Masri contends, however, that the facts that are central to his claim are not state secrets, and that the district court thus erred in dismissing his Complaint.

The heart of El-Masri's appeal is his assertion that the facts essential to his Complaint have largely been made public, either in statements by United States officials or in reports by media outlets and foreign governmental entities. He maintains that the subject of this action is simply "a rendition and its consequences," and that its critical facts—the CIA's operation of a rendition program targeted at terrorism suspects, plus the tactics employed therein—have been so widely discussed that litigation concerning them could do no harm to national security. Appellant's Br. 38. As a result, El-Masri contends that the district court should have allowed his case to move forward with discovery, perhaps with special procedures imposed to protect sensitive information.

El-Masri's contention in that regard, however, misapprehends the nature of our assessment of a dismissal on state secrets grounds. The controlling inquiry is not whether the general subject matter of an action can be described without resort to state secrets. Rather, we must ascertain whether an action can be litigated without threatening the disclosure of such state secrets. Thus, for purposes of the state secrets analysis, the "central facts" and "very subject matter" of an action are those facts that are essential to prosecuting the action or defending against it.

El-Masri is therefore incorrect in contending that the central facts of this proceeding are his allegations that he was detained and interrogated under abusive conditions, or that the CIA conducted the rendition program that has been acknowledged by United States officials. Facts such as those furnish the general terms in which El-Masri has related his story to the press, but advancing a case in the court of public opinion, against the United States at large, is an undertaking quite different from prevailing against specific defendants in a court of law. If El-Masri's civil action were to proceed, the facts central to its resolution would be the roles, if any, that the defendants played in the events he alleges. To establish a prima facie case, he would be obliged to produce admissible evidence not only that he was detained and interrogated, but that the defendants were involved in his detention and interrogation in a manner that renders them personally liable to him. Such a showing could be made only with evidence that exposes how the CIA organizes, staffs, and supervises its most sensitive intelligence operations. With regard to Director Tenet, for example, El-Masri would be obliged to show in detail how the head of the CIA participates in such operations, and how information concerning their progress is relayed to him. With respect to the defendant corporations and their unnamed employees, El-Masri would have to demonstrate the existence and details of CIA espionage contracts, an endeavor practically indistinguishable from that categorically barred by *Totten* and *Tenet v. Doe.* . . . Even marshalling the evidence necessary to make the requisite showings would implicate privileged state secrets, because El-Masri would need to rely on witnesses whose identities, and evidence the very existence of which, must remain confidential in the interest of national security.

Source: *El-Masri v. United States,* 479 F.3d 296 (4th Cir. 2007)

5.22 *Arar v. Ashcroft* (en banc decision of the U.S. Court of Appeals for the Second Circuit), 2009

Maher Arar was also a victim of "extraordinary rendition." A Canadian national, Arar was taken in 2002 from New York's Kennedy Airport during a stopover and eventually sent to Syria, where he was held in secret

*and tortured for ten months. His suit against the United States govern-
ment was also unsuccessful. Both El-Masri and Arar were ultimately
released and never charged with a crime, but they were denied relief in
court. The excerpt is from the decision by the Second Circuit. It affirmed
dismissal of Arar's complaint, ruling that a "Bivens-type" claim, which
involves allegations of constitutional violation by federal officials, should
not be permitted in this case.*

"He was interrogated for twelve days . . . and in that period was beaten
on his palms, hips, and lower back with a two-inch-thick electric cable
and with bare hands"

When he arrived in Amman on October 9, he was handed over to Jordanian
authorities who treated him roughly and then delivered him to the custody
of Syrian officials, who detained him at a Syrian Military Intelligence facility.
Arar was in Syria for a year, the first ten months in an underground cell six
feet by three, and seven feet high. He was interrogated for twelve days on his
arrival in Syria, and in that period was beaten on his palms, hips, and lower
back with a two-inch-thick electric cable and with bare hands. Arar alleges
that United States officials conspired to send him to Syria for the purpose of
interrogation under torture, and directed the interrogations from abroad by
providing Syria with Arar's dossier, dictating questions for the Syrians to ask
him, and receiving intelligence learned from the interviews.

On October 20, 2002, Canadian Embassy officials inquired of Syria as to
Arar's whereabouts. The next day, Syria confirmed to Canada that Arar was in
its custody; that same day, interrogation ceased. Arar remained in Syria, however, receiving visits from Canadian consular officials. On August 14, 2003,
Arar defied his captors by telling the Canadians that he had been tortured
and was confined to a small underground cell. Five days later, after signing a
confession that he had trained as a terrorist in Afghanistan, Arar was moved
to various locations. On October 5, 2003, Arar was released to the custody of
a Canadian embassy official in Damascus, and was flown to Ottawa the next
day. . . .

In the small number of contexts in which courts have implied a Bivens
remedy, it has often been easy to identify both the line between constitutional and unconstitutional conduct, and the alternative course which officers
should have pursued. The guard who beat a prisoner should not have beaten
him; the agent who searched without a warrant should have gotten one; and
the immigration officer who subjected an alien to multiple strip searches
without cause should have left the alien in his clothes. This distinction may or
may not amount to a special factor counseling hesitation in the implication of

a Bivens remedy. But it is surely remarkable that the context of extraordinary rendition is so different, involving as it does a complex and rapidly changing legal framework beset with critical legal judgments that have not yet been made, as well as policy choices that are by no means easily reached.

Consider: should the officers here have let Arar go on his way and board his flight to Montreal? Canada was evidently unwilling to receive him; it was, after all, Canadian authorities who identified Arar as a terrorist (or did something that led their government to apologize publicly to Arar and pay him $10 million).

Should a person identified as a terrorist by his own country be allowed to board his plane and go on to his destination? Surely, that would raise questions as to what duty is owed to the other passengers and the crew.

Or should a suspected terrorist en route to Canada have been released on the Canadian border—over which he could re-enter the United States virtually at will? Or should he have been sent back whence his plane came, or to some third country? Should those governments be told that Canada thinks he is a terrorist? If so, what country would take him?

Or should the suspected terrorist have been sent to Guantanamo Bay or—if no other country would take him—kept in the United States with the prospect of release into the general population?

None of this is to say that extraordinary rendition is or should be a favored policy choice. At the same time, the officials required to decide these vexed issues are "subject to the pull of competing obligations." Many viable actions they might consider "clash with other equally important governmental responsibilities." Given the ample reasons for pause already discussed, we need not and do not rely on this consideration in concluding that it is inappropriate to extend Bivens to this context. Still, Congress is the appropriate branch of government to decide under what circumstances (if any) these kinds of policy decisions—which are directly related to the security of the population and the foreign affairs of the country—should be subjected to the influence of litigation brought by aliens.

XIII

All of these special factors notwithstanding, we cannot ignore that, as the panel dissent put it, "there is a long history of judicial review of Executive and Legislative decisions related to the conduct of foreign relations and national security." (Sack, J., concurring in part and dissenting in part). Where does that leave us? We recognize our limited competence, authority, and jurisdiction to make rules or set parameters to govern the practice called rendition. By the same token, we can easily locate that competence, expertise, and responsibility elsewhere: in Congress. Congress may be content for the Executive Branch to exercise these powers without judicial check. But if Congress wishes to create a remedy for individuals like Arar, it can enact legislation that includes enumerated eligibility parameters, delineated safe harbors, defined review processes, and specific relief to be afforded. Once Congress has performed this task, then the courts in a proper case will be able to review the statute and provide judicial oversight to the "Executive and Legislative decisions [which have been made with regard] to the conduct of foreign relations and national security." . . .

BARRINGTON PARKER, Circuit Judge, joined by Judges calabresi, pooler, and sack, dissenting:

. . . Maher Arar credibly alleges that United States officials conspired to ship him from American soil, where the Constitution and our laws apply, to Syria, where they do not, so that Syrian agents could torture him at federal officials' direction and behest. He also credibly alleges that, to accomplish this unlawful objective, agents of our government actively obstructed his access to this very Court and the protections established by Congress. See *8 U.S.C. § 1252(a)(2)(D)* (providing for judicial review of constitutional claims or questions of law raised by an order of removal).

While I broadly concur with my colleagues who dissent, I write separately to underscore the miscarriage of justice that leaves Arar without a remedy in our courts. The majority would immunize official misconduct by invoking the separation of powers and the executive's responsibility for foreign affairs and national security. Its approach distorts the system of checks and balances essential to the rule of law, and it trivializes the judiciary's role in these arenas. To my mind, the most depressing aspect of the majority's opinion is its sincerity.

A primary theme of the majority's approach is deference to executive authority, especially in a time of national unrest, turmoil, or danger. The conduct of foreign policy and the maintenance of national security are surely executive and legislative powers. Yet those powers are not limitless. The bounds in both wartime and peacetime are fixed by the same Constitution. Where appropriate, deference to the coordinate branches is an essential element of our work. But there is, in my view, an enormous difference between being deferential and being supine in the face of governmental misconduct. The former is often necessary, the latter never is. At the end of the day, it is not the role of the judiciary to serve as a help-mate to the executive branch, and it is not its role to avoid difficult decisions for fear of complicating life for federal officials. Always mindful of the fact that in times of national stress and turmoil the rule of law is everything, our role is to defend the Constitution. We do this by affording redress when government officials violate the law, even when national security is invoked as the justification.

Notably, the majority opinion does not appear to dispute the notion that Arar has stated an injury under the Fifth Amendment of the Constitution. That is heartening, because, by any measure, the notion that federal officials conspired to send a man to Syria to be tortured "shocks the conscience." What is profoundly disturbing, however, is the Court's pronouncement that it can offer Arar no opportunity to prove his case and no possibility of relief. This conclusion is at odds with the Court's responsibility to enforce the Constitution's protections and cannot, in my view, be reconciled with [Bivens]. See also *Davis v. Passman* (declaring Bivens remedy for alleged Fifth Amendment violations). The majority is at odds, too, with our own State Department, which has repeatedly taken the position before the world community that this exact remedy is available to torture victims like Arar. If the Constitution ever implied a damages remedy, this is such a case—where executive officials allegedly blocked access to the remedies chosen by Congress in order to deliver a man to known torturers.

The Court's hesitation today immunizes official conduct directly at odds with the express will of Congress and the most basic guarantees of liberty contained in the Constitution. By doing so, the majority risks a government that can interpret the law to suits its own ends, without scrutiny. . . .

The majority discovers myriad reasons to "hesitate" in the face of Arar's complaint that federal officials conspired to send him to Syria to be tortured. Its principal reason, however, is that permitting such an action "would have the natural tendency to affect diplomacy, foreign policy and the security of the nation." Maj. Op. at 38. This view of the separation of powers, which confines the courts to the sidelines, is, in my view, deeply mistaken; it diminishes and distorts the role of the judiciary especially during times of turmoil.

Source: *Arar v. Ashcroft*, 585 F.3d 559 (2nd Cir. 2009)

5.23 Statement of President Barack Obama on the Release of Office of Legal Counsel Memos, 2009

In April 2009 President Obama made public some of the documents generated by the Office of Legal Counsel during the Bush administration, including reports on specific cases where coercive interrogation methods were used (documents 5.7, 5.13, 5.14, and 5.15). On the day the documents were released, Obama explained in a public statement the rationale for releasing them. He also reiterated his general commitment to executive secrecy in appropriate cases.

"A dark and painful chapter in our history"

The Department of Justice will today release certain memos issued by the Office of Legal Counsel between 2002 and 2005 as part of an ongoing court case. These memos speak to techniques that were used in the interrogation of terrorism suspects during that period, and their release is required by the rule of law.

My judgment on the content of these memos is a matter of record. In one of my very first acts as President, I prohibited the use of these interrogation techniques by the United States because they undermine our moral authority and do not make us safer. Enlisting our values in the protection of our people makes us stronger and more secure. A democracy as resilient as ours must reject the false choice between our security and our ideals, and that is why these methods of interrogation are already a thing of the past.

But that is not what compelled the release of these legal documents today. While I believe strongly in transparency and accountability, I also believe that in a dangerous world, the United States must sometimes carry out intelligence operations and protect information that is classified for purposes of national security. I have already fought for that principle in court and will do so again in the future. However, after consulting with the Attorney General, the Director of National Intelligence, and others, I believe that exceptional circumstances surround these memos and require their release.

First, the interrogation techniques described in these memos have already been widely reported. Second, the previous Administration publicly acknowledged portions of the program—and some of the practices—associated with these memos. Third, I have already ended the techniques described in the memos through an Executive Order. Therefore, withholding these memos would only serve to deny facts that have been in the public domain for some time. This could contribute to an inaccurate accounting of the past, and fuel erroneous and inflammatory assumptions about actions taken by the United States.

In releasing these memos, it is our intention to assure those who carried out their duties relying in good faith upon legal advice from the Department of Justice that they will not be subject to prosecution. The men and women of our intelligence community serve courageously on the front lines of a dangerous world. Their accomplishments are unsung and their names unknown, but because of their sacrifices, every single American is safer. We must protect their identities as vigilantly as they protect our security, and we must provide them with the confidence that they can do their jobs.

Going forward, it is my strong belief that the United States has a solemn duty to vigorously maintain the classified nature of certain activities and information related to national security. This is an extraordinarily important responsibility of the presidency, and it is one that I will carry out assertively irrespective of any political concern. Consequently, the exceptional circumstances surrounding these memos should not be viewed as an erosion of the strong legal basis for maintaining the classified nature of secret activities. I will always do whatever is necessary to protect the national security of the United States.

This is a time for reflection, not retribution. I respect the strong views and emotions that these issues evoke. We have been through a dark and painful chapter in our history. But at a time of great challenges and disturbing disunity, nothing will be gained by spending our time and energy laying blame for the past. Our national greatness is embedded in America's ability to right its course in concert with our core values, and to move forward with confidence. That is why we must resist the forces that divide us, and instead come together on behalf of our common future.

The United States is a nation of laws. My Administration will always act in accordance with those laws, and with an unshakeable commitment to our ideals. That is why we have released these memos, and that is why we have taken steps to ensure that the actions described within them never take place again.

Source: /www.whitehouse.gov/the_press_office/Statement-of-President-Barack
-Obama-on-Release-of-OLC-Memos

5.24 Executive Order of President Barack Obama, 2009

One of President Obama's first executive orders revoked all previous directives regarding terror-related interrogations and established the Army Field Manual (document 5.19,) as the uniform standard.

"Ensuring Lawful Interrogations"

By the authority vested in me by the Constitution and the laws of the United States of America, in order to improve the effectiveness of human intelligence-gathering, to promote the safe, lawful, and humane treatment of individuals in United States custody and of United States personnel who are detained in armed conflicts, to ensure compliance with the treaty obligations of the United States, including the Geneva Conventions, and to take care that the laws of the United States are faithfully executed, I hereby order as follows:

Sec. 1. *Revocation.* Executive Order 13440 of July 20, 2007, is revoked. All executive directives, orders, and regulations inconsistent with this order, including but not limited to those issued to or by the Central Intelligence Agency (CIA) from September 11, 2001, to January 20, 2009, concerning detention or the interrogation of detained individuals, are revoked to the extent of their inconsistency with this order. Heads of departments and agencies shall take all necessary steps to ensure that all directives, orders, and regulations of their respective departments or agencies are consistent with this order. Upon request, the Attorney General shall provide guidance about which directives, orders, and regulations are inconsistent with this order.

Sec. 2. *Definitions.* As used in this order:

(a) "Army Field Manual 2-22.3" means FM 2-22.3, Human Intelligence Collector Operations, issued by the Department of the Army on September 6, 2006.

(b) "Army Field Manual 34-52" means FM 34-52, Intelligence Interrogation, issued by the Department of the Army on May 8, 1987.

(c) "Common Article 3" means Article 3 of each of the Geneva Conventions.

(d) "Convention Against Torture" means the Convention Against Torture and Other Cruel, Inhuman or Degrading Treatment or Punishment, December 10, 1984, 1465 U.N.T.S. 85, S. Treaty Doc. No. 100-20 (1988).

(e) "Geneva Conventions" means:

(i) the Convention for the Amelioration of the Condition of the Wounded and Sick in Armed Forces in the Field, August 12, 1949 (6 UST 3114)

(ii) the Convention for the Amelioration of the Condition of Wounded, Sick and Shipwrecked Members of Armed Forces at Sea, August 12, 1949 (6 UST 3217);

(iii) the Convention Relative to the Treatment of Prisoners of War, August 12, 1949 (6 UST 3316); and

(iv) the Convention Relative to the Protection of Civilian Persons in Time of War, August 12, 1949 (6 UST 3516).

(f) "Treated humanely," "violence to life and person," "murder of all kinds," "mutilation," "cruel treatment," "torture," "outrages upon personal dignity," and "humiliating and degrading treatment" refer to, and have the same meaning as, those same terms in Common Article 3.

(g) The terms "detention facilities" and "detention facility" in section 4(a) of this order do not refer to facilities used only to hold people on a short-term, transitory basis.

Sec. 3. Standards and Practices for Interrogation of Individuals in the Custody or Control of the United States in Armed Conflicts.

(a) *Common Article 3 Standards as a Minimum Baseline.* Consistent with the requirements of the Federal torture statute, 18 U.S.C. 2340-2340A, section 1003 of the Detainee Treatment Act of 2005, 42 U.S.C. 2000dd, the Convention Against Torture, Common Article 3, and other laws regulating the treatment and interrogation of individuals detained in any armed conflict, such persons shall in all circumstances be treated humanely and shall not be subjected to violence to life and person (including murder of all kinds, mutilation, cruel treatment, and torture), nor to outrages upon personal dignity (including humiliating and degrading treatment), whenever such individuals are in the custody or under the effective control of an officer, employee, or other agent of the United States Government or detained within a facility owned, operated, or controlled by a department or agency of the United States.

(b) *Interrogation Techniques and Interrogation-Related Treatment.* Effective immediately, an individual in the custody or under the effective control of an officer, employee, or other agent of the United States Government, or detained within a facility owned, operated, or controlled by a department or agency of the United States, in any armed conflict, shall not be subjected to any interrogation technique or approach, or any treatment related to interrogation, that is not authorized by and listed in Army Field Manual 2-22.3 (Manual). Interrogation techniques, approaches, and treatments described in the Manual shall be implemented strictly in accord with the principles, processes, conditions, and limitations the Manual prescribes. Where processes required by the Manual, such as a requirement of approval by specified Department of Defense officials, are inapposite to a department or an agency other than the Department of Defense, such a department or agency shall use processes that are substantially equivalent to the processes the Manual prescribes for the Department of Defense. Nothing in this section shall preclude the Federal Bureau of Investigation, or other Federal law enforcement agencies, from continuing to use authorized, non-coercive techniques of interrogation that are designed to elicit voluntary statements and do not involve the use of force, threats, or promises.

(c) *Interpretations of Common Article 3 and the Army Field Manual.* From this day forward, unless the Attorney General with appropriate consultation provides further guidance, officers, employees, and other agents of the United States Government may, in conducting interrogations, act in reliance upon Army Field Manual 2-22.3, but may not, in conducting interrogations, rely upon any interpretation of the law governing interrogation—including interpretations of Federal criminal laws, the Convention Against Torture, Common Article 3, Army Field Manual 2-22.3, and its predecessor document, Army Field Manual 34-52—issued by the Department of Justice between September 11, 2001, and January 20, 2009.

Sec. 4. Prohibition of Certain Detention Facilities, and Red Cross Access to Detained Individuals.

(a) *CIA Detention.* The CIA shall close as expeditiously as possible any detention facilities that it currently operates and shall not operate any such detention facility in the future.

(b) *International Committee of the Red Cross Access to Detained Individuals.* All departments and agencies of the Federal Government shall provide the International Committee of the Red Cross with notification of, and timely access to, any individual detained in any armed conflict in the custody or under the effective control of an officer, employee, or other agent of the United States Government or detained within a facility owned, operated, or controlled by a department or agency of the United States Government, consistent with Department of Defense regulations and policies.

Source: www.whitehouse.gov

5.25 Executive Order of President Barack Obama, 2009

Immediately after taking office, President Obama announced that the detention facility at Guantanamo would be closed. However, as of late in 2010, Guantanamo remained open, with no plans for its closure.

"The detention facilities at Guantánamo for individuals covered by this order shall be closed as soon as practicable"

By the authority vested in me as President by the Constitution and the laws of the United States of America, in order to effect the appropriate disposition of individuals currently detained by the Department of Defense at the Guantánamo Bay Naval Base (Guantánamo) and promptly to close detention facilities at Guantánamo, consistent with the national security and foreign policy interests of the United States and the interests of justice, I hereby order as follows: . . .

Sec. 2. Findings.

(a) Over the past 7 years, approximately 800 individuals whom the Department of Defense has ever determined to be, or treated as, enemy combatants have been detained at Guantánamo. The Federal Government has moved more than 500 such detainees from Guantánamo, either by returning them to their home country or by releasing or transferring them to a third country. The Department of Defense has determined that a number of the individuals currently detained at Guantánamo are eligible for such transfer or release.

(b) Some individuals currently detained at Guantánamo have been there for more than 6 years, and most have been detained for at least 4 years. In view of the significant concerns raised by these detentions, both within the United States and internationally, prompt and appropriate disposition of the individuals currently detained at Guantánamo and closure of the facilities in which they are detained would further the national security and foreign policy interests of the United States and the interests of justice. Merely closing the facilities without promptly determining the appropriate disposition of the individuals detained would not adequately serve those interests. To the extent practicable, the prompt and appropriate disposition of the individuals detained at Guantánamo should precede the closure of the detention facilities at Guantánamo.

(c) The individuals currently detained at Guantánamo have the constitutional privilege of the writ of habeas corpus. Most of those individuals have filed petitions for a writ of habeas corpus in Federal court challenging the lawfulness of their detention.

(d) It is in the interests of the United States that the executive branch undertake a prompt and thorough review of the factual and legal bases for the continued detention of all individuals currently held at Guantánamo, and of whether their continued detention is in the national security and foreign policy interests of the United States and in the interests of justice. The unusual circumstances associated with detentions at Guantánamo require a comprehensive interagency review.

(e) New diplomatic efforts may result in an appropriate disposition of a substantial number of individuals currently detained at Guantánamo.

(f) Some individuals currently detained at Guantánamo may have committed offenses for which they should be prosecuted. It is in the interests of the United States to review whether and how any such individuals can and should be prosecuted.

(g) It is in the interests of the United States that the executive branch conduct a prompt and thorough review of the circumstances of the individuals currently detained at Guantánamo who have been charged with offenses before military commissions pursuant to the Military Commissions Act of 2006, Public Law 109-366, as well as of the military commission process more generally.

Sec. 3. Closure of Detention Facilities at Guantánamo. The detention facilities at Guantánamo for individuals covered by this order shall be closed as soon as practicable, and no later than 1 year from the date of this order. If any individuals covered by this order remain in detention at Guantánamo at the time of closure of those detention facilities, they shall be returned to their home country, released, transferred to a third country, or transferred to another United States detention facility in a manner consistent with law and the national security and foreign policy interests of the United States.

Sec. 4. Immediate Review of All Guantánamo Detentions.

(a) *Scope and Timing of Review.* A review of the status of each individual currently detained at Guantánamo (Review) shall commence immediately.

(b) *Review Participants.* The Review shall be conducted with the full cooperation and participation of the following officials:

(1) the Attorney General, who shall coordinate the Review;

(2) the Secretary of Defense;

(3) the Secretary of State;

(4) the Secretary of Homeland Security;

(5) the Director of National Intelligence;

(6) the Chairman of the Joint Chiefs of Staff; and

(7) other officers or full-time or permanent part-time employees of the United States, including employees with intelligence, counterterorism, military, and legal expertise, as determined by the Attorney General, with the concurrence of the head of the department or agency concerned.

(c) *Operation of Review.* The duties of the Review participants shall include the following:

(1) *Consolidation of Detainee Information.* The Attorney General shall, to the extent reasonably practicable, and in coordination with the other Review participants, assemble all information in the possession of the Federal Government that pertains to any individual currently detained at Guantánamo and that is relevant to determining the proper disposition of any such individual. All executive branch departments and agencies shall promptly comply with any request of the Attorney General to provide information in their possession or control pertaining to any such individual. The Attorney General may seek further information relevant to the Review from any source.

(2) *Determination of Transfer.* The Review shall determine, on a rolling basis and as promptly as possible with respect to the individuals currently detained at Guantánamo, whether it is possible to transfer or release the individuals consistent with the national security and foreign policy interests of the United States and, if so, whether and how the Secretary of Defense may effect their transfer or release. The Secretary

of Defense, the Secretary of State, and, as appropriate, other Review participants shall work to effect promptly the release or transfer of all individuals for whom release or transfer is possible.

(3) *Determination of Prosecution.* In accordance with United States law, the cases of individuals detained at Guantánamo not approved for release or transfer shall be evaluated to determine whether the Federal Government should seek to prosecute the detained individuals for any offenses they may have committed, including whether it is feasible to prosecute such individuals before a court established pursuant to Article III of the United States Constitution, and the Review participants shall in turn take the necessary and appropriate steps based on such determinations.

(4) *Determination of Other Disposition.* With respect to any individuals currently detained at Guantánamo whose disposition is not achieved under paragraphs (2) or (3) of this subsection, the Review shall select lawful means, consistent with the national security and foreign policy interests of the United States and the interests of justice, for the disposition of such individuals. The appropriate authorities shall promptly implement such dispositions.

(5) *Consideration of Issues Relating to Transfer to the United States.* The Review shall identify and consider legal, logistical, and security issues relating to the potential transfer of individuals currently detained at Guantánamo to facilities within the United States, and the Review participants shall work with the Congress on any legislation that may be appropriate.

Sec. 5. Diplomatic Efforts. The Secretary of State shall expeditiously pursue and direct such negotiations and diplomatic efforts with foreign governments as are necessary and appropriate to implement this order.

Sec. 6. Humane Standards of Confinement. No individual currently detained at Guantánamo shall be held in the custody or under the effective control of any officer, employee, or other agent of the United States Government, or at a facility owned, operated, or controlled by a department or agency of the United States, except in conformity with all applicable laws governing the conditions of such confinement, including Common Article 3 of the Geneva Conventions. The Secretary of Defense shall immediately undertake a review of the conditions of detention at Guantánamo to ensure full compliance with this directive. Such review shall be completed within 30 days and any necessary corrections shall be implemented immediately thereafter.

Source: www.whitehouse.gov

CONCLUSION

> The sovereign always has a double relationship with the community.
> It promises well-being, but it asserts the right to claim a life.

PAUL KAHN

Violence and State Development

The documents reproduced in this book show that torture and associated practices of state violence have continued uninterrupted in the United States from colonial times through the present. Any claim that torture has decreased during a given period is true, at most, in relative terms. To be sure, slavery, "settlement" of the frontier, and world war, among other events, provided increased opportunities for torture, but there is always one or more segments of the population facing such treatment no matter what larger-scale conflicts are occurring. Thus, commentators like Louis Hartz, who see liberal principles guiding U.S. political development throughout the nation's history, must explain the co-presence of liberal ideas and strikingly illiberal practices.[1] I noted in the introduction that Rejali believes democracy (and, more specifically, the human rights monitoring that democracy brings about), paradoxically, is *productive* of a certain kind of torture (i.e., "clean" torture). In other words, the oversight and accountability that come with democracy make it problematic for states to use force that bruises. They rely instead on less detectable violence. Here, Rejali assumes that the impulse to torture is always there. The next question is *why* that violent impulse is ever-present, even in liberal-democratic regimes.

Contemporary thinkers have theorized the link between modern law and violence by viewing law as subject to certain internal tensions. Žižek explains that all regimes begin in violence. In order for a government to constitute itself, it must break (and break with) the law of the preceding order. As Jodi Dean puts it, interpreting Žižek, "Law begins in trauma. From the standpoint of the old law, the violent establishing of something new is crime."[2] Thus, state violence is inescapable—it "haunts" or "stains" the political order from the founding moment forward, and it shadows the formal law as *transgression*. Transgression of the law, in Žižek's psychoanalytic schema, helps to bind individuals more tightly to the law, and therefore to the regime: "Transgression can provide the common link, the libidinal support that binds a collective together—our collective dirty secret. Here superego tells members there is more to law than its official face, that they, the members, know what to do, that the official rules do not apply to them; they should go ahead, violate the laws, harass, assault, kill."³ Law itself (through superego, according to Žižek) licenses people to transgress it. The injunction to enjoy through transgression is delivered implicitly, disavowed publicly. Put another way, this disavowed aspect of law "is the criminality necessary for its own functioning."⁴ Thus, law itself is bound to its necessary criminality, and individuals are bound to law by their enjoyment of that criminality.

We might ask whether the Rule of Law can eliminate or control this transgressive enjoyment. The Rule of Law means in part that the legitimacy of state action is judged against the specific laws that govern and establish a particular state. Under a liberal-democratic form of government, the state risks losing legitimacy when it appears to violate its principles (individual rights, respect for human dignity, limits on state power). If the violations occur in secret, of course, there is no conflict. But when evidence of violence is made public, it must be explained. Does certain state behavior constitute an exception or can it be explained away as nonviolation of principles? In the preceding documents there are examples of both exception and nonviolation of principles: "This is an extraordinary situation" suggests a state of exception, and "These terrorists/prisoners/slaves aren't entitled to the same rights as others" suggests the principle is not violated. Both explanations—exception and nonviolation—operate as post hoc justifications for actions that might otherwise threaten legitimacy. Rule of Law, then, does not always function to expose and correct transgression.

Another explanation for the deep-seated presence of violence within law involves the concept of the *sacred* as applied to political communities.⁵ While citizens are committed to seeing the state as legitimate, they are also committed (in an even deeper sense) to the "sacredness" of the political order in which they live. The community's self-understanding, which reflects its aspirations and dreams, centers on this notion of sacredness. Transcendent and enduring, the sacred must be preserved in order for the community to hold together. And it is preserved through sacrifice. The symbolic relationship between sacredness and sacrifice is familiar to us in other settings (e.g., religious traditions), but it is more likely to be overlooked in the context of political orders. Nonetheless, it is present—both in premodern times and in contemporary states as well. In the United States, "there is a never-ending thirst for new books, movies and accounts of national political history—the narrative of sacrifice—from the founding through the victory in the Cold War and now, of course, the war on terror."[6] This narrative is comprehensible to those on the inside of the community of shared meaning; to outsiders it often does not make sense, as Kahn notes. Members of the community will understand why a certain sacrifice is necessary; they will share a sense of the sacredness that sacrifice preserves.

In the "social imaginary of sovereignty," the sacred-sacrifice relationship produces terror and torture. The terrorist is sacrificed to preserve the state.[7] Kahn sees a reciprocal relationship between torture and terror. Both are communicative practices; both are "political performances that inscribe meaning on bodies through pain and the threat of pain."[8] Torture, of course, takes the logic of state violence to its extreme by completely dominating the victim, negating the victim's will, and making the victim an instrument of the will of the state. Torture is "the ultimate act of state power. In arrogating to itself the capacity to torture its citizens, the state has assumed absolute power over them."[9] The temptation for those holding state power to resort to violence is always there; the practice of torture is its fullest realization.

Social philosopher Jürgen Habermas asks what binds society once the "metasocial guarantees" of the sacred have broken down.[10] It is a combination of law's facticity and validity that performs this binding, Habermas believes. The facticity of law enjoins subjects to obey, but in the end they commit to law because it has been validated discursively. In other words, legitimation occurs through subjecting potential rules to substantive critique. Kahn, on the other hand, sees a space of sovereignty *beyond* law. In this space, the sovereign, who is now the people, "pursu[es] a sacrificial politics of killing and being killed."[11] If we accept the notion that the modern government "rests on the oldest form of realizing meaning in the West: sacrifice," then we have a basis for finding attachments deeper than those which arise from the discursive legitimation process Habermas describes.[12] It is not that the affective replaces the rational but rather that they are co-present. The state no longer *guarantees* the sacred, but political communities remained attached to it, and ready to sacrifice for it, nonetheless.

Continuities

Compulsions to confess and justify can be seen repeatedly in the documents examined in the preceding chapters. The president or other state official condemns torture in the Philippines, or at Abu Ghraib, as if each case can be "closed" simply by stating what occurred and then "putting it away." Sometimes, as in Nixon's handling of the My Lai massacre, there is no explicit condemnation. Either way, incidents fade from public memory no matter how brutal, how oft repeated, or how similar to previous cases.

Rhetoric of violence links marginalized groups in a number of ways. First, the justification of adopting the tactics of a "savage" enemy appears repeatedly: in fighting the British in the War of Independence, killing noncombatant Native Americans, and torturing Filipino insurgents, for example. Moreover, some of the same racialized language is used to dehumanize targeted groups, as in the case of Native Americans, Filipinos, North Vietnamese, Arabs, and African Americans.

A second theme in the rhetoric of violence is the logic of exception, which I have referred to a number of times. The logic of exception is not entirely dissimilar from the theme of adopting the enemy's tactics: both are employed rhetorically to suggest that a necessary deviation from the norm has occurred—that the event in question is to be understood as unusual, aberrational, nonconstitutive.

What can one conclude from the limited sampling of documents represented in this collection? First, the continuity of state violence through U.S. history is shown by a variety of official sources. Second, I want the reader to make what she will of the continuities in state discourses of torture. If state actors say the same thing across time periods and geographical settings, we may want to pay attention, especially when those repeated statements have to do with justifying objectionable state behavior. Justifications can take the form of legal doctrines (such as the jurisprudence of "cruel and unusual punishment," discussed here), in which case they actually gain precedential significance, but close reading of official statements of any kind can lead to better understanding of state violence: past, present and future. Inaugural addresses by governors and presidents exhibit similarities;[13] legal arguments too come through history remarkably unchanged. Louis Fisher has noted that the "unlawful enemy combatant" concept originated in the 1942 military tribunal proceedings that tried eight Nazi saboteurs (and executed six of them), and then was resuscitated after 9/11 to justify stripping procedural and substantive rights from terror suspects.[14] Thus, the language of the Roosevelt administration facilitated detainee treatment in the Bush administration. Similarly, Dayan's treatment of the law of "cruel and unusual" makes clear the way justifications for brutality became fixed in precedent. We can see those same justifications employed in the post-9/11 context just as effectively as they were in the nineteenth-century slavery-related cases and the twentieth-century capital punishment cases. In the realm of law, such formulations assume, literally, life and death significance. If a justification is offered by the state and accepted by a court, the original defendant loses, and subsequent defendants as well lose their challenges to the state's decision to put them to death.

Another continuity in the documents is the presence of dissenting voices. The Wickersham Report (chapter 3) and the Soufan testimony (chapter 5) are two of many examples of state officials challenging violent state practices. To say that violence occurs repeatedly is not to say that it always goes uncontested. In the face of state violence, it is tempting to conclude in hindsight that the state's project was irresistible and inevitable; that way, individuals might be excused or at least forgiven for their participation. When Hannah Arendt submitted her famous report on the Eichmann trial, she challenged the world to think about the way monstrous acts were committed by ordinary, even dull individuals carrying out their appointed duties in service of the state. What Arendt called the "banality of evil" was a chilling discovery for her readers worldwide because it is harder to accept the fact that a bureaucrat facilitated genocide than it is to see a fascist leader as the embodiment of evil. There is another lesson, though, to be drawn from Arendt's study of state crime. As she reported the implementation of Hitler's plan to expel and murder European Jews, Arendt proceeded by examining the process in each individual country. There was variety of pace and method among the various nations, and there were also records of Nazi officials and government officials from occupied states taking bribes and disobeying orders. Officials allowed some Jews to escape after payment of a bribe; some officials refused to carry out orders and went unpunished.[15] There is no question, of course, that the regime was governed and guided by violence or that its project was genocide. But it is easier to assume that all individual choice was foreclosed by totalitarian rule; then, questions of individual moral choice are harder to raise. Arendt shows us that this was not the case—and certainly, for state officials in the U.S. context, even more space for resistance was available.

Torture and Morality Revisited

Commentators have gone on record to say that we must acknowledge that torture will be used—and should be used—in certain circumstances. Judge Posner even suggests that "only the most doctrinaire civil libertarians (not that there aren't plenty of them) deny that if the stakes are high enough, torture is permissible. No one who doubts that should be in a position of responsibility."[16] Others, too, though not perhaps in terms so strong as these, have defended torture as a "last resort," a "lesser evil," to be engaged in reluctantly as an abhorrent practice, but engaged in, nonetheless, at the end of the day when certain circumstances exist. Well-intentioned commentators who express repugnance at the thought of torture, and who genuinely seek to regulate and punish it, arrive at the moment, not without anguish, when they are prepared to say torture is necessary. Such good-faith arguments are an unavoidable part of the discursive process of understanding torture and making policy, but I cannot join those opinions or endorse where they wind up at the end of the day. For me, the problem is this: arguments justifying last-resort torture proceed from counterfactuals that make the pro-torture arguments appear compelling to some, but it is misguided to deal in counterfactuals when relevant *factual* conditions are at hand. To put it somewhat differently, counterfactuals ask the listener to assume a set of facts, then admit that under those facts the speaker's conclusion is warranted. Thus, a limit point is instantiated, and we work backward from there to see if a slightly altered counterfactual also supports the speaker's conclusion. In the context of torture, such what-if scenarios suggest, wrongly, that torture has no history, no established sets of practices, no already-existing motivations. The United States has long resorted to torture. Its torture practices sit on a spectrum of violent state practices that all have long histories. There is no real dispute about this. Thus, the question is not whether to resort to torture in the future but whether to *continue* torturing, given what we know about its efficacy, its costs, the feasibility of controlling "mission creep," and, last but not least, the plausibility of "ticking bomb" situations. This point might seem obvious, but I find it remarkable the way torture is constructed in U.S. popular discourse as something-we-might-have-to-do-someday even when there is no doubt that we are doing it now.

I resist granting the conditions of the ticking bomb scenario for the reasons McCoy does: the sheer implausibility of it, and its dissimilarity from actually occurring interrogation scenes that repeat themselves endlessly, throughout modernity.[17] As I have said, I do not think that scenario usefully advances the discussion of torture and morality. But rejecting the ticking bomb scenario does not remove the question: *Is it ever justified to inflict pain on one person in order to save numerous others?* Kahn sees this conflict, at least in part, as one between "the two great Western traditions of deontological and utilitarian ethics."[18] But he refocuses this debate by asking where the choice arises. It arises within a community of shared meaning, in which subjects are willing to make sacrifices for those they care about. Their regard for fellow citizens (or children, or partners) is the context in which the question of sacrifice arises. The background conditions, too, give shape to a particular question of sacrifice. Kahn compares the nuclear question during the Cold War to the torture question now and suggests that neither question can be addressed effectively in the abstract, without a sense of how the community experiences those conditions, without a sense of who and what the community cares about, or what its concerns are.[19]

But there is still more to say about the choices a moral agent might make. In her critique of Alan Dershowitz's position, Elaine Scarry notes a further problem—with the construction of the moral agent—in Dershowitz's argument. He asserts that the "ticking bomb" scenario demonstrates the need for judicially approved torture through "torture warrants." But this reasoning posits a morally defective agent. The agent is defective, Scarry says, because the agent needs legal immunity before she will commit an act of torture. An appropriately functioning agent would not need absolution; she would act even if she knew she would be punished legally, provided that she believed her action to be justified, as Antigone did when burying her brother.[20] In other words, any reasoning subject who would wait for "clearance" by the state before acting on what she determined to be the right course of action is a defective moral agent. This argument is compelling. If torture remains outside the law, never justified, then the person who resorts to torture (knowing all that we know about torture and why it is abhorrent) does not expect to be absolved. This is not a matter of a loose prohibition, which would go under-enforced. Instead, it poses a clearer moral choice and asks the agent to make an agonizingly difficult decision without indemnification from the state.

With regard to the disconnect between ticking bomb scenarios and actual situations where torture is contemplated (and used), the voluntary release of torture records by the Obama administration is an encouraging trend. The secrecy protecting torture practices in the United States has actually helped to mystify the public about when torture is "necessary," why it is used, and how effective it is. The more we know about what is being done "in our name," the better able we are to assess the justifications.[21] When secrecy reigns, we are left to rely on government spokespeople and television fantasy scenarios.

Remembering the Victims

In his lengthy study of torture, Rejali mentions a 1939 conversation between a Jewish guerrilla and a Palestinian Arab who share a jail cell. The guerilla shows the wounds he has suffered at the hands of his British captors; the Arab brings him food and condemns the man's torturers. The point of the story is to show how torture creates a "common political space" where people relate and try to understand what each other's lives have been.[22] Here, Rejali is arguing against discourses of torture that cordon such experiences off from the rest of human life.[23] While it is readily understandable that readers and observers would want to avert their eyes from torture scenes, it is misguided to allow such impulses to generate discourses that separate, exoticize, or (worst, perhaps) occlude torture from discussions of politics, separating the normal from the aberrational.

In preparing this study, I read of incidents I knew about but wanted to forget (My Lai, Sand Creek), and I learned of others for the first time. I read about torture techniques and policies that literally sickened me. In the course of processing written information, one naturally tries to visualize the written description; when reading descriptions of extreme pain, this becomes difficult for several reasons. Of course, part of the difficulty is the sheer horror of it. Beyond that traumatic element, however, is another aspect of the problem. The mind tries to take the measure of what different tortures actually *feel* like but it cannot. Sanford Levinson suggests, "It is perhaps a dreadful play on words to describe torture as too painful to think about."[24] But I think this is exactly the point. We ought to try and think about it; when we find ourselves unable to contemplate certain acts done by humans to other humans, that failure of imagination should tell us something about the chasm separating the acts from everyday understanding. There is a saying to the effect that whatever can be thought can also be enacted. Here in the case of torture we have a strange reversal: things that *cannot* be thought have nonetheless been enacted. We retreat into the safety and security of our own lives—that is, if we have access to such safety and security. We cannot know what another person's pain feels like (although some people have voluntarily submitted to tortures as a gesture at this kind of understanding); separation and inaccessibility of one from another of us is one of the given conditions of being human. We can learn about what others experience, but we cannot make their experiences our own.

A question emerges, though, from thinking about this struggle between confronting and forgetting. What kind of policies would emerge from a "common political space" where we tried to communicate, to understand, what torture actually feels like, what it *does* to the victim and the torturer? What if these questions were asked not in a flippant way—as when Donald Rumsfeld dismissed complaints about forced standing by saying that he himself stood eight to ten hours per day—but in a serious effort to communicate.[25] What would become of the "necessity defense" as justification of torture? How would our perspective of the "ticking time bomb" scenario change? On the one hand, opponents of torture rightly want to show how much of a departure it (torture) is from the legitimate use of state power. This, as I have said, is one impulse for the treatment of torture as a departure point, a deviation. At the same time, though, apologists for torture often move in the same direction, albeit for a different reason. The torture apologist constructs a hypothetical of extreme and unusual danger where torture is "necessary." For example, one oft-posited scenario involves a terrorist in custody who knows the location of a bomb that is about to explode and thereby kill a large number of civilians. The apologist then presumes that torture saves the day by eliciting the location of the bomb, and with that she rests her case. But we are left, in this account, without much consideration of what is actually done to make the prisoner divulge the needed information. Television fills in the gap, as, for example, when the interrogator shoots the prisoner in the leg. Whether we dehumanize the prisoner (he deserves what he gets) or stylize the violence to a form we are inured to (a gunshot wound on a TV or movie set), the focus is not on the torturing but rather on the reason for torturing. The focus is not on the psyche of the torturer but on the torturer's heroism. Thus, we are led, by prevailing treatments of the topic, away from the topic itself.

It has been said that "the lesson of torture" is the silence meeting the victim's screams. The torturer assures the victim, "No one will ever hear you, no one will ever know, no one will ever discover," confirming the victim's isolation.[26] It is my hope that the documents presented in this book will aid us in building a conversation about what has been done, what is being done, and what will be done through exercise of state power—and that in such a conversation the voices of the victims will assume a prominent place.

Notes

1. See, e.g., Louis Hartz, *The Liberal Tradition in America* (New York: Harcourt Brace, 1955).

2. Jodi Dean, *Žižek's Politics* (New York: Routledge, 2006). Paul Kahn, too, argues that to explain torture as a political phenomenon, it is necessary to "examin[e] the manner in which violence creates and sustains political meaning." See Kahn, *Sacred Violence* (Ann Arbor: University of Michigan Press, 2008), p. 4. Both theorists see violence playing a role in creating and reinforcing group identity.

3. Dean, *Žižek's Politics*, p. 35.

4. Ibid., p. 34.

5. Kahn, *Sacred Violence*.

6. Ibid., p. 175.

7. Ibid. Here, Kahn intends *terror* more broadly than simply to describe a twenty-first-century terrorist. *Terror* stands for *all* threats (real or imagined) to destroy the existing political order; such threats are met with torture, and that is why terror and torture are twinned in social-political imaginary.

8. Ibid., p. 6.

9. Kate Millett, *The Politics of Cruelty* (New York: Norton, 1994), p. 18. Luban sees this stance of absolute power as providing the primary basis for liberal objections to cruelty. David Luban, "Liberalism, Torture, and the Ticking Bomb," 91 *Virginia Law Review* 1433 (2005).

10. Jürgen Habermas, *Between Facts and Norms* (Cambridge: Polity Press, 1996), pp. 23–25.

11. Kahn, *Sacred Violence*, p. 86.

12. Ibid., p. 98.

13. See document 2.17 in chapter 2.

14. Louis Fisher, *Nazi Saboteurs on Trial* (Lawrence: University Press of Kansas, 2003), p. 158.

15. Hannah Arendt, *Eichmann in Jerusalem* (New York: Penguin Books, 1994). See, e.g., pp. 181–93 ("Deportations from the Balkans").

16. Richard Posner, "Torture, Terrorism and Interrogation," in Sanford Levinson, ed., *Torture: A Collection* (Oxford: Oxford University Press, 2004), p. 295.

17. Alfred McCoy, *A Question of Torture* (New York: Holt, 2006), p. 195.

18. Kahn, *Sacred Violence*, p. 70.

19. Ibid., pp. 78–81.

20. Elaine Scarry, "Five Errors in the Reasoning of Alan Dershowitz," in Levinson, *Torture: A Collection*, p. 281.

21. Levinson, in *Torture: A Collection*, p. 38.

22. Darius Rejali, *Torture and Democracy* (Princeton: Princeton University Press, 2007), pp. 30–31.

23. Rejali also makes it a point to note, wherever possible, the identities of the victims, because he believes those identities are all too easily forgotten. *Torture and Democracy*, p. xxiii.

24. Levinson, in *Torture: A Collection*, p. 38.

25. Richard Leiby, "Donald Rumsfeld, A Real Stand-Up Guy," *Washington Post*, June 24, 2004, C3.

26. Millett, *The Politics of Cruelty*, p. 301.

BIBLIOGRAPHY

Arendt, Hannah. *Eichmann in Jerusalem.* New York: Penguin Books, 1994.

Bekerman, Omer Ze'ev. "Torture: The Absolute Prohibition of a Relative Term; Does Everyone Know What Is in Room 101?" 53 *American Journal of Comparative Law* 743, 751 (2005).

Blackmon, Douglas. *Slavery by Another Name.* New York: Anchor Books, 2008.

Blanton, Thomas, and Peter Kornbluh. Entries in the National Security Archive. www.gwu.edu/~nsarchiv/NSAEBB/NSAEBB122/ (accessed June 16, 2010).

Conroy, John. *Unspeakable Acts, Ordinary People.* New York: Alfred A. Knopf, 2000.

Cover, Robert. *Justice Accused: Antislavery and the Judicial Process.* New Haven: Yale University Press, 1984.

Crocker, Thomas P. "Overcoming Necessity: Torture and the State of Constitutional Culture." 61 *Southern Methodist Law Review* 221, 230 (2008).

Dayan, Colin. *The Story of Cruel and Unusual.* Cambridge, MA: Boston Review Press, 2007.

Dean, Jodi. *Žižek's Politics.* New York: Routledge, 2006.

Dershowitz, Alan. *Shouting Fire: Civil Liberties in a Turbulent Age.* New York: Little Brown, 2002.

Fisher, Louis. *Nazi Saboteurs on Trial.* Lawrence: University Press of Kansas, 2003.

Frankenberg, Gunter. "Torture and Taboo: An Essay Comparing Paradigms of Organized Cruelty." 56 *American Journal of Comparative Law* 403, 407 (2008).

Gilroy, Paul. *The Black Atlantic: Modernity and the Double Consciousness.* Cambridge, MA: Harvard University Press, 1993.

Greene, Jerome, and Douglas Scott. *Finding Sand Creek.* Norman: University of Oklahoma Press, 2004.

Habermas, Jürgen. *Between Facts and Norms.* Cambridge: Polity Press, 1996.

———. "Constitutional Democracy: A Paradoxical Union of Contradictory Principles?" *Political Theory* 29, no. 6 (2001): 766–81.

Harbury, Jennifer. *Truth, Torture and the American Way.* Boston: Beacon Press, 2005.

Hartz, Louis. *The Liberal Tradition in America.* New York: Harcourt Brace, 1955.

Jaffer, Jameel, and Amrit Singh. *Administration of Torture: A Documentary Record from Washington to Abu Ghraib and Beyond.* New York: Columbia University Press, 2007.

Kahn, Paul. *Sacred Violence.* Ann Arbor: University of Michigan Press, 2008.

Koh, Harold Hongju. "A World without Torture." 43 *Columbia Journal of Transnational Law* 641, 647 (2005).

Kramer, Paul. *The Blood of Government: Race, Empire, the United States and the Philippines.* Chapel Hill: University of North Carolina Press, 2006.

Levinson, Sanford. "Fighting Terrorism with Torture: Where to Draw the Line?" 1 *Journal of National Security Law and Policy* 231, 234 (2005).

———, ed. *Torture: A Collection.* New York: Oxford, 2004.

Luban, David. "Liberalism, Torture and the Ticking Bomb." 91 *Virginia Law Review* 1425, 1432 (2005).

McCoy, Alfred. *A Question of Torture.* New York: Henry Holt, 2006.

Michelman, Frank. "Brennan and Democracy." 68 *California Law Review* 399 (1998).

Millett, Kate. *The Politics of Cruelty.* New York: Norton, 1994.

Pallitto, Robert, and William Weaver. *Presidential Secrecy and the Law.* Baltimore: Johns Hopkins University Press, 2007.

Parry, John T. "Fighting Terrorism with Torture: Where to Draw the Line?" 1 *Journal of National Security Law and Policy* 253, 276 (2005).

———. "What Is Torture, Are We Doing It, and What If We Are?" 64 *University of Pittsburgh Law Review* 237, 251 (Winter 2003).

Peters, Edward. *Torture.* New York: Basil Blackwell, 1985.

Rejali, Darius. *Torture and Democracy.* Princeton: Princeton University Press, 2007.

Report of the Joint Committee on the Conduct of the War: Massacre of the Cheyenne Indians. Washington, DC: Government Printing Office, 1865.

Rogin, Michael. *Fathers and Children: Andrew Jackson and the Subjugation of the American Indian.* New Brunswick, NJ: Transaction Books, 1991.

Rosenblum, Nancy, ed. *Liberalism and the Moral Life.* Cambridge, MA: Harvard University Press, 1989.

Rothenberg, Daniel. "Commentary: 'What We Have Seen Has Been Terrible': Public Presentational Torture and the Communicative Logic of State Terror." 67 *Albany Law Review* 477 (2003).

Salter, Mark. "The Global Visa Regime and the Political Technologies of the International Self: Borders, Bodies, Biopolitics." *Alternatives: Global, Local Political* 31, no. 2 (2006): 167–89.

Scott, George Riley. *The History of Corporal Punishment.* London: Torchstream Books, 1948.

Storey, Moorfield, and Julian Codman. *Marked Severities: Secretary Root's Record in Philippine Warfare.* New York: George Ellis, 1902.

Stroud, George. *A Sketch of the Laws Relating to Slavery in the Several States.* Philadelphia: Henry Longstreth, 1856.

Svaldi, David. *Sand Creek and the Rhetoric of Extermination: A Case Study in Indian-White Relations.* Lanham, MD: University Press of America, 1989.

Torture by Proxy: International and Domestic Law Applicable to "Extraordinary Renditions." Report by the New York City Bar Association and NYU Law School (2004), www.nyuhr.org (accessed December 12, 2007).

Waldrep, Christopher. *Lynching in America: A History in Documents.* New York: New York University Press, 2006.

Waldron, Jeremy. "Torture and Positive Law: Jurisprudence for the White House." 105 *Columbia Law Review* 1681 (2005).

INDEX

Rumsfeld, Donald, 188–9, 193–4, 262
Rutledge, Wiley, 133

sacred, 256–7
sacrifice, 257
Sanchez, Ricardo, 193, 195
Sand Creek, Colorado, 1, 12, 262; U.S. Army at, 7
savage, 258
Scarry, Elaine, 261
Schley, William, 61
Schmitt, Carl, and "state of exception," 3–4, 12, 258
Schumer, Charles, 210
segregation, 63
September 11, 3, 7, 14, 22, 184, 186, 197–9, 200–201, 219, 221, 223, 225, 258
Shackleford, James, 64
ships, wartime seizure of, 32
Shklar, Judith, 1, 2
shocking the conscience, 138, 163, 202, 204, 206, 246
shotgun, 105
skeleton, as device of intimidation, 113
slaves: laws regarding, 30–1, 45–51, 58–61, 64, 256, 258; trade in, 165; in war, 77, 79, 80, 127
Smith, John, 68
Soufan, Ali, 217, 259
South Carolina, state of, 32–5, 47–8
Southeast Asia, 130
Soviet Union, 130; fall of, 7
Spain, 36
Star Chamber, 119, 207
starvation, 76
state secrets, 240–2
State v. Mann, 57
State v. Nagle, 111
Stevens, John Paul, 181, 202, 204
stocks, 86, 88
stomach pumping, 137–8
Storey, Moorfield, 96
straitjacket, 101–2
stress positions, 195, 216–7, 229
summary killing, 140
superego, 256
Supreme Court, 4, 6, 15, 153, 163, 181
sweat-box, 110

sweating, process of, 87

Taguba Report, 209–10
Taliban, 184
Tenet, George, 223, 240–2
Tenet v. Doe, 242
Tennessee, state of, 43, 52, 58, 61
terrorism, 190, 202, 218, 247
terrorist, 185, 218, 222, 229, 256–7
Texas, state of, 113, 154–5
third degree, 73, 110
Thomas, Clarence, 181, 202
ticking bomb hypothetical, 210, 222, 261, 263
Tombs, the, 161, 164
torture, 116, 121, 133, 158, 165–73, 184–8, 207, 210, 211, 213, 224, 228, 229, 234, 238, 239, 240, 246, 249–50, 255–63; by beating, 243; by burning, 174–8; chamber, 119; chemical, medical and electrical, 141, 174, 180, 230; "clean," 2, 255; condemnations of, 19; in confinement box, 226–7; Convention Against, 9, 11, 31, 171–3, 184, 211, 215, 249, 250; by death threat, 174, 180, 189, 198 (*see also* mock execution); defense to charges of, 227; as distinct from "cruel, inhuman, and degrading treatment," 5, 31–2, 36, 90, 99, 127, 170–4, 185, 215, 226–7, 233–5, 239, 240; electroshock, 174–8, 230; as a form of state violence, 8, 12, 258; by hooding, 189, 212–3, 237; judicial and political, 7, 130; justifications for, 3; by loud music, 194; necessity of, 17; psychological, 8; by sleep deprivation, 167, 194, 213–4, 229, 230; by smothering, 174; "stealthy," 2–3; as taboo, 5; using dogs, 194, 207–8; using phobias and fear, 189, 191, 197–8; warrants, 261; by water dousing, 216; in U.S. Code, 180
Trop v. Dulles, 158
truth serum, 178
tying up by the thumbs, 87

Uniform Code of Military Justice, 15, 22, 209, 231
United Nations, 126–7, 165, 170–1
United States v. Bailey, 187
United States v. Carter, 186
unlawful combatant, 189, 190, 231–2, 237–8